ARTHUR MILLER'S AMERICA

Theater & Culture in a Time of Change

Edited by Enoch Brater

The University of Michigan Press
Ann Arbor

First paperback edition 2005

Published in the United States of America by
The University of Michigan Press
Manufactured in the United States of America
∞ Printed on acid-free paper

2008 2007 2006 2005 5 4 3 2

A CIP catalog record for this book is available from the British Library.

Library of Congress Cataloging-in-Publication Data

Arthur Miller's America : theater & culture in a time of change / edited by Enoch Brater.
p. cm. — (Theater—theory/text/performance)
Includes bibliographical references and index.
ISBN 0-472-11410-7 (cloth : alk. paper)
1. Miller, Arthur, 1915—Criticism and interpretation. 2. Miller, Arthur, 1915—Stage history—United States. 3. Theater—United States—History—20th century. 4. National characteristics, American, in literature. 5. Miller, Arthur, 1915—Knowledge—America. I. Brater, Enoch. II. Series.

PS3525.I5156Z53 2005
812'.52—dc22 2004063695

ISBN 0-472-03155-4 (pbk. : alk. paper)

For Miller students, past, present & future,
at the University of Michigan and elsewhere

Preface

Arthur Miller was born north of Central Park in Manhattan on October 17, 1915. Nineteen years later, after two rejection letters and a successful appeal to the dean, he arrived on the University of Michigan campus as one of a cadre of East Coasters who left home to try their luck at one of America's great Midwestern centers of higher learning. He hitchhiked part of the way. That journey from New York to Ann Arbor and back again has become the subject of legend, part, indeed, of Miller's own mythmaking; but as the essays in this volume should make clear, that journey would have considerable repercussions on the shape of theater and American culture in the second half of the twentieth century.

To mark the occasion of the playwright's eighty-fifth year in 2000, and his long association with Michigan, the university sponsored a hugely successful international symposium, bringing together a group of scholars, critics, students and theater professionals who had in one way or another been attracted to his work. It is fair to say that not one of us suspected the level of discourse and discussion that was to follow. *Arthur Miller's America: Theater and Culture in a Time of Change* is an attempt to share with a much wider audience the rich exchange of ideas that took place during those fall days in the seminar halls of the Horace H. Rackham Building. In each case the seminar participants returned from Ann Arbor determined to rework their presentations; their contributions, rethought and retooled in light of what took place during the conference, now appear for the first time in finished, printed form.

Part of the excitement of Michigan's tribute to Miller was the series of events mounted to supplement the strictly academic side of things. These included a major photography exhibit at the University Museum of the work of Inge Morath that focused on both the figure of Miller and his stage plays. Of particular interest here was the considerable documentation of the playwright's association with such personalities as the controversial director Elia Kazan, the Rev. Sloan Coffin, and the novelist William

Styron, among many others. Morath's artful photographs also gave us entry into Miller's private world in Roxbury, Connecticut: the small study where he works, the table that he made (the playwright is also a master carpenter), the landscape that he sees from his front porch. Further insights into the world of Arthur Miller were provided by the staff of the University of Michigan Library, who shared with the community a revealing collection of exhibition materials: letters to and from Miller's playwriting teacher Kenneth Rowe; samples of his prize-winning entries to the Hopwood Awards Committee (and evaluations from the national judges); early writings from the student humor magazine; and original programs and designs for *Up from Paradise,* which premiered at the Power Center for the Performing Arts. Under the direction of Darryl V. Jones, the Department of Theater and Drama also presented an extremely forceful, sold-out production of *A View from the Bridge.*

Miller, who had planned to attend the conference, was in the final moment unable to do so. Two weeks before the date for this conference he fell in London on a sidewalk curb and broke several ribs; his doctor ruled flying from New York or Connecticut out of the question. Undaunted by this sudden turn of events, the Office of the Vice President for Communications arranged to have Miller "appear" by live video hookup. A production team based in Hartford arrived in a large truck on Miller's driveway, set up a satellite dish, and prepared for broadcast. Three larger-than-life MTV-like screens were installed in the Rackham Auditorium for a "live feed" with the editor of this volume. And it must be reported in this preface that several Michigan undergraduates admitted to me that seeing Miller on a huge screen was "a whole lot better than seeing him real." Time bends in strange ways.

That interview, a discussion really, appears in slightly altered form in this volume, as does a separate discussion with Pulitzer Prize composer and Michigan faculty member William C. Bolcom, whose operatic adaptation of *A View from the Bridge* played in Chicago and New York (Bolcom also wrote the music for the original Broadway production of *Broken Glass,* one of several collaborations with the playwright). A third interview, also previously unpublished, appears in the pages that follow: Toby Zinman's lively discussion with the actor Patrick Stewart, who played the lead role in the well-publicized New York production of *The Ride Down Mt. Morgan.*

Miller's place, along with Eugene O'Neill and Tennessee Williams, as one of the big three of twentieth-century American theater is well reflected in the following series of essays, interrogations that often take as their point of departure masterful works like *Death of a Salesman* or popular ones like *All My Sons.* The discussions also include searching examinations of the more problematic late plays, and suggest a number of reasons why they remain so. Pedagogically, too, whether in studio workshops like Stella Adler's or more predictable venues like college classrooms, Miller's work continues to play a central part in the training of young professionals as well as new audiences for an ever-emerging American theater. Readers of this volume will have the opportunity to consider—and perhaps reconsider—why studying and performing Miller still plays this essential role.

Even beyond questions of theater, or even the politics of theater, this playwright's public posture as committed citizen raises disturbing questions about the responsibility of the artist in a changing and always volatile society. Miller has rarely shirked the task. From picket line to op-ed piece in the *New York Times,* from protest to petition, from letter to the editor to commentary in *The Nation,* he remains to this day the closest thing America has to a public intellectual. And it should not be forgotten that Miller's speaking out against injustice began a long time ago—when it took guts. Miller, then, both in and out of the theater, as both icon and agitator, is therefore a tempting subject for vast cultural commentary, as several essayists display here.

Ruby Cohn observed during the symposium that perhaps we were lucky that Miller wasn't "really" there with us: it allowed us to question the work from perspectives, not always flattering, we might have been too timid or far too polite to entertain in his presence. Looking back on it now, she may have been right. Miller told me more than twenty years ago, surprised as he was by my attachment to the difficult task of trying to understand the late work of Samuel Beckett, that he, personally, "never wrote a play my Uncle Max couldn't understand." When I reflect on the diversity of approaches my colleagues offer for consideration in this book, I now realize something that seems to have eluded me for far too long a time: that his Uncle Max, like his famous nephew, must have been quite a guy.

Acknowledgments

This project on Arthur Miller would not have been possible without the generous support of the University of Michigan. Official sponsors for the symposium on which this book is based included the Office of the President, the Office of the Provost, the LS&A Enrichment Fund, the Horace

H. Rackham School of Graduate Studies, the University of Michigan Alumni Association, the Office of the Vice President for Communications, the Department of English Language and Literature, the University Musical Society, the Department of Theater and Drama, the University Museum of Art, the School of Music, the Hopwood Writing Program, the School of Education, the University of Michigan Libraries, and the University of Michigan Press. Many individuals contributed to our success: Lee C. Bollinger, Chacona Johnson, Patrick Naswell, Lisa Rudgers, Richard Gove, James C. Steward, Carole C. McNamara, Kathryn L. Beam, Donna K. Johnston, Jonathan P. Brater, and the late Inge Morath. My colleagues at Michigan, Darryl V. Jones, Zelma Weisfeld, Glenda Dickerson, Bert Cardullo, Leigh Woods, and Linda Gregerson, chaired sessions; and the students in the Arthur Miller Seminar worked hard as conference facilitators. Linda Ben-Zvi of Tel Aviv, John Dorsey of Tokyo, Laura Cerrato of Buenos Aires, Kirsten Herold from Denmark, and Louis Marks from the BBC in London brought an international dimension to the proceedings in a panel led by Hersh Zeifman of York University in Toronto. Greatly enriched by studies written by scholars in Spain, Germany, South Africa, Italy, and China, their work is scheduled to appear soon in *Global Miller,* a second volume based on the conference to be published by the University of Michigan Press. Vicki Lawrence and LeAnn Fields were instrumental in transforming the conference papers into publishable form. *Arthur Miller's America: Theater and Culture in a Time of Change* is the result, therefore, as these acknowledgments should make abundantly clear, of both a university and a world-wide event.

Contents

Enoch Brater

Early Days, Early Works
Arthur Miller at the University of Michigan

I

Arthur Miller's long association with the University of Michigan actually began with a rejection letter—two of them, in point of fact. When he graduated from Abraham Lincoln High School on Ocean Parkway in Brooklyn, New York, in 1933, he needed four faculty members to write letters of recommendation; he could find only three. He had flunked algebra three times, and the rest of his record—both at Lincoln and at James Madison High School, where he spent two years playing football (a serious leg injury later kept him out of military service)—was similarly lackluster, and that is putting a good face on it. Turned down in 1933, he applied again in 1934 because, as he told me informally in October 2000, Michigan was one of the few places that took writing seriously.[1] When he received a disappointing second letter of rejection, he was emboldened to respond to the dean of the college, telling him that he had been working hard and "had turned into a much more serious fellow." Years later, writing for *Holiday* magazine in 1953, Miller remembered that the dean said he "would give me a try, but I had better make some grades. I could not conceive of a dean at Columbia or Harvard doing that."[2] Looking back at this probationary period from his eighty-fifth year, Miller commented, "I still can't believe Michigan let me in."[3]

What brought a New Yorker like Arthur Miller to a Midwestern college town like Ann Arbor? First and foremost, tuition was cheap; and these were, after all, some of the toughest years of the Depression. Tuition was free, of course, at a more likely choice for someone from Miller's background: City College, now part of the City University of New York. This had long been the intellectual center for boys and girls born to immigrant parents like Miller's, Polish Jews who made whatever fortune they had at the *schmata* trade in Manhattan's Garment District on Seventh

Avenue. Isidore Miller, the playwright's father, actually owned and ran a coat factory there, but what had once been a thriving manufacturing business went belly-up after the crash of '29. "I did go to City College for about three weeks in the evening," Miller said, "because I was working during the daytime. But I couldn't stay awake."[4] After a few weeks, he dropped out. Miller's father, a practical-minded businessman, was amazed to hear of a faraway school called Michigan that would actually pay students money for writing. His son told him about the prestigious Avery Hopwood Awards, built from a legacy given by another Michigan alumnus who had made a fortune on Broadway with such slight bedroom farces as *Getting Gertie's Garter* and *Up in Mabel's Room;* plays like *The Best People* (revived in a Michigan student production in February 1998, directed by Philip Kerr) brought in huge box office receipts in the 1920s. Miller's father was impressed, but he reminded his son that he had to make some money first—before trying his hand at the Hopwoods.

Miller worked in New York for two years at Chadwick-Delamater, a gigantic warehouse for automobile parts located on the site that was later to become, in 1963, the Lincoln Center for the Performing Arts. He made fifteen dollars a week and worked for a "very dour, pasty-faced, very neat" boss named Wesley Moulton. "The area was a kind of slum," he wrote in the *New York* magazine (December 18–25, 2000), "with a lot of saloons, working-class bars, and boarded-up houses." They had never hired someone who was Jewish before, and at first wouldn't hire Miller when he answered their ad in a newspaper. But his old boss in Brooklyn intervened and told Moulton in no uncertain terms that Miller knew "more about parts than most of you guys, so if you don't give him a job there's only one reason." At Chadwick-Delamater Miller remembered that he "was the only Jew. The guy who worked there after me was an Italian. They hated him, too."[5]

In the years before superhighways, and even before the landmark Pennsylvania Turnpike was constructed, it took a long time to get from New York to southeastern Michigan. But once he arrived in Ann Arbor after a circuitous bus ride and a hitchhike, he said, quite simply, "I felt at home."

> It was a little world, and it was man-sized. My friends were the sons of diemakers, farmers, ranchers, bankers, lawyers, doctors, clothing workers and unemployed relief recipients. They came from every part of the country and brought all their prejudices and special wisdoms. It was always so wonderful to get up in the morning. There was a lot learned every day. I recall going to hear Kagawa, the Japanese philosopher, and how, suddenly, half the audience

> stood up and walked out because he had used the word Manchukuo, which is Japanese, for the Chinese province of Manchuria. As I watched the Chinese students excitedly talking outside on the steps of Hill Auditorium, I felt something about the Japanese attack on China that I had not felt before.[6]

As an undergraduate at one of the great publicly supported institutions of higher learning in America, Miller was attracted to the spirit and opportunity of what we would now call diversity in progressive, liberal education. The University of Michigan, for example, provided a far less hostile environment to students from Miller's own background (the writer Norman Rosten, the CBS television anchorman Mike Wallace, and future MIT president Jerome Wiesner were there at the same time)—especially when compared to Ivy League institutions back East, where quotas against Jews and other "others" were strictly enforced. H. Porter Abbott reports that his grandfather, who was in the university administration at the time, specifically encouraged an admission policy based on merit. Picking up students who were barred from "restricted" Wasp strongholds like Harvard and Princeton, it was, he said, simply the best policy for building a strong, ambitious, egalitarian and hardworking undergraduate class.[7] Yale, it should be remembered, did not have a tenured Jewish faculty member until 1956.

As a first-year student at the University of Michigan, Miller lived in a rooming house on South Division Street run by Mrs. Elnora Nelson, the widow of a dentist (she made all of her residents store their luggage in a large wooden barrel in the attic containing old teeth; the future playwright soon discovered that none of them had any gold crowns). Miller's housemates included Harmon L. Remmel and Henry Carl Reigler, both from Little Rock, Arkansas; Keith and Bob Dubey from just north of Ann Arbor; Paul B. Cares, a doctoral student; Charles S. Cook, who was killed in World War II; Bob Danse; and William and Mary Tommy Lee from Kentucky, who occupied an apartment on the first floor. "They were great bridge players," recalls Remmel, "and all of us living in the Nelson house got to play bridge there with them." That first year Miller and several of his housemates took their meals at a small mom-and-pop restaurant around the corner run by a family named Helper.[8] Later, when Miller moved to another house at 411 North State Street, where he paid $1.75 a week, he took some of his meals at the Wolverine Eating Club in the basement of Lane Hall. The club's cook, Anna Panzer, recalled in a 1983 interview that they fed about 250 people three meals a day. She was assisted by John Ragland, who later became Ann Arbor's only African American lawyer. About 40 students, including Arthur Miller, helped with the prep and cleanup in exchange for free meals, while the rest paid $2.50 a week.[9] At the time Miller earned $15 a week feeding past-prime vegetables to thousands of mice at 4:00 P.M. every day in Professor Frank H. Clark's genetics laboratory, which was housed on the edge of town near the old Ann Arbor Coal Yard. In his autobiography, *Timebends,* Miller recalls trudging two miles each way.[10]

II

Although most Miller studies trace the beginning of his literary career at Michigan to his undergraduate submissions to the Hopwood Awards Committee, he first made his mark in Ann Arbor as a writer for the *Michigan Daily.* Housed, as it still is today, in the Student Publications Building at 420 Maynard Street, the *Daily* was even in those days one of the country's most notable student newspapers, along with the *Columbia Spectator* and the *Harvard Crimson.* A review of the future playwright's work as a young journalist allows us to trace his progress from cub reporter to sometimes fiery editorial columnist.[11]

The name "Arthur A. Miller" first appeared in the *Michigan Daily* staff box on Tuesday, May 21, 1935 (the "A" stands for Asher, Miller's middle name). In the thirties the *Daily* was printed in seven-column format; Miller had his first byline on May 24, 1935. Based on an Associated Press source, the article is ripe with dramatic foreshadowing: "Anti-Red Bill Sent to Senate." Reporting on the Dunckel-Baldwin antiradical bill, making it a felony to advocate the overthrow of the government, Miller begins his coverage of events in Lansing, the state capital, as follows: "Before a gallery packed with more than 400 protesters . . . some of whom were university students, the house passed the anti–violent overthrow measure while representatives on opposing sides nearly came to blows." The bill passed 61-28, but not before demonstrators in the gallery were heartily rebuked for disorder by the speaker pro tem. "The spectators," Miller wrote, "were mostly opposed to the measure, many of them wearing tags with the slogan, 'Don't pass 262,' on them. . . . Immediately before its passage, the sponsors of the measure seemed to be acceeding [*sic*] to the negative pressure, since they offered arguments only spasmodically."

Miller's reporting for the *Michigan Daily* falls rather neatly into two separate categories: one dealing with campus events and information of a nonpolitical nature, the other reflecting his growing commitment and attraction to progressive causes. His first byline for an original story appeared on October 11, 1935, when he reports on "Mice of Many Colors," an article based on his part-time work feeding rodents in Professor Clark's research laboratory. On November 9 of the same year he covers a story about the Medical School under the headline, "Scientists See and Hear What Dog's Brain Cells Are Doing." Four months later there is a distinct shift in his assignments. On March 1, 1936, he reports on the National Education Association meeting in St. Louis, Missouri. The lead paragraph reads: "Should a teacher bring into [the classroom] controversial social and economic questions?" Two days later he covers the looming 20 percent reduction in state contributions to local relief, unless local governments can make up for the shortfall—a setback for the WPA program that was part of the Roosevelt administration's New Deal. And on March 12, 1936, Miller's byline appears above the fold for the first time as he reports on the Michigan Student Alliance symposium "Fascism, Naziism, and Hearst."

Miller's college buddy Harmon Remmel recalled that in his early years at Michigan the playwright was "always involved with one cause or another." And it was at the *Daily* that Miller soon found it possible to reconcile his journalistic and political interests. That opportunity would come in a signed editorial published on October 11, 1936. Here Miller responds to the following remarks made at the Michigan Union by the vice chairman of the board of Chrysler Corporation, identified only as one "Mr. Zeder": "Hitler is doing a great job, he's carrying on, he's getting his house in order." Fred Morrell Zeder's remarks bring out Miller's sharp irony and social commitment. It was unusual for an editorial to be signed by one member of the *Daily* staff, or to be signed at all, and Miller made the most of the occasion. "In other words," Miller writes, "you mean labor in concentration camps working for whatever you choose to pay them. You mean that labor strikes and efforts of labor to make a living wage under decent conditions are 'crimes against the state.'" When Zeder told the president of the university that he preferred fascism over communism, President Alexander Grant Ruthven (to his credit) responded, "We are not confronted with a choice between fascism and communism, but we cannot survive, we cannot achieve peace without the recognition of our responsibility for the welfare of others." Miller also elaborates and editorializes on Ruthven's remarks: "Fascism has not one iota of 'responsibility for the welfare of others.' So thanks again, Herr Zeder. But we advise if we may, that you change your opinion of the college man. HE is not a sap!"

Miller's final entry in the *Michigan Daily* appeared as a letter to the editor on May 31, 1937, when he was no longer a member of the staff.

Writing in support of a sit-down strike organized by labor representatives in Washtenaw County, Miller lampoons the right-wing position taken by "C.B.C" published the day before: "I think his logic rears up and kicks him in the face." Assuring his audience that they are all "good Americans," Miller concludes this letter by remarking that "good Americans, like good elephants, never forget tea parties, especially the Boston kind. But with one reservation under the belt. The Boston Indians never even built the tea."

One of Miller's stories that did not make it into the *Michigan Daily* concerned an ugly racist incident that took place in sports-minded Ann Arbor in 1934–35. The Michigan football team, which then included an undergraduate from Grand Rapids who would later become President Gerald R. Ford, was scheduled to play against Georgia Tech.[12] The team from Atlanta refused to play on the same field with Ford's African American teammate, Willis Ward. The official story was that Ward chose not to play after Georgia Tech protested his presence and Michigan administrators didn't back him. The actual story was a bit more complicated. Miller's friends from Arkansas, Harmon Remmel and H. C. Riegler, who actually knew one of the Georgia Tech players named "Pee Wee" Williams from high school back in Little Rock, took Miller with them to meet with members of the team, to protest but also to appeal to the athletes' sense of fair play. "Miller was right in the middle of this," Remmel recalls. Not only did the visiting team rebuff "the Yankee" Miller "in salty language," but they told him they would actually kill Ward if he set one foot on the Michigan gridiron. "The Georgia Tech team was wild." Miller was furious. He "went immediately to the office of the *Michigan Daily* and wrote an article about it, but it was not published." Coach Harry G. Kipke quietly sent Willis Ward off to scout another Michigan game in Wisconsin. Remmel said that Miller "could not believe that the Georgia Tech team would have tried to *destroy* Willis Ward—but, I am sure they would have."

Not all of Miller's journalistic writings at Michigan were weighted with so much local political history. He also contributed to the *Gargoyle,* a humor magazine written and published by students on the Ann Arbor campus. Founded in 1909, the *Gargoyle* remains one of the oldest college humor magazines still in circulation. Miller contributed two articles. The first, entitled "You Simply Must Go to College," appeared in October 1937. The second appeared a few months later, in January 1938. "The Rosten" is a satirical piece about his friend and fellow writer Norman Rosten, who was a year ahead of him at Michigan. Revealing a facility for the kind of ironic edge we might associate with a mature Miller work like *The Price,* the undergraduate writer characterizes his reclusive and bohemian colleague as someone who "practically lives on paper clips."

III

The most important writing Miller did as an undergraduate at the University of Michigan was his work on early playscripts, including *No Villain, Honors at Dawn,* and *The Great Disobedience.* Paul Mueschke, the English instructor who was impressed by Miller's response to the classical Greek plays they studied in his class, also noticed his student's remarkable facility as a writer, a talent that seems to have eluded his high school teachers back in Brooklyn. Mueschke referred Miller to his colleague Kenneth Rowe, a popular Michigan professor who taught a number of courses in dramatic literature and playwriting. Rowe was also the author of a book called *Write That Play!,* a manual scrupulously adhered to by students, Miller among them, who chose to enroll in his writing class. Rowe, Miller said, "may not have created a playwright (no teacher ever did), but he surely read what we wrote with the urgency of one who actually had the power to produce the play."[13] It was from Professor Rowe that Miller learned the mechanics of the trade, including such elementary principles as narrative exposition, character development, delayed entrance of a central character, the surprise ending, and the virtue of carefully calibrating the rising action of a play. Rowe made his students read a lot of Ibsen. "You may not have heard of this Norwegian playwright," Rowe told one of his bright-eyed undergraduates ten years later. "But by the time you leave here you will know who he is."[14]

Miller switched his major from journalism to English in 1936, about the same time he enrolled in Professor Rowe's drama course. Set alongside his writings for the *Michigan Daily,* the plays he wrote as an undergraduate display the same commitment to questions of social justice that can be observed in his early journalistic endeavors: only in the early plays Miller struggles to represent the question of social justice within a wide network of moral responsibility. *No Villain,* which Miller wrote during six days holed up in his rooming house at 411 North State Street, is, as Christopher Bigsby notes, the first in "a series of plays in which [Miller] tested his skills and explored his response to private and public issues." The play concerns Abe Simon, a coat manufacturer like Miller's own father, who is faced with financial ruin when a strike of shipping clerks prevents him from delivering his goods. The bank is about to call in his note of credit. Bigsby, who read the unpublished typescripts of Miller's early plays held at the Harry Ransom Center of the University of Texas and the Theater Collection of the New York Public Library at Lincoln Center, efficiently sums up the plot of *No Villain* as follows:

> One son, Ben, who has grudgingly gone into business, supports him, despite his own left-wing convictions. Another son, Arnold, back from college and imbued with Communist theory, will not. . . . The conflict, in essence, is that between private interest and the general well-being, but there are, as the title suggests, no villains; the characters are all victims of a system which alone is evil. This sets man against man and places material rather than human values at the centre of human affairs. Thus, Abe insists . . . that "If you don't get them they'll get you. You gotta be on one side or the other in this business. In any business . . . [i]t's dog eat dog." His son, Arnold, sees things differently: "You've got to get out and on top and look down and see. See what one thing is worth against another. The world is different now than when you were young. It's not there to be made now. Now we've got to change the world!"[15]

Speaking years later to a group of acting students about a scene from *All My Sons,* Stella Adler would characterize this same conflict-in-the-making as "business vs. civilization."[16] In *No Villain* Miller's handling of this crisis is still somewhat tentative, thesis too often upstaging dramatic revelation. But the play securely sets in motion the direction of Miller's work to come. And in one of the most memorable passages in *Timebends,* the playwright remembers the exhilaration of that week back in 1936 when he stayed in Ann Arbor during spring break to work on *No Villain.* When he finished the last page of his manuscript, he ran through the streets of Ann Arbor and then through the Diag, as he felt for the first time "what it meant to be a writer." Crossing the Law Quad and North University Avenue, "my head in the stars," there was for the young Arthur Miller the "magical force of making marks on a paper and reaching into another human being, making him see what I had seen and feel my feelings—I had made a new shadow on the earth."[17]

Jim Doll, the son of Miller's landlord on North State Street, who also lived in the house, was a theater costume designer who answered many of Miller's innocent questions about the practicalities of stage space when the novice playwright was working on *No Villain.* He was also the first person Miller asked to read his play, and he gave him crucial encouragement. Miller submitted the play to the Hopwood Awards Committee that spring under the pseudonym "Beyoum" (all submissions must be anonymous, and to this day students exercise considerable eccentricity in fashioning a nom de plume). *No Villain,* Miller's first submission, won $250 and the Minor Award for Drama. One of the national judges, Alfred Kreynmborg (1883–1966), wrote on May 13, 1936, that the play had "an excellent modern theme, handled with a tender insight into character." He predicted that "Beyoum" was one of the contestants that year "who should be heard from." The two other external judges, Edith J. R. Isaacs and Alexander Dean, wrote similarly encouraging comments about *No Villain.* Miller revised the play a year later and gave it a new title, *They Too Arise,* and entered this version of the play in the national contest sponsored by the Theatre Guild's Bureau of New Plays. He won a scholarship of $1,250. The play was subsequently produced in Ann Arbor and Detroit by the B'nai Brith Hillel Foundation. Directed by Frederic O. Crandall, the Hillel Players presented *They Too Arise* at the Michigan League's Lydia Mendelsohn Theatre on March 12 and 13, 1937. The program for the play featured an ad from Kruger's Kosher Delicatessen and Restaurant located at 233 South State Street, with the motto "Home Cooked Meals Away from Home." But the restaurant, like Miller's play, had only a short run in Ann Arbor. According to Kenneth Rowe, the playwright returned to *No Villain* for a third time during the period from April 1938 to March 1939. This time the play, retitled *The Grass Still Grows,* is a comedy, described by Rowe as "a happy blend of serious and hilarious, sentiment and philosophical reflection." Professor Rowe was now referring to his student's plays as "the Abe Simon Trilogy."[18]

In 1937 Miller won a second Hopwood for *Honors at Dawn,* a play he submitted using the pseudonym "Corona." Mueschke, his old English professor, who served as the internal judge, wrote that "Corona's manuscript is superior to the other entries and compares quite favorably with other full-length proletarian plays of recognized merit. *Honors at Dawn* should be carefully revised and given a campus production if possible." This is another strike play. The conflict advanced here, with its steady emphasis on working-class values and workers' solidarity, resembles some of the best-known drama presented in the twenties and thirties by established New York playwrights like Sidney Kingsley, Elmer Rice, and especially Clifford Odets, whose *Waiting for Lefty* is the strike play above all other strike plays. In writing *Honors at Dawn* Miller draws upon both his experience of university life and the time he spent working in an automobile parts warehouse in Manhattan:

> Once again there are two brothers, representing different responses to life and adopting radically different stances with respect to an economically and socially divided country. Harry celebrates the American dream. The son of a Polish immigrant, he embraces the myths and prejudices of a society whose chief virtue seems to lie in the economic rewards which it offers to those with the energy and ruthlessness to claim them. His brother, Max, seems uninterested in the siren call of success. He is a practical man who takes pleasure in his ability to maintain and improve machinery. . . . [His workmates] are involved in a fight for higher pay and union recognition and persuade Max to assist them by distributing leaflets. When he is seen doing this he is offered a bribe to inform on his fellow workers but refuses, joining his brother at university as a means of avoiding the dilemma. When precisely the same offer is made to Harry by the university authorities, themselves under pressure from the factory owner whose donations to the university give him a hold over the institution, he readily agrees in return for a loan to finance his extravagant lifestyle. His job is to report back on radical students and on a professor whose views have brought him into conflict with the same factory owner.[19]

Bigsby's careful summary of the plot line reflects in part the narrative potential and energy that impressed the external judges for this play, Yale theater scholar Allardyce Nicoll and playwrights Susan Glaspell and Percival Wilde. "Corona has the ability to work out an idea interestingly, logically, and dramatically," wrote Wilde in his report to the Hopwood Committee. Although Glaspell's judgment was far less favorable, the awards committee was eventually persuaded by Wilde's assessment that the "writing is honest, fresh, and stimulating . . . [and] there is a definite illusion of life brought about by good character observation."

Miller entered the Hopwood competition for a third time in 1938 with a prison play he called *The Great Disobedience,* but the judges thought it was "too turgid" to merit further consideration (though the play did come in second). Written as an assignment for one of Rowe's playwriting classes, *The Great Disobedience* stems from the weekend visits Miller made to Jackson State Penitentiary, where his former classmate Sid Moscowitz, having taken only one course in elementary psychology, served as psychologist for the entire prison. His job was to keep "six thousand inmates from going crazy." The visits elicited a strong emotional response from Miller, and he returned to Ann Arbor each time determined to write a crusading social protest play about prison reform. *The Great Disobedience,* Miller said, "was the first I ever researched; I wanted to get out of myself and use the world as my subject. And here was the system's malign pressure on human beings waiting to be exposed."[20]

In Miller's play Victor Matthews, who works as a doctor for a rubber company, is sent to prison for performing an abortion. But the real reason for his incarceration is his failure to protect the interests of his employer. *The Great Disobedience* sees the prison system as "intimately involved in capitalism's efforts to protect its profits and maintain its control."[21] Miller continued to work on his prison play after he left the university; at one point he was even thinking of a streamlined version of *The Great Disobedience* as a possibility for the soon-to-be-dismantled Federal Theatre Project, where his friend Norman Rosten was already working. Professor Rowe, however, urged Miller to move in a different direction, away from the agit-prop mechanics he felt were a dead end for the young playwright. Miller believed he might still be able to save the play if, as he wrote to Rowe, I can "do it direct, clean, Greek-like." He toyed with the idea of working with "levels, lights, two choruses, and verse." Lee Strasberg (whose name Miller misspells) looked at the play and, according to Miller, "praised it." For a time it seemed as though it might "go to [the actor] Maurice Evans." But nothing came of this project and Miller, discouraged, reluctantly abandoned the play.

Arthur Miller's involvement with theater at Michigan does not end with his three famous entries to the Hopwood Awards Committee between 1936 and 1938. Two nontextual instances are particularly revealing: as a recently arrived freshman from New York, he played a nonspeaking role as a bishop in a student production of Shakespeare's rarely performed *King Henry VIII;* and in his senior year he was one of several student members of an ad hoc "Laboratory Workshop Committee." Joining Ellen Rothblatt, Marian Smith, Norman Kiell, and Morlye Baer, he was one of five student signators on a petition—a manifesto, really—they addressed to the university's oversight Committee on Theater Practice and Policy. Their letter, now on file at the Rare Book Collection at the University of Michigan Library and dated January 21, 1938, outlines a series of student-initiated suggestions for strengthening training in technical aspects of theater production. The Rare Book Collection does not contain the committee's response, if indeed there was any.

IV

Armed with his B.A. in English, two Hopwood Awards, and a generous stipend from the Theatre Guild, Miller returned to New York in 1938. He did so with a strong letter of recommendation from Kenneth Rowe addressed to his connections at the Federal Theatre Project. Miller was soon put to work writing radio plays, coauthoring one with Norman Rosten called *Listen My Children.* Unknown to Miller, who felt he was lucky to have a job, the FTP's days were numbered, despite Hallie Flanagan's visionary direction. Her organization was designed to put theater practitioners back to work during the Depression; and it did so by mounting now legendary performances across the United States, including an all-black *Macbeth,* the premiere of T. S. Eliot's *Murder in the Cathedral,* and Marc Blitzstein's fabled musical *The Cradle Will Rock.* Conservative—and provincial—legislators in Washington, D.C., were never really comfortable with federal support for the arts, and it was only a matter of time before what they saw as a left-leaning theater collective had its funding cut off. Miller, among many others, was out of a job almost as soon as he started it. In 1940 the Federal Theatre Project was abolished and Miller went on relief.[22]

It was during these first postgraduate years that Miller embarked on a long correspondence with his mentor Kenneth Rowe. The letters, given to the University of Michigan Library by Rowe's nephew after his uncle died on October 27, 1988, detail the playwright's early experiences back in New York, his attempts to break into the professional theater world, as well as his nostalgia for the support and encouragement he received as an enterprising student at the University of Michigan:

> I can see every square foot of Ann Arbor in my head and it's prettier than this city, but I'm glad I'm not back there. Here one knows the maximum opposition and a man can confront it and learn more precisely what his place is in the world. In Ann Arbor one is a little shy of taking oneself seriously because one suspects that the whole business of collegeism is not quite bedrock secure and that it is a mock-serious game played within an outer world of deadly earnestness. There are no makeup examinations here . . . happily.

During the next two years Miller continued to devote himself to his writing. He was supported in part by the woman who would become his wife on August 5, 1940, Mary Grace Slattery, a Catholic from Ohio he met when they were both activist students in Ann Arbor. She worked as an editor and a waitress while he completed his play about Montezuma and Cortez called *The Golden Years.* Miller wrote to Rowe that since June 1938 he had been struggling with "two plays, a revue, four or five radio scripts, short stories, and three post cards. . . . Of it all, a 4-minute radio sketch and a half-hour radio play have been accepted and produced. Net receipts, $200 less 10% commission, plus $75 for a movie, equaling $255.00." Yearning for success, but down on luck, contacts, and networking, Miller complains, "O the stink of it would pollute the heavens." By 1941 he is working in a box factory, as a scriptwriter for the sale of U.S. war bonds, and as a shipfitter in the Brooklyn Navy Yard.[23]

All the while, between shifts, Miller was developing a series of radio scripts. He preferred working at night, for this left his days free for writing. Between 1941 and 1942 he completed *The Pussycat and the Expert Plumber Who Was a Man, William Ireland's Confession,* and *The Four Freedoms.* None of his fellow workers, a rough-and-tumble group at the Brooklyn Navy Yard, could believe he was a playwright, and Miller mostly kept this information to himself. He was also writing poetry. "I needed it for my plays," he said in a letter to Kenneth Rowe. "Poetry requires a deep feeling for speech rhythm. . . . The only other time in my life when I felt like this is when I mastered geometry."

By the mid-1940s, as Miller became more secure as a writer, and especially after the success of *All My Sons* in 1947 and *Death of a Salesman* in 1949, the correspondence with Rowe began to taper off. But this by no means spells the end of Miller's ongoing relationship with the University of Michigan. On December 15, 1947, he wrote a report from his home at 31 Grace Court in Brooklyn Heights for the Hopwood Awards Committee, this time as one of the national judges for the competition that had first acknowledged him as a young writer. Miller never forgot that. In his 1953 piece for *Holiday,* a magazine assignment designed to trace the change that had taken place on college campuses during the complacent Eisenhower years, Miller looks back fondly on the passion for art, activism, and ideas that characterized his own college experience. The retrospective is reprinted in *Echoes Down the Corridor: Collected Essays, 1944–2000,* edited by Steven R. Centola. Miller takes his title from his stage direction in *The Crucible.*

Miller made the first of his many triumphant returns to his alma mater in 1956 (the same year he married Marilyn Monroe in a quiet ceremony in White Plains, New York), when he was honored as Doctor of Humane Letters. On May 23, 1963, he returned to Ann Arbor to do what he once said he would never do, deliver a lecture at the Hopwood Awards presentation ceremony; why draw out a long speech when aspiring young writers were squirming in their seats and longing to hear about cash prizes? He wrote to Professor Arno Bader, who asked him to speak at the ceremony, as follows: "I swore that if I were ever asked to, I would never speak on the occasion of the award ceremonies."[24] Miller actually used this as the opening line in "On Recognition," the speech he presented that spring at Rackham Auditorium. In 1965 Miller was back in Ann Arbor again, and this time for a very different reason: a well-publicized teach-in that closed down the University of Michigan for three days, part of the nationwide college protests against the war in Vietnam. Miller's daughter Jane, born on September 7, 1944, was a student at Michigan at this time.

In the year 1967, as part of the sesquicentennial celebration marking the University of Michigan's founding in 1817, the college mounted an Arthur Miller Festival, which ran from January through March. Miller served as playwright-in-residence, offering a public address on February 28. And for one week in late November–early December 1973 he was again back on campus, teaching a minicourse on his own plays as adjunct professor of theater; his students were given the rare opportunity of performing scenes from *The American Clock.* Miller's *Up from Paradise,* the musical based on *The Creation of the World and Other Business,* had its world premiere in Ann Arbor the next year; it opened on April 23, 1974, at the university's new Power Center, where it ran for five days. The playwright wrote a program note for his new show:

> I have felt for a long time that Universities were potentially capable of opening exhilarating perspectives for modern theatre, and not as academic exercises. The central fact is that they contain an audience which is seeking rather than jaded, open to fresh experience rather than nostalgic for what it has comfortably known. . . . the problem has been their separation from the professional artists, a separation that impoverishes both.

On April 9, 1981, the Hopwood Awards celebrated its fiftieth anniversary in the presence of an alumni list that included, among others, Dennis McIntyre, Norman Rosten, John Ciardi, Dorothy Donnelly, X. J. Kennedy, Max Apple, Nancy Willard, Ted Solotaroff, John Malcolm Brinnin, and Chad Walsh. Miller, Hopwood's most distinguished honoree, delivered a formal address to a standing-room-only audience in Rackham Auditorium. Before he flew back to New York the next day, Miller spent the afternoon with a now very frail Kenneth Rowe. They both knew it would be the last time they would meet.

Miller was back home in Ann Arbor for two additional university events, once during the inaugural year of the Institute for the Humanities (1987–88); and again in 1999, when the Festival of New Plays under the direction of Frank Gagliano moved for a few years from Carnegie-Mellon University in Pittsburgh to Ann Arbor. To mark the occasion, the provost of the university and the dean of the College of Literature, Science and the Arts created the Arthur Miller Award, a prize of three thousand dollars given for the outstanding new play presented during the festival. Miller was on hand in the Trueblood Theater to present the first annual award: "What young playwrights need most," Miller observed, "is money."

Recovering from a fall, Miller was unable to travel as he had planned with his wife Inge Morath to the University of Michigan symposium marking his eighty-fifth year. Undaunted, he "appeared" via live satellite hookup for an interview with this author in the Rackham Auditorium at 3:00 P.M. on Thursday afternoon, October 26, 2000.

Over the years, of course, there have been many other visits. The most recent took place on April 1, 2004, when he appeared on a panel with Mark Lamos, who staged the Los Angeles premiere of *Resurrection Blues* and was in town to direct students in scenes from Miller's rarely performed plays. What I have outlined here are only the most prominent and more official ones. They speak for themselves—and should make clear that Miller still carries with him the early days he spent at the University of Michigan, and the chance this great public university gave him to become the writer he always wanted to be. When he left Michigan in 1938, he rode back to New York with a young salesman of riding equipment who had sold a lot of saddles in Ann Arbor. The salesman left with the impression that Michigan was a fairly ritzy school; Miller said he had not known a single soul in four years who had mounted a horse:

> As we drove east, through Toledo and Ashtabula, the red-brick roads through Ohio farmlands, I tried to tell him what Michigan really was. It was the professor who, with selected members of his class, held seances during which the spirits of Erasmus, Luther and other historical figures were summoned and listened to. It was the fraternity boys on the porches of their mansions, singing nostalgic Michigan songs as in a movie, and it was three radicals being expelled. It was, in short, the testing ground for all my prejudices, my beliefs and my ignorance, and it helped to lay out the boundaries of my life.[25]

Notes

1. Arthur Miller to this author, October 18, 2000. Telephone conversation.
2. Arthur Miller, *Echoes Down the Corridor: Collected Essays, 1944–2000,* ed. Steven R. Centola (New York: Viking, 2000), 14.
3. Arthur Miller to Enoch Brater, telephone conversation, October 20, 2000.
4. See Enoch Brater, "Conversation with Arthur Miller," October 26, 2000, which appears as a subsequent chapter in this book.
5. Arthur Miller, "Arthur Miller," *New York,* December 18–25, 2000, 122. See also Arthur Miller, *Timebends: A Life* (New York: Grove Press, 1987), 213–22.

6. Miller, *Echoes Down the Corridor,* 16.

7. I am grateful to Professor H. Porter Abbott of the University of California, Santa Barbara, for sharing this information with me.

8. I am grateful to Arthur Miller's classmate at the University of Michigan, Harmon L. Remmel of Fayetteville, Arkansas, for generously relating his memories of Ann Arbor in the 1930s to me in two letters dated October 26, 1999, and April 16, 2000.

9. See Grace Shackman, "Lane Hall: From the YMCA to Women's Studies," *Ann Arbor Observer,* November 2000. I want to thank Jean Ledwith King of Ann Arbor, Michigan, for bringing Miller's connection with the Wolverine Eating Club to my attention.

10. Miller, *Timebends,* 212ff.

11. My information about Miller's writing for the *Michigan Daily* is taken from the archives of the newspaper, which are housed in the Student Publications Building, 420 Maynard Street in Ann Arbor.

12. President Ford recalled this same incident when he spoke in support of the University of Michigan's affirmative action policies in Ann Arbor, April 2000.

13. Miller, *Echoes Down the Corridor,* 15.

14. Dr. Giles G. Bole, Jr., Dean Emeritus of the University of Michigan Medical School and a Michigan undergraduate in the late 1940s, to Enoch Brater in July 2001.

15. Christopher Bigsby, "The Early Plays," in *The Cambridge Companion to Arthur Miller,* ed. Bigsby (Cambridge: Cambridge University Press, 1997), 22.

16. "Stella Adler: Awake and Dream" (1989), produced by WNET for the PBS Series *American Masters;* distributed by Home Vision.

17. Miller, *Timebends,* 213.

18. My information about Miller and Professor Kenneth Rowe is taken from their correspondence; the letters are preserved in the Rare Book Collection of the Harlan Hatcher Graduate Library at the University of Michigan.

19. Bigsby, "The Early Plays," 32–33.

20. Miller, *Timebends,* 91, 93.

21. Bigsby, "The Early Plays," 36.

22. See Hallie Flanagan, *Arena: The History of the Federal Theater* (New York: Duell, Sloan and Pearce, 1940; rpt. New York: B. Blom, 1965).

23. On Miller's work at the Brooklyn Navy Yard, see Brater, "Conversation with Arthur Miller."

24. Letter from Arthur Miller to Professor Arno Bader, Rare Book Collection, Harlan Hatcher Graduate Library, University of Michigan.

25. Miller, *Echoes Down the Corridor,* 30.

Frank Gagliano

The *Timebends* World
Prospect for Performance

I am a playwright. And, from the very first time I read *Timebends,* I thought it would make a wonderful theater piece.

I'll briefly try to lay out how I've been wrestling with the elements in the book—to find some shape that, at the least, could be performed on the stage of my mind's eye; and, at the most, could actually be produced for a live audience. After all, what better way to honor this country's greatest living playwright than to make a play of his life; especially since such a theatrical blueprint as *Timebends* exists to help construct such a piece.

From the start I felt that the collage form of the book—with its fragmenting of time—was perfect for an epic theater presentation. *Timebends* details, and at times dramatizes, a particular life against a sweep of American and world history, and seems to me to render a central character's odyssey to overcome external and internal obstacles, in his search for connections; and in his resistance to, and need to transcend, despair. It also deals with a subject that increasingly intrigues me: the making and sustaining of an artist in an increasingly corrupt, corporate-influenced, American commercial theater.

Among the characters included—and I imagine a dozen or so actors playing all of them—are Brooks Atkinson, Clifford Odets, Elia Kazan, Molly Kazan, Lee J. Cobb, Lee Strasberg, Paula Strasberg, Lillian Hellman, Saul Bellow, Harry Cohn, Marilyn Monroe, Norman Mailer, Orson Welles, Alexander Calder, Harold Clurman, Spyros Skouras, Clark Gable, Montgomery Clift, Laurence Olivier, Kermit Bloomgarden, Brendan Behan, Peter Brook, Robert Whitehead, Tennessee Williams, Mordecai Gorelik, Bobby Lewis, John Huston, Robert Lowell, Sidney Lumet, Marcello Mastroianni, Maya Plisetskaya, Dimitri Shostakovich, Louis Untermeyer, Kurt Weill, Ernie Pyle.

Some of the characters on this list I got to know a bit, later on in my career; most I didn't. But I certainly knew *of* them; and in *Timebends* they appear in scenes and have dialogue and take part in back-story events that reveal much about Arthur Miller, the times he lived in, and his plays. In addition, some of these scenes have pressured beginnings, journeys, and consequences, often in one dramatic arc, and just need to be dropped into the stage epic—almost without editing.

I'm thinking, for example, of the scene where Miller and his *All My Sons–Death of a Salesman* director, Elia Kazan, are attempting to get the famous and notorious head of Columbia Pictures, Harry Cohn, to back Miller's waterfront rackets screenplay, *The Hook.*[1] It is at once a scene that involves a larger-than-life character of authority, a scene of large wants and obstacles—and all of it mired in the oppressive politics of the day. The event journeys to the following consequence: Miller withdraws the screenplay in the face of political censorship and pressure from Cohn. In addition, it's the first scene where Marilyn Monroe appears; standing on the periphery (she'll be a major character later on), but dramatically active *in* the scene because Miller keeps viewing her out of the corner of his eye and because she has to endure Harry Cohn's leering and boorish behavior.

And I'm thinking of the great and terrible and sad scene (332–35) when Elia Kazan (whom Miller loved as a brother) tells Miller that he's going to name names to the House Un-American Activities Committee; and Miller comes to the horrible discovery that had he been part of Kazan's earlier life, when Kazan had dabbled in American Communism—brother-like or not—Kazan would have handed Miller over to the committee. By the way, this same scene appears in Kazan's memoir, *A Life,* and the outline of the event is identical; with Kazan, in *his* book, feeling that what he did was right; but Kazan, to his credit, is also saddened by the breakup. Miller, at that point, was on his way to Salem to do research for *The Crucible;* and there is a final moment in the scene when Kazan's wife, Molly, realizes that Miller is equating what her husband is doing with the witch hunt madness of Salem. It is a horrific moment of dramatic discovery for a character, and one can see and hear the earth opening for Molly, as it had for Miller throughout the confrontation.

There are many great scenes with the arts community elite:

The American playwright Clifford Odets, one of Miller's earliest idols, making an embarrassing and depressing speech at the Waldorf-Astoria Peace Conference (239–43)

A soiree at the salon of the imperious, left-leaning American playwright, Lillian Hellman, with young Yugoslavian diplomats from the United Nations, who plead with Hellman to understand Tito's break with Stalin (254–59)

Spyros Skouras, president of 20th Century Fox, trying to get Miller to cooperate with the House Un-American Activities Committee (again, a scene that includes Marilyn Monroe but by this time, she's Miller's wife and a major world celebrity) (401–5)

So many scenes of character, of confrontation, and of American and world history.

It's logical, I suppose, that I would gravitate toward these—what?—showbiz scenes for inclusion in the epic, since that is my professional interest. And, of course, I also turned to the purely political scenes (those I would head "Such Were the Times")—because I, too, lived through those McCarthy years; and because trial scenes are surefire on stage, and these are some of the best. But, when I returned to the book, I was astonished to gravitate toward a whole other area that involved events that included Miller's family and friends and acquaintances—a rich tapestry of human characters who were later to inform all of Miller's plays and all of whom had lives of their own and often were rendered—again—within dramatic events in the book. They—especially now—had to be in this stage epic.

This list of characters includes Augusta and Isidore Miller (Arthur Miller's mother and father), grandfather Louis Barnett, brother Kermit Miller, uncles Moe and Hymie Barnett, Mikush (the frightening apartment house super), Bill Fox, Mungy the masturbator, Vinnie Longhi, Ezio Tedei, Lucky Luciano, Ipana Mike, Sammy Gasalino, Homer Fickett, G. Mennen Williams, Aunt Betty (the family seer, who predicts Arthur Miller will flunk out of the University of Michigan), Mr. Franks, Sid Franks, Hedda Rosten, Joe Feldman, Mr. Glick, Sammy the Mongoloid, Grandma Slattery—all of whom I had neglected in my first read-through of *Timebends.*

As a playwright I tend to see—really see—characters only when I hear them talk. Generally, in *Timebends,* it's the men who do most of the talking, so I tended to see them most clearly. However, there are moments when, in a single stroke, a female character is nailed to the stage. Here's Miller's mother, Augusta, relating her arranged marriage:

Augusta[2]: Grandpa [Barnett] and Grandpa Miller went into our living room and compared their account books. They were there for four hours, and finally they came out and said I was getting married.

(She laughs—then suddenly clenches her jaw and mutters) Like a cow! (18)

With that—what I call a "pressure shift"—Miller dramatizes a character's ironic humor, bitterness, rage, and subtext, and suggests all sorts of possible dramatic gestures for the actor—and with incredible stage economy. (Miller is, after all, a born dramatist.)

But it's Isidore (Izzy) Miller, the father, an uneducated, self-made man, that I see most clearly; partly because he talks like my late Jewish father-in-law used to talk. Here's a sample: Isidore is describing a play he saw on the road (obviously *King Lear,* starring the great Yiddish actor Jacob Adler):

> *Isidore:* He played some kind of king. You know, it was the olden days. And he had these three or four daughters. I think it was three, maybe four. And he's going to give each one some of his money, and the one that really loves him the most he thinks don't love him. So he ends up half out of his mind looking for his buttons, and he's got nothin' and he's left standing there in the rain, it was some story. But that Adler, there was an actor. He put it over, I tell ya. I seen that show, must've been over forty times, because he was touring for years in it. What I would do, I would go past the theatre and ask them when the last scene goes on, because that was the best scene, when he's out there in the rain. He would belt out a roar that you couldn't bear to look at him. (60)

And here's University of Michigan fellow student Joe Feldman—a firebrand, right out of Clifford Odets—in the 1930s haranguing a *Michigan Daily* student editor:

> *Joe Feldman:* What is this about Nazi planes "allegedly" flying for Franco? Are you trying to become the *New York Times,* for Christ's sake? Do we not have photographs showing the wreckage of shot-down fighter planes with Nazi German identification on the engines?
>
> *Editor:* Anybody could take a picture of anything; and how do we know the picture hadn't been snapped in Hamburg?
>
> *Joe Feldman:* You mean they crash planes on purpose in Hamburg? *Erwachen Sie!* Rouse yourself from the protofascistic funk you're in, stop playing with yourself and turn this into a newspaper. So what if you don't get tapped by the *Times?* Aren't you too young to be so corrupt? (98)

But also effective are those scenes without dialogue. When Miller's mother tells her father, Louis Barnett (who is living with them during the Great Depression), that Arthur is marrying a gentile girl, Mary Slattery, Louis says nothing. Instead, he picks up a clock and throws it at his daughter—just missing her head (5).

And then there is the death scene of great-grandfather Barnett. He is a character of biblical size who would take young Arthur to shul. On his deathbed he calls for a young, new rabbi, who comes to the bedside, leans over the grandfather, and accompanies him in prayers. The rabbi leaves, Grandfather falls asleep, and he seems to be fading. Then great-grandfather awakens, feels under his pillow for the little stash of diamonds he has saved to distribute to his family. They're gone. He bolts out of his deathbed, goes to the synagogue, grabs the young rabbi by the throat, and demands his diamonds back. The young rabbi does so. Great-grandfather goes home, back to bed—and dies (40–42).

Regarding Miller's first marriage: some of the great series of scenes—that I had failed to take interest in during my first reading of the book—take place in the Midwest with Mary Slattery's family (72–84). As soon as Arthur and Mary receive dispensation from the Catholic Church, and in order to satisfy Mary's family, there is to be a Catholic ceremony in Ohio. We are into Horton Foote territory, and are introduced to a new array of rural, conservatively political characters, who are in sharp contrast to the New York Jewish characters we've met. Besides the rich moments that come from the clash of such disparate people—never condescending, by the way (and the sketch of Grandma Slattery is a gem of a portrait in quick strokes; 79–81), there are myriad connections. Shocks of recognition. Scenes against exotic backgrounds. Scenes with major world celebrities and politicians; scenes at the violent 1968 Democratic National Convention, where Miller is part of a delegation from Connecticut; University of Michigan scenes; Miller involved in world headlines. Miller musing about art, about his plays; scenes at rehearsals of his great plays; scenes with cab drivers, young punks, and major hoods; scenes of fall-down humor and even shtick. The small scenes. And the big scenes. Sadness and humor. The twentieth century, with Miller at its creative and moral center—trying to bring it all together; being guilty about it, joyous about it, perplexed by it; having epiphanies; confronting the scoundrels; dealing with failure; with dismissal by the critical elite of his own country; plagued by trying to hold onto his natural status as the perpetual outsider, while compelled to become engaged, the active insider, to fight the fights; at once the observer *and* the participant. And with an ability to articulate it all. And dramatize it.

A hell of a protagonist. No question.

I said earlier that I really get to see characters when I hear them speak. Here's one final example of a speech from the book that gets at the "center of pain" that every stage dramatic character needs (and this is a speech

I'm already recommending to my student actresses, as an audition piece). (Marilyn Monroe is riffing on the death of her beloved Aunt Ana):

> *Marilyn Monroe:* I went and lay down in her bed, the day after she died . . . just lay there for a couple of hours on her pillow. Then I went to the cemetery and these men were digging a grave and they had a ladder into it, and I asked if I could get down there and they said sure, and I went down and lay on the ground and looked up at the sky from there. It's quite a view, and the ground is cold under your back. The men started to try to fool around, but I climbed out before they could catch me. But they were nice and kidded me. And then I went away. (371)

Yes, it would make a hell of a theater piece, this "Timebends World of Arthur Miller" (again—if only in my mind's eye). Perhaps I'll be able to elaborate on my vision as I continue to wrestle with the book's elements, to find its stage shape—and its center.

All this despite the following letter:

> Dear Frank,
>
> About your "Timebends" theatre idea; first of all I wouldn't have either the time or, quite frankly, the inclination to participate in putting it together. In any case, as I am sure you will understand, having already written it once I couldn't hope to confront it all a second time with any excitement. I hate being so disappointing when you are obviously enthusiastic, but I think I would rather the thing remain a piece of prose than picked apart and acted out. I am afraid I can't see an esthetic purpose in it, a hope for a piece that—apart from a certain curiosity that it might evoke—would stand on its own as a theatre work. God knows, maybe—despite appearances—I am really too bashful to welcome a public acting-out of what I packed away between covers, but there it is.
>
> I hope this doesn't set you back too much, but I know you understand that I can't help but give you my real reaction. At the same time I want you to know how much I appreciate your admiration for my work, not least "Timebends." Sincerely
>
> Arthur Miller

Notes

1. Arthur Miller, *Timebends, A Life* (New York: Penguin, 1995), pp. 302–9. Subsequent quotations from this edition.

2. Since the subject of this discussion is Arthur Miller's biography as theater piece, I have taken the liberty of setting some quotes in play-dialogue format.

Mike Sell

Arthur Miller and the Drama of American Liberalism

Though it is generally acknowledged that Arthur Miller is a Liberal, that his writings consistently reflect Liberal concerns, and that his plays find their dramatic sources in the Liberal tradition of modern drama initiated by Ibsen, little has been said about exactly what kind of Liberal Miller is.[1] He's a very stubborn and active one, certainly, as his refusal to name names when called before the House Un-American Activities Committee in 1956, his work with PEN after being elected president in 1965, his vocal opposition to the American military presence in Vietnam, his public support of Soviet dissidents in the 1970s and 1980s, and his opposition to censorship in all forms and at all times demonstrate. That said, we need to draw distinctions within the liberal political tradition, a tradition that is as varied, rich, and contradictory as any long-lived vital tradition will tend to be.

Liberalism is a complex, contested, and situated set of political and social beliefs. The complexity and flexibility of this belief system were the traits that allowed it to survive and ultimately win its running battles with feudalism, anarchism, fascism, socialism, and communism. For example, the term *Liberal* (the general category here indicated by capitals) can be applied to both "conservatives" and "liberals" (subcategory indicated by the lower case) in the United States. The majority of American conservatives and liberals would appropriately characterize themselves as the heirs to a tradition of political thought born from the bourgeois revolutions of the late eighteenth century, a tradition that emphasizes the rights of the individual against state and society, an egalitarian vision of the human species, and a meliorist philosophy of history. In other words, both American conservatives and American liberals are "Liberal" despite their often intense disagreements about the status of specific individual rights, the role of the state and/or social mores in expanding or hedging those rights, the limits of egalitarianism, and the mechanisms that promote and conserve the achievements of historical progress.[2]

Struggles over the meaning and destiny of Liberalism were particularly acute during the Cold War (1945–91), no more so than in the first two decades of the conflict, when Miller established himself as both a significant playwright and as a public intellectual. Needless to say, as a Liberal playwright and activist for many decades, Miller has repeatedly found himself on treacherous, shifting terrain—terrain that has forced him periodically to reassess and reshape his role in the American Liberal society of which he is a committed and undaunted citizen. "This desire to move on," he writes, "to metamorphose—or perhaps it is a talent for being contemporary—was given me as life's inevitable and rightful condition."[3] It's difficult to find examples of Liberal schools of thought in which metamorphosis has been viewed as not simply something to be avoided or overcome, but to be claimed as the very principle of political thought and action. In this respect, Miller's comments mark him as an original Liberal thinker, a decidedly *dramatic* Liberal thinker. Thus, I call Miller a "Liberal playwright," using the capital, to indicate that, though he has generally refused to toe the line of any specific variant of Liberalism, he has continually sought not simply the rights due to the citizen but also the aesthetic and experiential foundations of a truly vibrant, dramatic Liberalism, a Liberalism that would goad and prod society to embrace fully and finally individual freedom, universal empowerment, and progress.

What I wish to explore in this essay is the critical relationship to American Liberalism that Miller maintains. Specifically, I wish to explore how Miller's dramatic texts attempt formally—dramatically—to solve the problems faced by American Liberalism during the Cold War. Throughout this period, the basic principles of Liberalism—individualism, universalism, progressivism—underwent a profound depressurization, threatening to become simply irrelevant to political struggle. Stalinism and the reduced militancy of the American working class seemed to put the lie to the well-worn myth of progress, for example, since progress cannot occur without an agent of progress; moreover, the equally well-worn myth of technological progress proved mated to annihilation, whether that of the Nazi camps, of nuclear missiles, or of the poisoning of the environment. The Liberal individual was no less threatened in an era of mass marketing, mass media, and mass man. Lastly, the "end of ideology" pronounced by Daniel Bell in 1962, the popularization of Freudian notions of the unconscious, and the crisis in the American political process caused by the rise of new social movements during the mid- and late-1960s undermined Liberalism's most crucial principle:

stable, universal standards of moral judgment. It is to this concern that I will turn first.

Liberalism's "preoccupation" with moral foundations, as John Gray describes it, a preoccupation that cannot "rest content with a self-image in which it was only an episode in the adventure of modernity" (45), ensures that Liberal thought will always exist in a state of crisis and, therefore, will always afford rich material for dramatic treatment. Francis W. Coker points out that Liberalism is a tradition dominated at least in part by the notion of negative freedom (the belief that freedom is defined by the *absence* of coercion). Thus, "the particular freedoms called for have changed as the denials of freedom have changed . . . [However,] the constant concern has been with pleas for deliverance from restraints . . . regarded, by some in the community, as unnatural and intolerable."[4] Liberalism is, therefore, a tradition bound paradoxically both by concern for timeless values and by the abiding belief that such values can only be defined in the concrete political contexts and constraints of the moment.[5]

Ibsen's Dr. Stockmann—and Miller's—of *An Enemy of the People* is the dramatic manifestation of this paradox. Like Stockmann, and like Ibsen and Miller themselves, many of Miller's protagonists are preoccupied with the search for moral foundations in situations in which, to quote Marshall Berman quoting Karl Marx, "all that is solid melts into air."[6] This can be said no less of *The Crucible*'s John Proctor than it can of *After the Fall*'s Quentin; no less of the long-separated brothers of *The Price* than of the paranoid salon-sitters of *The Archbishop's Ceiling.* And it can be said no less of the tradition of realism itself, whose fundamental belief in the moral force of individual judgment stands in almost perfect counterpoint to its skeptical attitude toward society, community, history, occasionally even language itself.

Though his work has on occasion pressed to the edge of realism (*A View from the Bridge* and *After the Fall* come immediately to mind), Miller has consistently created characters in the vein of Ibsen. Such characters are more than the sum of their environments while remaining always anchored in them.

Miller's first significant and most Ibsenesque work, *All My Sons,* dramatically hinges on the recognition by character and spectator of a dramatically intense moment of historical and moral coherence; specifically, on the fateful letter bequeathed to the Keller family by a son who recognized all too certainly the relationship of personal decision and community fate. The letter that reveals Larry's redemption-seeking suicide has received its share of criticism; it's a device that Miller himself viewed with skepticism only a few years after the play's premiere, though he has never considered it a flaw. Quite the contrary, Miller characterizes the letter as an emblem of the individual's effort to pronounce his judgments and a mark of Miller's allegiance to the "Greco-Ibsen tradition." As he puts it,

> Whenever the hand of fate reaches out of its grave, it is always somehow absurd as well as amazing, and we tend to resist belief in it, for it seems rather magically to reveal some unreadable hidden order behind the amoral chaos of events as we rationally perceive them. But that emergence, of course, is the point of *All My Sons*—that there are times when things do indeed cohere.[7]

And this coherence is more than a matter of dramatic form; Miller has described *All My Sons* as a "jurisprudence."[8] Though the play exhausted Miller's interest in Ibsenite dramatic structure, it rejuvenated his search for what might be called the "morality of form," a coherent principle of dramatic structure that, for Miller, makes possible an understanding of right action, of the place of right action in a specific conflict, and of the larger significance of righteous action and sectarian conflict to the human community.

In another context, Miller has written about the wrenching, absurd shifts in geopolitical alignments that he and the rest of the Liberal community experienced after World War II. In a comment germane to the topics of coherence, ethics, and judgment, Miller notes that his decision not to abandon his political beliefs came as a consequence not of his certainty concerning his own righteousness, "but because of a sense that there could be no aesthetic form without a moral world, only notes without a staff" (*Timebends,* 160). His musical metaphor benefits from careful consideration; Miller explicitly links morality to the coherent aesthetic and affective experience of music, an experience that is just as impossible to reduce to the textual composition as it is to separate from it. Having abandoned any specific political dogma, Miller has explored a variety of dramatic architectures that would fulfill the classic function of drama described by Aristotle—to create profoundly *affective* links between history and philosophy—while responding to the changing dramatic contexts of his moment. In a 1972 *New York Times Sunday Magazine* interview, Miller told Josh Greenfield that when he wrote *All My Sons,* he thought of "writing as legislating," as though the world was to be ordered by the implications in his work.[9]

That said, there is also an echo of the Liberal concept of negative freedom in Miller's belief in the importance of defining right and wrong through the dramatic exploration of crisis and resolution. Individualism without crisis is incomprehensible to him. In a 1969 interview with Richard Evans, Miller criticized the trend within the New Left that celebrated irrationality as a harbor for individualism. "It is not a promising attitude," he says. "A viable viewpoint—must also include, and have at its center, really, the fact that man deprived of the habit of making real decisions is lessened and can, as we know, effectively vanish."[10]

This negative notion of freedom is not merely a concern of character; it is also a formal concept in the plays. In a notebook containing an early version of *Death of a Salesman,* the young Miller writes that "restrictions, like all tyrannies, exist by default of revolutionary resistance."[11] As Helge Normann Nilsen points out, at first glance this might seem to be a general commentary on the nature of freedom; however, it is in fact a complaint concerning the dramatic conventions of Broadway after World War II, conventions against which Miller struggled. It can be difficult, in a post-post-avant-garde era, to understand just how innovative *Salesman*'s theme and Jo Mielziner's set design were in 1949. Despite the efforts of Eugene O'Neill, Sophie Treadwell, Susan Glaspell, Gertrude Stein, e. e. cummings and the more experimental, if no less moralizing, productions of the Federal Theatre Project, Broadway in the late 1940s was, in Miller's words, in a "classical phase—absolute definite rules" that considered entertainment a priority, moral vision a flaw.[12] Miller has always desired to communicate not just to a coterie; he wants to be truly popular. But how to communicate untimely ideas to an audience that expects merely the frivolous?

The crux of the problem for Miller is *value.* Though his plays reflect a naturalist urge to place characters within a tightly woven net of personal, social, political, and historical forces, they also reflect an essentially tragic commitment to the articulation of transcendent principles based in specific stories of individual and community resistance to fate. The Greco-Ibsen elements in *All My Sons* and *Salesman* are the consequence of a studied resistance to Broadway philistinism grounded in the most high-minded regions of the dramatic tradition—regions shaped by the effort to wed a realistic appraisal of human struggle to a transcendent realm of values. But transcendent values have a tendency to warp perception—Miller's realism is by no means realistic. As he wrote in 1957, the "real" in Ibsen's realism was rooted in a firm belief in a causality too complex to be fully ascertained, a belief that compelled the Norwegian to be "as much a mystic as a realist." "Which is simply to say," Miller continues, "that while there are mysteries in life which no amount of analyzing will reduce to reason, it is perfectly realistic to admit and even to proclaim that hiatus as a truth."[13] *All My Sons,* in particular, emblematizes this realism; as Enoch Brater comments, "All of its mythological paraphernalia is entirely integrated within a naturalistic set."[14] Much the same is true of *The Wild Duck* or Chekhov's *The Seagull,* exemplary realistic dramas that include symbolic elements in their sets in order simultaneously to suggest and delimit a transcendent realm beyond the quotidian details of sitting room and small talk. We can trace an interesting connection here between Miller's take on Ibsen and his efforts to revise Liberalism to account for the changing conditions of the American scene. Just as freedom can sometimes (and *must* sometimes) be defined only negatively, so truth in drama can be defined sometimes only in the delimited absence of rational understanding. In the hiatus of analysis, naturalism gives way to realism, one tradition of Liberalism gives way to another.

If we can assume some sort of significant connection between Miller's Ibsenism and his revisioning of Liberal principles, then we need to pay careful attention to exactly how the mythological or symbolic elements work in Miller's plays, elements that seem to put the lie to the essential rationalism of Liberalism but that may, in some way, serve as the dramatic equivalent of negative freedom. In brief, these elements are almost never more than counterpoint, accent, or negative condition in Miller's work. Continuing his discussion of Ibsen's mysticism, Miller writes that the Norwegian "sought to make a play as weighty and living a fact as the discovery of the steam engine or algebra. This can be scoffed away only at a price, and the price is a living drama."[15] In other words, realism must not be trapped in the realistic, but it must be situated in reality. Examples abound in Miller's work of such nonrealistic elements: the siren-like melody of the flute sounding over the Lomans' quavering Brooklyn, the broken harp in *The Price,* the almost surrealist spurt of feathers in *Incident at Vichy.* However, while these all link the interpersonal anguish and discovery of the plays to the nonrealistic but truthful "hiatus" described by Miller, it is notable that they mostly serve to illustrate specific problems or dramatic conflicts that will either be discussed and debated at some point by the characters (as in *The Price*) or justified by dialogue or dramatic revelation (as is the case with *Salesman*'s flute and the ephemerality of the walls within which the hopelessly nostalgic Willy goes mad). *Vichy*'s feathers drifting about the stage, noticed only briefly by the next group of prisoners, but never discussed by the characters and never juxtaposed to a clarifying stage image or action, are an exception in Miller's work. Even in the putatively antirealistic *After the Fall,* the nonrealistic dramaturgy is framed by Quentin's self-analysis—as if it were his duty to make comprehensible the moments of irrational, almost-but-not-quite surrealist conjunctions and systematic betrayals of his life. Like the analysand in therapy, Miller's characters—Quentin first among them—confront their own confusion and try to make sense of the world and their place in it.

If values have lost their universality in a relativistic age, Miller's plays suggest that the struggle to define and defend them has not. Quentin's talkative refusal of uncertainty and silence is typical; Miller's protagonists never simply resist their environments or bewail their lack of understanding (as Tennessee Williams's so often do, despite the beauty of their laments). They judge themselves and they judge others, often ruthlessly and, as the peripatetic ironies of Miller's plots prove, often naively.

Incident at Vichy thematizes this search for coherence. As the participants in what is basically a debate about solidarity and activism are in ones and twos forced off stage and onto the steam-engined trains of the Holocaust, the remaining characters are gradually compelled to stop talking and act. Here, dramatic movement outspeeds self-recognition, and the play ends in a sudden, jarring act of self-sacrifice and an agonizing tableau: a compromised Nazi officer and an Austrian aristocrat who has just sacrificed his life for a Jew stare at each other in mutual, silent incomprehension, as the next round of prisoners enters the stage. The tension of such a moment is possible only in performance; the traditional Liberal concern with the empowerment and protection of understanding and progressive action is, in *Vichy*'s final moments, put into surging, emphatically dramatic stasis. The incapacity to bring understanding and action into empowering alliance—a dramatic analogue to Liberalism's failure to halt absolutism—is given body and blood on the stage. Drama serves the ends of ideology in *Incident at Vichy* not as a vehicle of propaganda, but as a catalyst of sensibility, an emotional cognate to a political dilemma.

Miller places great value on the role of emotion as a vital corollary to the struggle for liberty and as a vital safeguard against the excesses of reason. He articulates a universal, egalitarian-minded vision of human society based in sympathy (but never sentimentality, which he characterizes as "a leak in the dramatic dike,"[16] and never, ever irrationality). Such sympathy is not only intended to be felt by the audience; Miller's characters, too, must be willing to confront emotional bonds with others, often through harrowing exploration of the self-serving misdeeds they have committed in the spirit of mad love. In *The Price,* the brothers' conflict is in no way resolved by the end of the play—the furniture is still to be sold at a price hardly equal to its sentimental value, and their relationship to their father is no less paradoxical, no less strong for the revelations of the father's greed and dishonesty that have occurred during the course of the play. But they have come to understand how the other experienced and survived the paradox. This allows some degree of sympathy to temper the frustration and resentment they both feel. As a Liberal struggling to articulate the relationship between nature and law (recall Alfieri in *A View from the Bridge:* "I'm warning you—the law is nature. The law is only a word for what has a right to happen"[17]), Miller banks on pity, terror, and sensibility. And he exploits one of the key strengths of realism: the capacity to utilize a highly flexible, but basically naturalistic, dramaturgy to inspire intense emotional responses in audiences.[18]

The struggle for clarity and the necessity of deep feeling—these are the dramatic corollaries of Miller's metamorphosing Liberalism. And they are, as I've suggested, innovative if not atypical contributions to Cold War Liberalism's rethinking of individualism, egalitarianism, and progress. Miller struggled through the same parched landscape as his fellow political activists and afforded Liberalism dramatic form for its practical and categorical crises. Miller has never intended his plays as anything less than public-minded efforts to change the course of American—if not global—political and social life. *Death of a Salesman, All My Sons, Incident at Vichy, After the Fall* and *The Price* stand as more than just significant plays by one of the world's leading dramatists. They are historical documents of the struggle of Liberalism to make coherent sense of itself in response to the political, social, and cultural crises of the Cold War. Miller, in short, is not just a Liberal playwright; he is a public intellectual fully engaged in the continuing debate concerning the Liberal foundations and future of his nation.

As I have mentioned, the tradition of Liberal thought is a tradition that emphasizes the rights of the individual against state and society, an egalitarian vision of the human species, and a progressivist philosophy of history. While it is the lattermost emphasis that I find most interesting as a way of looking at Miller's well-shaped dramas, individualism and egalitarianism are just as significant to the plays. It might be more appropriate to say that individualism and egalitarianism are just as *problematic,* because it is difficult to discover any clear definition of these ideas in Miller (and undesirable to expect any from a dramatist). Quite the contrary, and much like the symbolic elements on his stages, these notions often have served Miller as the very objects of conflict, concern and articulation. *Death of a Salesman* is, as Thomas Porter notes, a subversion of the potent myth of American individualism and its exemplum, Horatio Alger. As he puts it, "The plot structure of *Salesman* dramatizes the failure of the myth by depicting the past and present failures of the salesman."[19] This failure is not simply the failure to sell well and achieve the mythic stature of the successful entrepreneurial capitalist symbolized by Willy's brother Ben; it is also the failure to preserve the magnetic bonds of the family against the depredations of individualism, emblematized by Willy's adultery.

Commenting on *All My Sons,* Tom Driver writes, "Miller's . . . moralism is a good example of what happens when ideals must be maintained in an atmosphere of humanistic relativism. There being no objective good and evil, and no imperative other than conscience, man himself must be made to bear the full burden of creating his values and living up to them."[20] This is hardly new to drama—Oedipus and Antigone had to bear the full burden of their values, didn't they?—but it does remind us to keep an eye on the individuals in Miller's plays because they represent both the foundation of and the threat to the progressive community. Because the family is such an emotionally loaded, magnetic symbol for American society, and because it enables a dramatically economic environment for realism's exploration of crisis and resolution, Miller's ruminations on individuality and community often take place within family couples (brothers, sons and fathers, husbands and wives) strained by the individualistic assertions of one or both of the pair.

In *After The Fall,* Quentin's ability to articulate the contradictions inherent to the relationship of the individual to his society is anchored in the burgeoning feelings he has for Holga, a female character who is both a lover and a friend (a rare find in Miller's work) and a unified expression of commitment to a collective future (the traditional role of women in the Western dramatic tradition). Ultimately, Quentin's willingness to relive the harrowing last days of his marriage to Maggie in order to achieve a more perfect union with a woman who has herself witnessed the greater betrayal of the Holocaust is true to Miller's basic vision of democratic society, "a system that requires a certain basic trust in order to exist."[21] The nasty, brutish society criticized by Thomas Hobbes and embraced by Adolph Hitler creep around this blasted landscape. The terror of untrammeled individualism and self-serving conformity haunts Miller's Liberal landscapes almost as tenaciously as individualism and love (of spouses, of friends, of families) do.

Samuel Yorks notes a similar tension in *All My Sons'* Chris Keller and in the play as a whole. While the older generation in the play is reproached by Chris for its "devotion to private and familial loyalties," loyalties that lack what he discovered among the men with whom he served in combat, "Chris fails to distinguish whether his men were ultimately loyal to the announced ideal or to one another" and so reproduced "the more limited clan loyalty after all. Nor does Miller: his play never resolves its basic conflict."[22] This lack of resolution can be seen as more than the desire to portray a crisis; it is the dramatic equivalent of negative freedom, the singular moment of crisis against which his characters and his audience must define and defend their principles. What is in conflict here has as much to do with ethics and politics as it has to do with the bonds of family, friends, the couple and the community.

What Miller has described as the "magnetic force of the family relation,"[23] a force no less present in the passionate, confusing relationships of men and women in his work, is a force about which the playwright harbors profound concerns, and which marks Miller's work as rooted in the age of Freud. In *After the Fall,* Miller mercilessly compares and contrasts the magnetic force of family and heterosexual love with the magnetic force of the Nazi *Volk*. This isn't as odd as it sounds; Miller brutally dissects the tendency of family, friends, and lovers to betray and victimize the individuals for whom they harbor such deep, irresolvably contradictory feelings. This is why Miller puts on stage a "blasted stone tower" which is, unmistakably, a ruinous, rotted phallus towering over the pits, hollows and crevices of Quentin, who's a kind of modernist Everyman. While fellow Liberals such as Irving Howe were calling for freedom of expression and celebrating the difficult works of the modernists as a harbor from Soviet realism's formal prescriptiveness, Miller was delving into the unconscious—and, according to the principles of Freudian analysis, universal—paradoxes of love, hope, lust and hatred. Hope that trust and love can grow in the hiatus of reason sets Miller's men to work on self-definition in the company of loved ones.

Miller's exploration of the cul-de-sacs of Liberal individualism in the age of Freud and Holocaust, of an individualism that never forsakes its commitment to community, compelled him to take his drama to the border of reason and unreason (to, in short, the emotional intensity of performer in performance). But as his comments on the necessity of decision making and shared standards for the defense of responsible individuality demonstrate, Miller doesn't only rely on sensibility. Miller's commitment to the Liberal vision of historical progress in an era that cast doubt on the very notion of history, let alone progress, compelled him to the more stable, orderly realms of dramatic form. Just as he rejected the Brechtian recoil from emotional identification, Miller also rejected the antidramatic trends that grew around him in the 1960s and placed him, or so some critics would have it, in the rearguard, particularly after the rise of performance art and performance studies. Michael Vanden Heuvel has argued that "critical aversion to textuality" in recent performance work is the consequence of drama's "process of endowing the perceived world with the attributes of a traditional text—the activity of fabricating master emplotments of history, for example, or of constructing holistic integrative frames of reference between people, events, and objects."[24] As a Liberal, Miller can have no truck with this rejection of textual drama; his quest for moral form is precisely the search for a universal emplotment, for a dramatic, coherent, and coincident ripening of self, sensibility and historical understanding.[25]

Though he ultimately rejected Ibsen's plays as a model for his own work, Miller has stayed true to realism's occasionally self-destructive urge to endow the world with the determinant shape of a dramatic plot while endowing it with mythological and symbolic elements that reflect the unique qualities of the individual's perceptions and the specific qualities of theatrical productions. One imagines Miller paying all due respect to the antitextual movements of recent years, but insisting that there can be no freedom in the absence of the textual traditions of the law and the interpretation of the law. The plots of Miller's plays move resolutely toward either the coherent articulation of values or toward the equally articulate delineation of the limits of language. On stage, the plays often demand a combination of stylized and realistic performance from their actors, a demand (as Janet N. Balakian notes in special regard to *After the Fall*) that is rooted in Miller's efforts to present dramatically the links between the private and the public, the past and the present, the textual and the performative.[26] As both a realist who cannot abide the realistic and a Liberal who can abide neither the self-made man nor the conformist, the coincident and coherent ripening of consciousness, values, images and events in the dramatic plot marks for Miller the possibility of a truly humanized history. Fully conscious of the absurdity of the human condition made manifest by the Cold War; fully conscious of the theater of images that seemed to put the lie to the necessity of dramatic resolution and unification; fully conscious of the crisis in individualism, egalitarianism and progressivism in the post–World War II Liberal-capitalist state, Miller has maintained his commitment to the mainstream of the Western dramatic tradition. The consistently strong curtain falls of his plays are symptomatic; they mark Miller's desire to create a dynamic, dramatic climax in honor of the initiation of a just, intelligent and absolutely contingent community.

Notes

1. One exception is Arthur Todras's "The Liberal Paradox: Clifford Odets, Elia Kazan, and Arthur Miller," Ph.D. diss., University of Michigan, Ann Arbor.

2. See John Gray, *Liberalism* (Minneapolis: University of Minnesota Press, 1986), x. Subsequent citations from this work are given in the text.

3. Arthur Miller, *Timebends: A Life* (New York: Grove Press, 1987), 4.

4. Francis W. Coker, "Some Present-Day Critics of Liberalism," in *Political Thought since World War II,* ed. W. J. Stankiewicz (New York: Macmillan, 1964), 377.

5. This is not only true of the Liberal tradition of negative liberty. The positive tradition of liberty, represented by the tradition of political thought stemming from Hegel, has itself had to contend with the shifting nature of political power, exemplified best by its continual efforts to pronounce the "death of history" (as both Daniel Bell in the 1950s and Francis Fukuyama in the 1990s attempted to do). Michel Foucault, in virtually all his writings, also described an end to history; this is why he is often considered "structuralist." His cartographies of crucial Liberal institutions such as law, literature, psychiatry, and the penal system both short-circuit the myth of progressive liberation of all peoples and emphasize the importance of moment-to-moment struggle.

6. Marshall Berman, *All That Is Solid Melts into Air* (New York: Penguin 1982).

7. Miller, *Timebends,* 134–35.

8. Qtd. in Barry Gross, "*All My Sons* and the Larger Context," in *Critical Essays on Arthur Miller,* ed. James J. Martine (Boston: G.K. Hall, 1979), 10.

9. Qtd. in Gross, "Larger Context," 14.

10. Richard I. Evans, "The Writer and Society," in *Conversations with Arthur Miller,* ed. Matthew C. Roudané (Jackson: University Press of Mississippi, 1987), 155.

11. Quoted in Helge Normann Nilson, "From *Honors at Dawn* to *Death of a Salesman:* Marxism and the Early Plays of Arthur Miller," *English Studies* 75, no. 2 (1994): 153.

12. Miller, *Timebends,* 103.

13. Arthur Miller, "The Question of Relatedness," in *Modern Critical Interpretations: Arthur Miller's "All My Sons,"* ed. Harold Bloom (New York: Chelsea House Publishers, 1988), 13.

14. Enoch Brater, "Ethics and Ethnicity in the Plays of Arthur Miller," in *From Hester Street to Hollywood: The Jewish-American Stage and Screen,* ed. Sarah Blacher Cohen (Bloomington: Indiana University Press, 1986), 126.

15. Miller, "The Question of Relatedness," 14.

16. Miller, "The Question of Relatedness," 14.

17. Miller, *A View from the Bridge* (New York: Viking Press, 1966), 65.

18. Brecht recognized the coincidence of emotion and politics in the Liberal

drama and its place in the foundations of the Liberal state; his Marxist dramaturgy consistently and coherently rejected emotional identification because it helped maintain the myth—and by extension, the institutions—of bourgeois individualism.

19. Thomas E. Porter, "Acres of Diamonds: *Death of a Salesman,*" in Martine, *Critical Essays,* 27, 32.

20. Quoted in Michael Graebner, *The Age of Doubt: American Thought and Culture in the 1940s* (Boston: Twayne, 1991), 34.

21. Miller, *Timebends,* 330.

22. Samuel A. Yorks, "Joe Keller and His Sons," in Bloom, *Modern Critical Interpretations,* 20.

23. Quoted in Gross, "Larger Context," 16.

24. Michael Vanden Heuvel, *Performing Drama/Dramatizing Performance: Alternative Theater and the Dramatic Text* (Ann Arbor: University of Michigan Press, 1991), 4.

25. It should be noted that Miller has never been hesitant about revising his texts in the service of effective performance and design. Mielziner's set design for *Salesman* and the tap-dancing Ted Quinn in Peter Wood's 1986 National Theatre production of *The American Clock* have both been given permanent place in the texts.

26. Janet N. Balakian, "The Holocaust, the Depression, and McCarthyism: Miller in the Sixties," in *The Cambridge Companion to Arthur Miller,* ed. Christopher Bigsby (Cambridge: Cambridge University Press, 1997), 120.

Bruce J. Mann

Teaching the Unseen Presence in Miller's Plays

My students enjoy reading Arthur Miller's plays. They are especially drawn to his characters ("Willy's just like my father") and to his intense dialogue and the meaningful conflicts he dramatizes. But class discussion rises to a higher level once students are aware of a striking effect evident in many of his plays. Again and again, Miller creates an unseen presence in the dramatic world—an inescapable force that hovers over the action and haunts his characters, who struggle with it. In *Death of a Salesman,* for example, it is the modern American dream. In *The Price,* it is the regret over life choices made years before. These forces are carefully chosen by the playwright to resonate on several levels—personal, social, political and universal—and as we use them to analyze the behavior of his characters, students begin to see that there is more to a Miller play than meets the eye, that the playwright is attempting to illuminate the moral dimensions of human experience.

In this essay I would like to explore the nature of the unseen presences in *Death of a Salesman, All My Sons, After the Fall* and *The Price.* I will discuss how Miller achieves this remarkable effect and to what purpose. Miller told Enoch Brater in a passage not included in the interview printed in this volume of essays that his poetry emerges in the empty space between speeches. "What we can't see," he said, "is even more important than what we can see." He added that his characters search for God or some sense of "order in the invisible world," a comment also directly related to this study.

The effect of an unseen presence in these plays became apparent to me early in my teaching career when I started an introductory drama class with *Death of a Salesman,* intending it to serve as a touchstone for analyzing our other plays. We then turned to Sophocles' *Oedipus the King* and Shakespeare's *Macbeth.* In the former, I emphasized the invisible but pervasive presence of Apollo, the ancient Greek god of the sun and prophecy, evoked by numerous references to him and to his oracle at Delphi and by the sun itself shining on the audience in the outdoor theater. In *Macbeth,* I discussed the presence of irrational forces, akin to those in the Freudian id, evoked by the witches, whose prophecies fascinate and tempt Macbeth. The effect in each play was of some overarching supernatural force that permeated the dramatic landscape and influenced the destiny of the main character. "Doesn't the American dream in *Death of a Salesman* work like Apollo and the witches?" asked a perceptive student. Yes, the forces are similar, I agreed, and I looked for this distinctive element in other Miller plays.

I found that Miller repeatedly uses suggestive dialogue, props, situations and other aspects of the setting to bring alive these almost supernatural forces that call his characters to account. In *All My Sons,* the hovering presence is Larry's death, which links everyone in the play and serves as an emblem of buried truths that the characters try unsuccessfully to suppress. In *The Price,* the force is evoked primarily by the dead father's chair, an emblem of the choices his sons made and now refuse to accept. In *After the Fall,* the force emerges in part from the expressive image of a concentration camp guard tower that glows in the background at key moments, an emblem of our capacity for evil that Quentin cannot yet acknowledge. These forces are used by Miller to test and measure the moral strength of his characters, whose conflict is less with each other than with the unseen presence working on their minds.

As we study these plays, my students come to realize that Willy Loman, Joe Keller and Quentin, among others, are involved with these forces because of what they seek—a kind of innocence, a state of being that frees them not only from responsibility to others but also from pangs of conscience and awareness of their imperfections. They are essentially selfish, wishing to live in an Edenic world, a paradise. As the plays demonstrate, however, such innocence is an illusion, a false vision of security and integrity that cannot be achieved in a world that exists "after the Fall." Nevertheless, Miller's characters continue to seek it, and the unseen forces in each play reveal their personal strategies—chasing the American dream, burying unsavory truths that threaten their illusory innocence, failing to accept the past and move on, and refusing to assume responsibility for hurting other people. As we read or watch the characters struggling selfishly, we see our own shortcomings mirrored. But by exploring the implications of their actions, we realize the dangers of trying to achieve innocence and the need to take our place in a world in which we are connected to others.

In *Death of a Salesman* (1949), the unseen presence of the modern American dream functions like the witches in *Macbeth*.[1] Willy Loman is drawn to the tempting promises of the mythic dream just as Macbeth is enraptured by the prophecies of "the weird sisters." Allusions to such American figures as Edison, Goodyear, Dale Carnegie, and J. P. Morgan pepper the dialogue. However, it is more Willy's personal influences, the men who most shaped his imagination, that bring the American dream alive: Willy's flute-selling father; Dave Singleman, the old salesman; and Ben, Willy's financially successful brother. These men suggest such archetypes of American myth as the pioneer, the rugged individualist, and the self-made man,[2] and Willy worships them, refusing to see that each is a flawed model (see Hadomi 114). His father abandoned the family; Dave Singleman was one of a kind, as his name implies, and Ben's ruthlessness suggests his lack of humanity.

Throughout the play, a deluded, exhausted Willy clings to the promise of the American dream—an ideal fulfillment that will lift him out of reality (his perceived failure) into Heaven on Earth, a paradise. Even at the end, talking with the ghost of Ben, Willy decides to kill himself so that he can leave a financial legacy for his son, Biff, and thereby reclaim the only time in his life that seemed innocent, the years when young Biff idolized him. "Ben," cries Willy, "he'll worship me for it!"

Biff was trained by his father to answer the siren call of the American dream. But during the play, he finally breaks his dependence on his father and realizes that the dream is empty. In a turbulent scene, Biff explains what he has learned to an uncomprehending Willy, revealing that he has achieved an impressive self-knowledge. But at his father's funeral, he shows that he still has more to learn, that to leave his own innocent world, he must try to empathize and connect with his father by understanding what motivated his life and his suicide. The famous speech at the funeral by Charley, their neighbor ("Nobody dast blame this man"), makes this point, although Biff misses it. Charley represents the healthy attitude toward the American dream—understand it, know yourself and keep things in perspective.

Ironically, one character who is deeply affected by the American dream seems almost unaware of its mythic power. Linda, Willy's wife, has the final words in the play, and her inability to understand why Willy killed himself shows that her value scheme was never shaped by the dream. In the early memory scene with Ben, for example, she disapproves of Ben using force with Biff: "Why must he fight, dear?" What primarily guides her is devotion to her husband as a human being. While

Linda is hardly perfect—she is blind to an important dimension of Willy's life—she radiates human values uncorrupted by the American dream—love, devotion, compassion and empathy. She has never sought Heaven on Earth, only the final payment on the house.

Death of a Salesman demonstrates Miller's mastery at developing an evocative unseen presence. But it was not the first play in which he employed this technique. In *All My Sons* (1947), he created, perhaps unknowingly, just such a presence, and it took the designer of the first production, Mordecai ("Max") Gorelik, to explain it to him. Writing in *Timebends,* his autobiography, Miller recalls that Gorelik placed a small mound in the setting, and the playwright complained to him that the actors were having trouble maneuvering around it. Why was it there?

> "You have written a graveyard play," Gorelik said as categorically as if he were reading each word in lights behind my eyes, "and not some factual report. The play is taking place in a cemetery where their son is buried, and he is also their buried conscience reaching up to them out of the earth."

Actually, the play takes place in the backyard of the Keller house "in the outskirts of an American town." But Gorelik wanted to create a physical correlative for the inescapable force at work in the play; he understood that the death of Larry Keller in the war haunts every character and signifies the buried truths they try to suppress.

Joe Keller is a businessman who hides the fact that, during the war, he allowed cracked cylinder heads to leave his plant and that he placed the entire blame on his partner, Steve Deever. The mistake resulted in the deaths of twenty-one American pilots when their planes malfunctioned and crashed. A court exonerated him, and Joe continues to bury the truth by insisting on his innocence. "What have I got to hide?" he asks at one point. "I ignore what I gotta ignore," he says at another, a sign of his refusal to accept responsibility for the crime. Despite insecurities and feelings of guilt, Joe is determined to preserve his perfect, all-American world with his lovely backyard and friendly neighbors.

Joe's wife, Kate, knows what Joe did, but she loves him fiercely, even as she blames him, and she too hides the truth. Rather than face the possibility that Joe's actions killed their son, Kate clings to the irrational belief that Larry is still alive, since his body was never recovered. When lightning strikes the apple tree they planted in Larry's memory, Kate interprets it not as a sign of lost Edenic innocence but as a sign that the family memorialized him too soon, that he did not die. These supernatural touches

(Miller originally named the play *The Sign of the Archer*) contribute to our sense of an unseen presence, just as the angry orange apartment buildings in the background of *Salesman* suggest a powerful and menacing overarching force in this dramatic world.

Chris Keller, too, buries the truth about his father. He was the only survivor in the war of an extraordinarily unselfish company of men, and Chris feels guilty that he has survived. He decides that he must live up to the moral standard they set. However, he has failed. We learn that, at some deep level, Chris must know of his father's guilt, although he works for him in the factory, makes money tainted by Joe's crime and even assumes his father's values. He has become an idealist who holds everyone else to the highest standard, while he refuses to see any of his own or his father's imperfections. In his own mind, his father must have clean hands, or Chris will be forced to confront his own considerable moral failings.

Like the others, Ann Deever hides the truth. Ann is the daughter of Joe's partner, and she was once Larry's fiancée; she is an immensely likeable character who appears at first to be the play's moral center. But at the end of the play, Ann produces a letter she received from Larry, written the day he died, which proves he took his own life; he had heard about his father's actions and could not bear to live. The letter, which some critics have found too melodramatic, is really an emblem of the play's unseen presence—the buried truth rising to the surface. The letter also reveals that Ann has her own agenda, a selfish one. She has never felt a duty to share the letter's contents with the Kellers, nor has she visited her father in jail to find out what really happened. Instead, she tries to bury the truth about Larry, marry Chris and move away to start a new life that will somehow restore the innocence of her youth.

By the end of *All My Sons,* the truth emerges, and the masks come off. Joe must admit that he allowed the parts to leave the plant, that he lied in court and that he pretended to be sick at home the day of the catastrophe so he could place the blame on Steve. Kate, Chris and Ann must face the collapse of their worlds, too, although Chris, with his idealism, heaps blame unmercifully on his father, never once seeing that for years he helped Joe deny the truth. Confronted with Larry's letter and called to account by Chris, Joe learns the lesson implicit in the play's title, that Larry and the pilots who died were "all my sons" and that he must take responsibility for what he did. But Joe's suicide does not completely clear the air; it seems more a gesture demanded by Chris—not an expiation of the crime—and Chris himself realizes this, too late.

In Miller's expressionistic play *After the Fall* (1964), the looming presence emanates from the various betrayals we witness and from the guard tower of a German concentration camp that dominates the action: "Its wide lookout windows are like eyes which at the moment seem blind and dark; bent reinforcing rods stick out of it like broken tentacles." The playwright wants us to sense the presence of a dark side to our natures—the capacity to hurt, betray and even kill those who stand between us and our desired innocence. We are capable of evil acts, even though we blame others, insist we are innocent and refuse to take responsibility for the pain we cause. This is the lesson Quentin, a lawyer, must learn in the play as he reviews his life and decides whether or not to develop his relationship with Holga, a woman he met and fell in love with in Germany, who radiates strength, compassion and insight.

After the Fall unfolds in Quentin's mind as a kind of identity crisis. At midlife, Quentin has lost his sense of self, and he is haunted by memories, especially those of his two failed marriages to Louise and Maggie. These memories are literally staged before us, showing how Quentin works through his anguish, facing what happened, coming to terms with himself and others, and shaping a new, more mature self. The knowledge frees him to move forward in a relationship with someone who also realizes we live in a world "after the Fall."

At the concentration camp, Holga says, "Quentin, dear—no one they didn't kill can be innocent again," and perhaps this is what triggered the reexamination of his life. He recalls his mother, who recently died, and realizes his inability to mourn her is connected to memories of her betrayals, especially when she called his father an "idiot" and a "moron" after his financial losses in the Crash. Quentin is beginning to recognize that selfishness is at the core of betrayal and other evils, and he sees it in his marriage to Louise, too. In reenacted scenes, we see them hurting each other and refusing to accept responsibility for what they say. It is as if each were in a separate tower, looking at the other, and proclaiming his or her innocence as the relationship deteriorates. Similar selfishness marks his marriage to Maggie. Quentin tries to convince himself he is a Christ-figure, out to save Maggie, the naive entertainer, but he really sees her beauty as his ticket to Paradise. He does not realize until too late that Maggie is inherently selfish, too, a self-destructive victim of a society that overvalues physical beauty, and her addiction is her attempt to achieve a kind of innocence.

In a memory scene, Quentin tries to get Maggie to admit her failure, and in doing so he finally grasps what he himself needs to see:

> *Quentin:* . . . If you could say, "I have been kicked around, but I have been just as inexcusably vicious to others, called my husband idiot in public, I have been utterly selfish despite my generosity, I have been hurt by a long line of men but I have cooperated with my persecutors—"
>
> *Maggie:* . . . Son of a bitch!
>
> *Quentin:* "And I am full of hatred; I, Maggie, sweet lover of all life—I hate the world! . . . Hate women, hate men, hate all who will not grovel at my feet proclaiming my limitless love for ever and ever!" But no pill can make us innocent. Throw them in the sea, throw death in the sea and all your innocence. Do the hardest thing of all—see your own hatred and live!

From this experience, played out in his memory, Quentin finally realizes that seeking innocence is the great sin, that he must take responsibility for the hurt he caused others, and try to forgive himself and others, including his mother and his former wives, and accept his life as it happened.

At the end, Quentin greets Holga, and we sense that their relationship will be different from the others. She has empathy, hope, love and understanding and already knows what Quentin has just learned:

> Is the knowing all? To know, and even happily, that we meet unblessed; not in some garden of wax fruit and painted trees, that lie of Eden, but after, after the Fall, after many, many deaths. Is the knowing all? And the wish to kill is never killed, but with some gift of courage one may look into its face when it appears, and with a stroke of love—as to an idiot in the house—forgive it; again and again . . . forever? No, it's not certainty, I don't feel that. But it does seem feasible . . . not to be afraid.

With this speech, Quentin shows that he has developed a new sense of self. He sees the makeup of the world more fully and seeks love, not the illusion of innocence.

The hovering presence in *The Price* (1968) is suggested by the "overstuffed armchair" and the piles of old furniture packed into the living room of a New York flat. Sixteen years after the death of their father, Victor and Walter Franz meet to dispose of the furniture, and we learn that this is their first meeting since his death. The armchair, in particular, signifies the choices we make in life and how often we regret them and wish we had made different ones. When their father's fortunes collapsed during the Depression, Victor dropped out of college to take care of him, since he seemed paralyzed by his fate. In time, Victor became a policeman and married Esther, and as he approaches the age of retirement from the force, he still feels that his career opportunities were destroyed by his more successful brother, who initially refused him a loan when he asked for it. While Victor chose to stay home, Walter left to pursue a prosperous medical career; but we learn that he has divorced his wife, rarely sees his children, and recently suffered a nervous breakdown, in part because of guilt over leaving their father and his deep-seated anxieties about failing as he did.

The play shows that Victor and Walter want to reconcile, at some level, but the choices they made and their unwillingness to pay the price for them—hence, the title—keep them from overcoming their differences. Each clings to his version of what happened, because it renders him "innocent," free of blame or responsibility. Walter reveals, for example, that he was willing to give Victor the money, but he knew that their father had thousands of dollars in a bank account. Walter also says that he had called the father to ask him to provide the loan money. All this is news to Victor, who believed his father was destitute; but he feels Walter is avoiding blame for his refusal at the time. Every gesture from Walter—he offers Victor a job at the hospital—is turned down, and Walter's intervention in the furniture sale seems condescending to Victor. As the revelations continue to come, including Walter's contention that their family life was loveless and that Victor was afraid to return to school, the brothers' positions stiffen, until Walter stalks out angrily, unable to bridge the gap between them.

One character does grow and change, Victor's wife, Esther. At the beginning of the play, she hectors her husband about getting a good price for the furniture, because she feels cheated by Walter's success and Victor's self-sacrificial life. She "wants money," she says, so that they can finally live well after all these years. We also learn that she has taken to drink and that she is ashamed of Victor's profession; she is annoyed that he might wear his uniform to the show later that evening. However, at the end, Esther talks in a more knowing manner to old Solomon, the furniture broker. She tells him she had always expected that once the brothers met and aired their grievances, a transforming forgiveness would "lift up everyone." She adds: "When do you stop being so . . . foolish?" Such a comment suggests that Esther sees herself more clearly, that watching these two men hold onto their illusory versions of innocence has shown her how she has lived for a similar illusion, instead of accepting who she is. Leaving the room, she insists that Victor not change his uniform, and Miller gives her the following stage direction: "She walks out with her life."

Left alone on stage is the broker, eighty-nine-year-old Gregory Solomon. Part trickster, part wise old man, Solomon exemplifies the approach to life that Victor and Walter's father refused. He loves life and his daughter, whose death haunts him, and instead of the selfish, cynical laugh that Victor's father laughed when Victor asked him for college money, Solomon laughs openly and freely at the end, when he plays the "Laughing Record." Blame and innocence are not in his vocabulary; he maintains a realistic outlook on life and values such things as work, resilience, curiosity and other people. He has not closed himself off to life because of errant choices he made long ago.

My students, using the unseen presences as a measuring rod, probe the characters in Miller's plays in this way, especially to determine their motivations. However, I sometimes find that, in our final discussions, they make harsh judgments: Joe Keller, for example, was a bad father. Shouldn't he pay for his crime? And Willy Loman is not much better. I understand such conclusions, but I remind them that there is a reason Miller's characters resemble their own fathers, mothers, uncles and brothers, and that in the Requiem of *Death of a Salesman,* Charley tells Biff pointedly, "Nobody dast blame this man." I encourage students to consider the nature of the unseen presences again and investigate why they exist. What kind of a society promotes the irrational, unattainable modern American dream? What kind of society links profits with war materials? What kind of society promotes individual success more than community responsibility? What kind of world makes us avoid self-knowledge? While we should criticize individual characters, we should also criticize the society in which they live.

Like Fitzgerald's *Great Gatsby* and Steinbeck's *Grapes of Wrath,* Miller's plays take the shape of a jeremiad (see Bercovitch 3–16). As we have discovered, the unseen presences in *Death of a Salesman, All My Sons, After the Fall* and *The Price* reveal a selfishness that modern American mythology encourages, the desire for innocence. Miller's plays urge us to look at ourselves and our own world and strive to make it better by adopting such values as responsibility, community, love, compassion, empathy, understanding and self-acceptance. These, he argues, should be the unseen spiritual forces that guide our lives, not our desire for the dangerous illusion of innocence.

Notes

1. See "Finding Himself: Echoes of *Macbeth* in *Death of a Salesman,*" an unpublished master's project by Kathy S. Jegla, Oakland University, 1994.

2. For an extensive discussion of American individualism, see Robertson, 127–211.

Works Consulted

Bercovitch, Sacvan. *The American Jeremiad.* Madison: University of Wisconsin Press, 1978.

Griffin, Alice. *Understanding Arthur Miller.* Columbia: University of South Carolina Press, 1996.

Hadomi, Leah. "Dramatic Rhythm in *Death of a Salesman.*" *Willy Loman.* Ed. Harold Bloom. New York: Chelsea, 1991. 112–28.

Miller, Arthur. *After the Fall.* Final stage version. New York: Penguin, 1980.

———. *All My Sons.* New York: Dramatists Play Service, 1974.

———. *Death of a Salesman.* New York: Penguin, 1984.

———. *The Price* in *The Portable Arthur Miller.* Ed. Harold Clurman. New York: Viking, 1971.

———. *Timebends: A Life.* New York: Grove, 1987.

Robertson, James Oliver. *American Myth, American Reality.* New York: Hill and Wang, 1980.

Wells, Arvin R. "The Living and the Dead in *All My Sons.*" *Modern Drama* 7 (1964): 46–51.

Patricia D. Denison

All My Sons
Competing Contexts and Comparative Scales

For over half a century, Arthur Miller's *All My Sons* (1947) has served as an exemplary instance of melodramatic plotting and prototypical realistic setting.[1] With the action of the play set in Joe Keller's 1940s suburban backyard, the world "green with sod" is, indeed, a decidedly familiar one (5).[2] Here, family secrets, hidden in the past, eventually emerge into the light of the present day, aided by repeated coincidence in a linear plot that produces predictable resolution. When, in the final scene, Joe Keller judges his own terrible "mistake" in the past (28), it is as though the play has presented to a jury one self-evident truth: that the consequences of individual actions extend logically and seamlessly from the local context in which they occurred to the much larger social context that includes all of us.

In the onstage world, not until the last act is the evidence finally in on Joe Keller, businessman, and judgments are then made. In the offstage world, from the 1940s to the 2000s, the evidence has long been assumed to be in on Arthur Miller, playwright, and one judgment recurs: "Miller is willy-nilly a moralist—one who believes he knows what sin and evil are."[3] Numerous theatergoers, practitioners, and critics have agreed with this judgment, made in the 1970s by Harold Clurman, codirector of the Group Theatre in the 1930s and producer of *All My Sons* in the 1940s. For admirers and detractors alike, certainty rather than contingency dominates much of Miller's work. As Clurman observed, "It is the moral stance in Miller, with its seemingly punitive bent, which causes a certain resistance to his work in some quarters,"[4] and such resistance continues, even in the response to Howard Davies' splendid revival of *All My Sons,* which opened July 6, 2000, at the National Theatre, London. Most reviewers lavishly praised the production—"superb," "tremendous," "a revelation"[5]—yet some complained of a blatant "Miller Message" in the play. As Charles Spencer puts it, "'Will you stop talking like a civics book' says a character in *All My Sons,* but Miller, the self-proclaimed 'impatient moralist,' can't stop talking like a civics book."[6] Another reviewer grumbled, similarly, that Miller the moralist "lets us know that All Will Be Made Clear, and lets us know most of What Will be Made Clear."[7] Such comments need to be taken seriously, as diverse character viewpoints and differing moral perspectives in *All My Sons* do indeed appear to converge.

But what is often overlooked is that in *All My Sons* character, action, and set repeatedly invoke other, less ordinary, contexts. While foregrounding a familiar context, Miller invites us to consider less familiar contexts such as distant battlefields and invisible cosmologies. In a set supplemented with multicontextual meaning and a dialogue charged with competing values, the local realistic environment is not a final destination but a point of departure for realms in which other values are embedded and from which other perspectives emerge.

While discussing in 1989 "the question of what is real, how you measure the real," Miller refers us back to *All My Sons:*

> That play took great pains to create a veritable backyard, and people sitting around having very ordinary conversations—the well-known norms of suburbia. . . . I begin with an equilibrium and something tips that equilibrium and interprets it as a result.[8]

What tips the equilibrium for audience and characters alike are not just the revelations regarding Joe's business decision during World War II, but the information from a variety of sources that affects how we view it. Our challenge is to make sense of the verbal and visual dimensions of a drama that take us through the apparently ordinary to a variety of extraordinary contexts. Our task is to move within and among convergent and divergent perspectives that emerge through the characters and action in this "veritable backyard." The contexts range from familial to cosmological, from individual to communal, from peacetime to wartime, from national to international. What is important here is that every time the context changes, the "equilibrium" shifts, for the values brought to bear upon the situation have themselves changed along with the situation. And in a play that is very much about the process of interpreting and judging, this is a critical point. For this play, like many Miller plays, deals not with delayed judgment upon a single moral axis, but with emerging and evolving judgments on a variety of moral axes.

In effect, we, along with the characters, are invited to judge the judgment Joe Keller makes on his own "mistake": his decision to ship defective airplane parts from his factory to the war's airfields, resulting in the death of twenty-one pilots in Australia. From the outset, the action and setting of the play do two things simultaneously: they reveal the causal chain that leads to Joe's suicide, and they present the contextual complexity that puts that judgment in question.

Three and a half years before the action of the play begins, Joe and his partner were arrested for their wartime crime; a week later, Joe's oldest son, Larry, a pilot, was declared missing in a plane crash off the coast of China. As the play opens, lightning has struck a tree planted as Larry's memorial, and in the Kellers' back garden remains "the four-foot high stump of a slender apple tree whose upper trunk and branches lies toppled beside it, fruit still clinging to its branches" (5). The damaged tree, eminently visible on stage, disturbs the realism of the set by inviting characters and audience alike to consider whether it has symbolic significance.[9] Kate Keller, bolstered by a faith in astrology and cosmic forces, reaches to those larger contexts to insist that she is unquestionably "right" to read this storm damage as a certain sign that her son Larry is still alive. To the skeptical she replies, "Laugh, but there are meanings in such things" (20). Her younger son, Chris, sticking to the context of a local realism, counters, "The wind blew it down. What significance has that got?" (18). His question reverberates throughout the action of a play that anchors itself in a realism that repeatedly implicates other values.

In Howard Davies' revival, William Dudley's acclaimed set design paid precise attention to factual detail, yet also provided modes of access to other realms. With the dialogue charged with competing values, it seems entirely appropriate that the set should be saturated with multicontextual meaning. Paradoxically, the more realistic the set seemed, the more it gave access to realms that lie beyond the confines of that form of realism. With real parsley growing in the garden ready to be picked by Sue, with lawn chairs strewn on the real green sod, and with colorful decorative lanterns hung on the trellis, the Kellers' "veritable backyard" seemed cosy and familiar in the Cottesloe Theatre (the NT production extended its run in the much larger Lyttleton Theatre). Yet the scales of value invoked in that intimate space onstage implicated significantly larger frames of reference offstage. Davies' production took no time in transporting the audience from the local, realistic landscape to otherworldly spaces. By deciding to stage Kate's "so real" dream (18), even before a word of dialogue was spoken, Davies immediately introduced the audience to, and unsettled them with, the invocation of awesome cosmic forces. As a loud and eerie sound, much like the roar of an airplane engine, rumbled above, a strong wind rustled the weeping willows that hung from the balconies, much like Greek garlands or laurel wreaths honoring valiant soldiers. Kate walked below, in her bedroom slippers, in the darkness, on the lush green sod. She, and we, watched as lightning struck the tree planted in Larry's memory and a branch fell—into the lap of a startled member of the audience the night I was there. What significance, we wondered, has that got? The scene then shifted suddenly into the most commonplace of dialogue, with pipe-smoking Jim searching for his tobacco and Joe reading the Sunday want ads.

As the action approaches the suspenseful final moments of the play, connections between disparate domains have multiplied, and we have not attended well if we conclude that they have acquired only linear value. We learn not only that Larry is indeed dead, as Chris believes, but also that his death, rather than being accidental, is related to his father's "mistake" in a way that invites us to revisit the fallen tree in the family backyard. Is the basic causal factor in this chain of events human error or cosmological fate, or are there alternative answers to be found in the many other contexts invoked that lie between the human and the cosmological realms? The letter kept secret until now by Ann,[10] reveals that Larry, after reading in the papers that his father's "mistake" had caused the death of twenty-one pilots, purposefully crashed his plane into the sea. As the play opens, more than three years later, Joe is "exonerated" for his crime (26); his partner, Steve Deever, still remains in jail for Joe's "mistake," and Steve's daughter, Ann, and the younger Keller son, Chris, are contemplating the possibility of marriage. Not until Ann forces Kate to read Larry's letter does Kate finally admit that Larry is dead and thus let Chris go. And not until Joe reads Larry's letter does he accept responsibility for past action whose consequences extend beyond his own family. The sound of Joe's gun is heard offstage, but it is important to focus on the fact that the action does not conclude with that judgment and death. The play ends not with Joe's decision to kill himself, but with the decision of Ann and Larry's brother Chris to bridge their family differences and go on together. The final word of the play—Kate's "Live"—reminds us that the task of reclaiming the past and taking "up our lives again" has been taken on by Chris and Ann (69, 18). And their mode of commitment is consistent not with the apparently singular realism of the set, but with the competing values invoked by the play's action and dialogue, and with differing ways of relating them.

Miller himself has described *All My Sons,* with its suspenseful revelations of past secrets, with its high melodrama and understated realism, with its "consecutive" rather than concurrent "actions,"[11] as his "most Ibsen-influenced" work. Citing Ibsen's "methodical unravelling of motives and the interplay of social and psychological causation,[12] Miller credits his nineteenth-century predecessor for skillfully using a plot-dominated, well-made play structure in the service of a much more complicated psychological realism. A century after Ibsen's era, "the taste for 'real' plays . . . has begun to stir again," Miller asserts in 1992; yet "there are still old-fashioned critics who think that anything that has a beginning and end is out of date. . . . but life, of course, includes not only surprise but the consequences flowing from our actions."[13] It is the linking of predictability and surprise in a variety of ways that makes Miller's plays different from the melodrama whose surprises are merely mechanical. When Miller talks about playwriting, he interweaves issues of dramatic structure and social structure. When he links "social and psychological causation" to the "consequences flowing from our actions," he reminds us of the issue of "relatedness" in the context of variety that he has insisted is central to an understanding of *All My Sons* and many of his other works.

Not only have Miller's terms "relatedness" and "connection" become critical commonplaces,[14] but so has Miller's reference to the play's "Greco-Ibsen form."[15] Although some might hastily dismiss the form as merely old-fashioned, Miller, intrigued by the "important question of form and meaning,"[16] and well aware that critics and commentators, like most of the rest of us, are lazy people, challenges us to tease out the implications of forms that can incorporate both causality and contingency. Pointing out that he "has no vested interest in any one form," as the variety of forms he has used displays, he urges us not to overlook, let alone dismiss as "a wooden notion," Ibsen's "insistence upon valid causation." "This is the 'real' in Ibsen's realism," asserts Miller, "for he was, after all, as much a mystic as a realist."[17] This recognition that the mystic world of the extraordinary and the realistic world of the ordinary can coexist is fundamental to any attempt to understand and situate the realistic aspect of Miller's work. For a dramatist like Miller, as much interested in the mysterious as in the explicable, the challenge is "not to make complex what is essentially explainable; it is to make understandable what is complex without distorting and oversimplifying what cannot be explained."[18] We should not, therefore, be surprised to find Miller, whatever his investment in conventional realism, praising the mysterious "prophetic" Greek element of the Group Theatre. While acknowledging the "vagueness" of the term "prophetic," Miller nonetheless applauds the ensemble-based Group Theatre for its affinity with Greek drama, in which "religion and belief were at the heart of drama."[19] Here, as Miller reclaims an earlier form of drama, he seeks to reconnect the security of "belief" with the many contingencies brought to bear upon it by actors/characters, the audience and himself as a young playwright in the 1940s. Causality, contingency and belief are capable of being related in a variety of changing ways.

How, he muses, can a dramatist make visible not so much the ordinariness but the "wonder" of belief that was so common in prophetic Greek drama? How can one situate twentieth-century wonder in a world in which contingency and certainty seem so difficult to reconcile? How, indeed, can one locate wonder in the ordinary world?

In *The Man Who Had All the Luck* (1944)—the premiere closed on Broadway after a few days—Miller invested heavily in abstract "writing wonder," but as he later acknowledged, it did "not make sense to common-sense people." Yet Miller's fascination with wonder did not diminish, for he had, he insisted, "always been in love with wonder, the wonder of how things and people got to be what they are."[20] In his next play, *All My Sons,* painstakingly written over two years, in contrast to his earlier plays written in a matter of a few months, Miller gives concrete form to abstract wonder by having it emerge from the precise detail of a variety of ordinary world contexts. This methodical attention to detail won him the 1947 Drama Critics Circle Award, but the more important point is that the carefully crafted "geometry of relationships" in *All My Sons* enables wonder to "rise up like a mist, a gas, a vapor from the gradual and remorseless crush of factual and psychological conflict." His model here was not just Ibsen or the Greeks but also Dostoyevsky, *The Brothers Karamazov,* for in this "great book of wonder . . . one finds the thickest concentration of hard facts."[21]

Like a cultural anthropologist whose work entails "thick description,"[22] Miller displays, visually and verbally, a richly textured environment in the Keller's "veritable backyard." The house, "nicely painted, looks tight and comfortable, and the yard is green with sod" (5). In Davies' revival, Dudley's set includes a three-story white frame house, with Victorian glass in the windows and a rocking chair on the front porch, rising impressively above the real grass growing on the stage of the Cottesloe Theatre. In the opening scene newspaper-reading, pipe-smoking, coffee-drinking, and donut-eating men talk together on the grass, and the real grass carried such visual significance that one reviewer was convinced that "the dew began falling after the interval."[23] Indeed, "As twilight falls," after the interval, we see Chris "sawing the broken-off tree" and Kate crossing the dewy grass, carrying "a tray of grape-juice drink in a pitcher, and glasses with sprigs of mint in them" (35). But it is from this realistic "thick description" of one world that the wonder of worlds beyond it emerges, initially in prosaic terms, but with steadily extending implication.

From the very outset, detailed stage description itself draws our attention to the interconnected wonder and want of the characters. Though Joe Keller is "a heavy man of stolid mind and build," he reads the Sunday want ads "with wonder," hoping to discover "what people want." He is, we are told, someone "for whom there is still wonder in many commonly known things" (5–7). His son Chris, "like his father, solidly built, a listener," reads the book section "to keep abreast of [his] ignorance" while his father "shakes his head," marveling that new books, "all different," come out every week (10–11). On this slow-moving, sleepy Sunday morning, in a detailed realistic setting, a key question emerges about what lies beyond the setting: how is what you want and believe related to what others want and believe? Within the play's causal plot and linear structure, the "trouble" of belief rather than the security of belief gains greater and greater prominence:

> *Frank: (Peeved.)* The trouble with you is, you don't *believe* in anything.
> *Jim:* And your trouble is that you believe in *anything.* (8)

Between these two poles, Miller, and his characters, struggle to situate Greek-like prophetic belief. In its most trivial form, for Frank, it seems you simply need a horoscope and trust in cosmic forces to establish your beliefs. And Kate is more than ready to grasp at belief derived from Frank's reading of the stars to confirm her conviction that "it would be practically impossible for him [Larry] to have died on his favorable day" (7). But other neighbors in nearby spaces situate belief differently. Doctor Jim Baylis, for instance, the candidate for *raisonneur,* if there were one dominant context, scoffs at the possibility of discovering truth in the "stars," but, married to a "too . . . too . . . realistic" wife, he himself longs to discover worlds that lie beyond "the condition which prevails" (9). How far beyond is never clear to us and never reached by him. A successful doctor, he had hoped in his younger years to do "medical research. Discover things," but now he "always sees the bars in front of him" (37). And his wife Sue, a practical nurse, seems determined to limit not just his, but everyone's horizons to hers. She warns Ann that the Kellers' son Chris, whom Ann intends to marry, is a danger to everyone with his "phony idealism," which unsettles everyone by reaching beyond all practical horizons and making "people want to be better than it's possible to be" (38). Sue's defensive preference for making do with what one has at hand, rather than reaching toward what might challenge the status quo, makes her a voice in the play directly opposed to that of the two people whose actions provide the conclusion to the action: Chris and Ann. Ann, whom Sue later describes as a "female version" of Chris (39), responds to Sue's accusation that Chris "makes people want to be better than it's possible to be" by asking simply, "Is that bad?" (38). It is, of course, an unanswered question, emerging in a play whose various contexts invoke a variety of standards of value that invite complex judgments.

What do we make, for instance, of Chris when he valorizes the extraordinary behavior of his fellow soldiers in battle, but then concedes that only the "practical" ones came home alive? Is there, then, no place in this world for heroism and idealism? Is Chris clear-headed or confused when he eventually faults himself for becoming "practical" (66)? Is Joe then right when he defends himself to Chris, by asserting that "a man can't be a Jesus in this world!" (68). If Joe believes that it is impossible to be God-like in the human world, is Chris then right to argue that his father, having failed to be a Jesus figure, is therefore more bestial than an animal? When Chris accusingly demands of Joe, "Now tell me where you belong," we have a variety of domains and a variety of benchmarks to consider: those of the animal world (alley cats and big dogs), the human world (family and business), the national (home front and factory), the global (war front and international community), and beyond (cosmic fates and greater powers).

> *Chris: (With burning fury.)* For me! Where do you live, where have you come from? . . . Don't you have a country? Don't you live in the world? What the hell are you? You're not even an animal, no animal kills his own, what are you? . . . Jesus God, what must I do? (59)

Torn between fixed and changing standards, Chris looks "all night for a reason to make him suffer," and fails, unable to find a counter to his father's desperate plea, "Who worked for nothin' in that war? . . . Half the Goddamn country is gotta go if I go [to jail]!" (67). Between the idealism of self-sacrifice and the pragmatism of self-acceptance, Chris, Ann, and the audience seek a middle ground.

In a dialogue saturated with the claims of contested and contesting contexts, including the home front versus the war zone, the ordinary world versus the extraordinary world, and the human world versus the heavens, the audience can, in effect, see what some of the characters seem incapable of seeing—that contested and contesting spaces might be reconceived in complementary, rather than oppositional, relationships. And it is in the often overlooked character of Ann that this mode of thinking is gradually exemplified.[24] As we saw earlier, Miller is fascinated with the possibility of creating an evolving "geometry of relationships" in *All My Sons.* By situating abstract wonder in relation to "the thickest concentration of hard facts" in a variety of contexts, vague abstraction becomes accessible through concrete detail.[25] By placing belief on a wide-ranging continuum, Miller seeks to relate the trouble of belief to the wonder of belief. And it is the mobility of belief emerging from changing contexts that gives philosophy a role in the play it might not otherwise earn.

Initially, philosophizing, abstract thinking and idealism are all linked. In these terms, Kate compares Frank, who stayed at home during the war with his family deferment, to the three younger "Eagle Scouts," Larry, Chris and the Deevers' son, George, who went off to war. Instead of looking after themselves and their families, they thought big and lost big.

> *Mother:* You had big principles, Eagle Scouts the three of you; so now I got a tree, and this one, *(Indicating Chris.)* . . . Andy Gump has three children and his house paid off. Stop being a philosopher, and look after yourself. (52)

When George Deever sees his father in jail, then visits the Kellers and starts sounding like "The Voice of God," we see the danger of abstract thought, prematurely fixed belief and premature judgment. Here, the certainty of "big principle" thinking can blind rather than enlighten. And Miller, himself an acknowledged "impatient moralist,"[26] is well aware that a principle, no matter how admirable, can preclude rather than advance thought. "Nothing," Miller insists, "is as visionary and blinding as moral indignation."[27] But it is Ann who chiefly exemplifies the refusal to be bludgeoned by it. When sanctimonious George, who "knows" for certain what is right for his sister, declares, "Everything they [the Kellers] have is covered with blood. You're not the kind of girl who can live with that. Get your things" (47), Ann resists the simple picture. She "is twenty-six, gentle but despite herself capable of holding fast to what she knows," and she refuses to leave (21). But "what she knows" does not prevent her from moving beyond it.

In a play that grounds "prophetic" belief in everyday realism, we would be foolish to ignore the young woman who bluntly speaks her mind not only to idealistic philosophers and pragmatic realists, but to a family struggling with the substantial pain of bereavement. In this world in which "war has changed all the tallies" (10), "Larry's girl" is not only part of the change but also an enabler of further change (14). In this "veritable backyard" with "people sitting around having very ordinary conversations . . . something tips that equilibrium and interprets it as a result."[28] Ann Deever, whom Sue described as the "female version" of idealistic Chris Keller, demands our attention as an equilibrium-tipping "something." Attention is usually paid to Chris in that role, and rightly so in a play entitled *All My Sons,* but this "gentle" fiancée of both sons enters the play not only ready to speak bluntly but, with concealed letter in hand, to act if need be, to take on the role of an agent of change in the most complex of circumstances.

Kate had earlier put it directly, to Chris and George, that "the trouble with you kids is you *think* too much" (51). Her concern is with abstract philosophy, with unpractical belief. But thought can travel to realms beyond the here and now that have practical consequences. So when Kate declares, "certain things have to be, and certain things can never be," Ann "turns trembling" and replies firmly, "No, Kate" (24). When Ann's brother, the pontificating "Voice of God," bullies her, she responds directly, "Go, George!" And when Kate repeatedly refuses to listen and learn, Ann hands the letter to Chris, who demands, in turn, that Joe "listen!"

With the storm-damaged tree still visible on stage, we sit and listen too, ready to make our own judgments of the accumulating evidence, as Chris turns to his father and says:

> This is how he died, now tell me where you belong . . . You listening? . . . listen! (68)

In the context of the whole action of this play, to what realistic or symbolic realm does Joe indeed "belong"? To what historical context, to what community, on which scale of value and to which species? The title of an earlier version of the play, *The Sign of the Archer,* might give us some clue not only how to judge Joe's final judgment on himself but also how to shape our judgment of the play. In the earlier version, as Miller notes, Kate dominated the action; "more precisely, her astrological beliefs were given great prominence, but in the final version, mysticism gave way to psychology."[29] Kate commissioned Frank's horoscope in the hope that a predetermined pattern of inevitability would emerge, but in the action of this play it is never clear that a single factor (the day on which one is born) determines one's fate. When Frank asks, "Is it junk to feel that there's a greater power than ourselves?" the answer is possibly yes, and possibly no (56). Although Kate desperately longs for the apparently fixed truth of a horoscope, Ann is ready to live a life with moving variables and changing perspectives. When, in the final climactic act, Ann refuses to leave with her bag (a bag that Kate has, unbeknownst to Ann, already packed), attention shifts again to this enigmatic young woman who seems capable of making hard choices and capable, above all, of listening and learning. If Ann were to have an astrological model, it would be one of moving among constellations, many of them highly complex and all of them subject to unpredictable change. And it is important to recognize the analogies drawn here among dramatic structure, social structure and the structure of an individual life. Rather than living life like David Beeves in *The Man Who Had All the Luck,* who believes that a "law was written in the sky somewhere" (179),[30] or like Kate, who searches for a "sign of the archer" that will provide a definitive answer, Ann listens to and queries the comparative values of others and looks for ways of moving beyond them.

On a precisely detailed, ordinary summer day in "our era," this small garden space is inhabited not just by people situated in it, but by the memories, hopes, fears, desires and beliefs that they bring with them from other contexts. The apparently climactic letter that Ann carries from her dead fiancé is only one of many intrusions from other times and other places. The question of "where you belong" is thus as much an invitation to explore as a demand to identify a final home. And Ann, like the others, must locate provisional understanding on the road to more firm belief. Filled with scorn for her jailed father, she visits the Kellers unaware, at first, of Joe's "certain talent . . . for lying" and the consequences for her father (61). Determined, though, not to lead the "lonely life" that Kate has prescribed for her, Ann stays when George goes (64). For Ann and Chris, the either/or of oppositional thinking eventually gives way to comparative rather than absolute judgments. Chris replies to his father's "Why am *I* bad?" with, "*I* know you're no worse than most men but I thought you were better" (67).

Chris's use of the comparative term "better" is that of an idealist moving on beyond idealism. Like Ann, he is learning how to reposition himself in the midst of competing contexts and comparative values of the play. Rather than telling us what is bad or good, as Miller the moralist as absolutist might well have done, he leaves us, along with the other characters, to consider what "better" might mean. When the audience hears Joe's gun go off, his concluding shot is just his judgment. Joe may have found a decisive standard, but his judgment at the end is judged by the rest of the play. In a play that positions the making of judgment in the context of competing perspectives, we have seen that the mix of good and evil will look different according to how you situate it. Chris's "You've got to be a little better" asks us to look ahead with him to an unknown future with Ann in which they will be coauthors of a not-yet-written social contract, for lives undergoing change, in the context of values still gradually emerging (31).

In Davies' revival of *All My Sons,* the set provided for the possibility of a homogeneous moral perspective, but, as the fallen tree suggests, the setting is inhabited by other alternatives. Ann enters the "veritable backyard" with a letter and disposition both capable of activating the potential reconstitution of the Keller world. This is someone who listens and learns, someone who speaks rather than pontificates, someone who has recognized differing spheres of implication and competing standards of judgment. She is not only a "female version" of Chris's idealism, but a more flexible thinker and more sophisticated maker of value judgments. She is the one who tips the equilibrium of the Keller world and alters our interpretation of it and her in the process. The final word of the play, Kate's "Live," addresses the emerging equilibrium that Ann has precipitated and that she and Chris will establish together. Using an analogy to physics—"the act of measurement itself changes the particle being measured"—Miller illuminatingly describes the dynamics of his early plays, including *All My Sons.*[31] For Miller, dramatic structure and social structure often overlap, and such is the case here. Ann's renewal of the family "equilibrium" exemplifies the presence of the "new balance" that Miller hoped to achieve with all his plays:

> A new poem will appear because a new balance has been struck which embraces both determinism and the paradox of will. If there is one unseen goal toward which every [one of my plays] strives, it is that very discovery and its proof—that we are made and yet are more than what made us.[32]

Chris and Ann survive together because they are not trapped by the past that has shaped them. Recognizing anew the force of Miller's argument that a human being "is unpredictable beyond a certain point," and that the history of humanity "is a ceaseless process of overthrowing one determinism to make way for another more faithful to life's changing relationships,"[33] we sit, as a jury, in judgment on Chris's and Ann's judgment, Joe's judgment and Miller's judgment.

Notes

1. This "insistently 'realistic'" play—"which is, of course, what Miller meant it to be" (Gross 71)—"relies on coincidence and contrivance" (Schlueter 113). "Its melodramatic flavour reflected a public predilection for moral absolutes" (Bigsby 112). See Barry Gross, "*All My Sons* and the Larger Context," June Schlueter, "The Dramatic Strategy of *All My Sons,*" C. W. E. Bigsby, "Realism and Idealism," and other essays in Arthur Miller's *All My Sons,* ed. Harold Bloom (New York: Chelsea House Publishers, 1988).

2. Subsequent page references are to Arthur Miller, *All My Sons* (New York: Dramatists Play Service, 1974).

3. Harold Clurman, ed., introduction, *The Portable Arthur Miller* (New York: Viking Press, 1971), xiii.

4. Clurman, introduction, xiii.

5. Benedict Nightingale, *The Times,* July 8, 2000; David Benedict, *Independent,* July 8, 2000; Stephen Fay, *Independent on Sunday,* July 9, 2000. See collected reviews in *Theatre Record,* August 8, 2000, 870–78.

6. Charles Spencer, *Daily Telegraph,* July 10, 2000.

7. Alistair Macaulay, *Financial Times,* July 10, 2000.

8. Arthur Miller, "A Conversation with Arthur Miller: Interview by Janet Balakian," *Michigan Quarterly Review* 29 (Spring 1990): 158–70, rpt. in *The Theater Essays of Arthur Miller,* ed. Robert A. Martin and Steven R. Centola (New York: Da Capo Press, 1996), 486.

9. In Elia Kazan's 1947 production, near a "disarmingly sunny suburban house," a "low hump" rose in the middle of the grassy backyard—an emblem, for set designer Mordecai Gorelik, of "buried conscience" in Miller's "graveyard play." Arthur Miller, *Timebends: A Life* (New York: Harper and Row, 1987), 133–34, 274–75. On the multivalent stylistic aspects of this play, see Enoch Brater, "Miller's Realism and *Death of a Salesman,*" in *Arthur Miller: New Perspectives,* ed. Robert A. Martin (Englewood Cliffs, N.J.: Prentice-Hall, 1982), 115–26.

10. The letter is often cited as an instance of implausible coincidence; as Billington recently asserted, "Any Victorian dramatist would have blushed at such a device." Michael Billington, *Guardian,* July 8, 2000. Yet Miller has countered, "If the myth behind *Oedipus* allows us to stretch our commonsense judgment of its plausibility, the letter's appearance in *All My Sons* seems to me to spring out of Ann's character and situation and hence is far less difficult to accept than a naked stroke of fate." Miller, *Timebends,* 134.

11. Miller, *Timebends,* 129.

12. Arthur Miller, "Ibsen and the Drama of Today," in *The Cambridge Companion to Ibsen,* ed. James McFarlane (Cambridge: Cambridge University Press, 1994), 232.

13. Miller, "Ibsen," 232.

14. Arthur Miller, "Introduction to the Collected Plays," *Plays One* (London: Methuen, 1988), 18, 20.

15. Miller, *Timebends,* 144.

16. Miller, "Introduction to the Collected Plays," 52.

17. Miller, "Introduction to the Collected Plays," 21.

18. Miller, "Introduction to the Collected Plays," 21.

19. Miller, "Introduction to the Collected Plays," 16.

20. Miller, "Introduction to the Collected Plays," 15.

21. Miller, "Introduction to the Collected Plays," 15.

22. In fields as various as cultural anthropology, art history and literary criticism, "thick description," Clifford Geertz's borrowing of Gilbert Ryles's phrase, draws attention to local texture and its relation to its larger context. Clifford Geertz, *The Interpretation of Cultures* (New York: Basic Books, 1973), 6.

23. Georgina Brown, *Mail on Sunday,* July 9, 2000.

24. Although the action is "carried by the male characters" and the women are usually "played somewhat sentimentally," Miller claims "that isn't the way they [the women's roles] were intended." "An Interview with Arthur Miller: By Matthew Roudané," *Michigan Quarterly Review* 24 (1985): 373–89, rpt. in Martin and Centola, *Theater Essays of Miller,* 430. Noting that the original production of *All My Sons* focused on the father-son conflict, Miller then cites the dominant role of the mother Kate in other productions: Rosemary Harris as Kate in Michael Blakemore's 1981 London production and Hanna Marron as Kate in the famous 1977 Jerusalem production (*Timebends,* 135). In Davies' production, Julie Waters received strong reviews, some favorable and others less so, for her role as Kate. Reviewers consistently praised the subtle and compelling performance of Catherine McCormack as Ann.

25. Miller, "Introduction to the Collected Plays," 15.

26. Miller, *Timebends,* 145.

27. Writing of the catastrophic Depression and his youthful Marxism, Miller points out that he could hear, two decades later, in the Salem Historical Society "the voices of those hanging judges, whom it was only possible really to understand if one had known oneself the thrill of having been absolutely right" (*Timebends,* 115).

28. Miller, "Conversation with Arthur Miller," 159.

29. Miller, "Introduction to the Collected Plays," 20. See Miller's comments on this point in "A Conversation with Arthur Miller," printed in this book.

30. Arthur Miller, *The Golden Years and The Man Who Had All the Luck* (London: Methuen, 1989), 179.

31. Miller, "Introduction to the Collected Plays," 54.

32. Miller, "Introduction to the Collected Plays," 55.

33. Miller, "Introduction to the Collected Plays," 54.

Austin E. Quigley

Setting the Scene
Death of a Salesman and *After the Fall*

In his essay "*After the Fall* and After," Albert Wertheim makes a strong case for a decisive shift in Miller's career during the eight-year hiatus between the opening of his revised version of *A View from the Bridge* and the opening of *After the Fall* (1964). The latter, he suggests, in spite of an unenthusiastic critical response, marks the beginning of "the second flowering of Arthur Miller's playwriting career."[1] "Comparisons with Miller's earlier dramatic works can serve to cloud the discussion," he argues, and there is certainly some clarity to be gained by situating *After the Fall* largely in the context of the plays that succeed it.[2] But he also notes, in passing, Gerald Weales's remark that "*The Inside of His Head,* Miller's original title for *Death of a Salesman,* might well be an alternate title for *After the Fall.* . . . Since [the play] aptly locates its episodes within the convolutions of Quentin's brain, this is made manifest onstage through the use of free-form sculpted areas" in which the various scenes are situated.[3]

As *Death of a Salesman* was written fifteen years before *After the Fall,* the continuity in Miller's writing career might be every bit as important as the discontinuities, and a more detailed comparison of the two plays confirms this to be the case. Even the evident contrasts between the two plays suggest not so much the differences between mutually exclusive alternatives, such as those provided when we contrast "open" with "closed," but the kind that distinguish mutually implicating oppositions, like those of the two sides of a coin.[4]

It is in these respects that *Death of a Salesman* and *After the Fall* can shed some illumination not only on each other but also on the more general nature of Miller's dramatic work. It is in terms of structure and setting that the complementary function of the two plays becomes most clearly apparent. Their episodic configurations provide related settings for characters wrestling with issues at the outer limits of human experience; they also provide related problems for audiences seeking to grasp precisely what is at stake.

Structurally, both plays interweave scenes of the past and present, depicting events in a sequence at odds with their chronological progression. The most obvious consequences of this departure from a linear chronological structure become evident if we recall the characteristic structure of the well-made play, with its linear structural pattern of exposition, complication, crisis and resolution. In such a structure the crisis scene, coming late in the narrative, is one capable of redirecting the drama by enacting or reporting a decisive causal event for which someone is clearly responsible. In effect, chronology, linearity, causality and responsibility are aligned with each other along a single axis, and the work of the audience is correspondingly simple. But the equivalent scene in *Death of a Salesman* is the eventual dramatization, late in act 2, of the frequently signaled event in Boston that occurred when Biff, aged seventeen, discovered his father with a woman in a hotel room. But this is not a new event that turns the action in a new direction, nor is it a newly revealed event for any of the characters, as Willy and Biff already know of it and neither Linda nor Happy learns about it when it is finally dramatized on stage. Its causal status is thus rendered problematic by its structural deployment, and even more problematic if we ask ourselves about its thematic implications. Was Willy simply the victim of some bad timing and, without this chance encounter, would all otherwise have been well, or at least tolerable, for Willy, Biff and the rest of the family?

Causality, in fact, is one of the most problematic features of *Death of a Salesman*. The key problem is not the shortage of causal factors but their sheer number and variety, so much so that the play, with its episodic structure, has at times been criticized for failing to make them cohere. At various points in the play, Willy's radical discontentment is explicitly linked to a variety of causes: the rootlessness and alienation of an urban rather than rural way of life (stage set, 11; Ben, 85; Biff and Happy, 22–23, 61; Willy, 122); the growing population with consequently increased competition and reduced space (Willy, 17–18); the changing values of American society (Willy, 81); the underlying economic system (Happy, 24–25); the early loss of a guiding father figure (Willy, 51); Willy's failure as a husband (Willy, 107); his failure as a father (Willy, 93); his failure as a salesman (Willy, 37); his old age (Linda, 57); his lack of self-knowledge (Biff, 138); his misguided ambitions (Charley, 89); his excessive self-pity (Biff, 56); his unimpressive appearance (Willy, 37); and so on.[5] This diffusion of the causes of Willy's disenchantment with his life can invite us to dismiss the play as one depicting a disgruntled failure, full of hot air and foolish dreams, whose frequent complaints and evident limitations fail to converge into any coherent pattern. The episodic nature of the play, in these terms, serves more to conceal than clarify the implicit structure of the action.

The counterargument, however, is that Willy is, as Biff defiantly asserts, "a dime a dozen" (132) in every respect except the one that Biff cannot quite comprehend: his desire and determination not to be. The diversity of negative evidence and hostile circumstances then serves not so much to muddy the thematic waters as to clarify the scale of Willy's determination to hold onto an aspiration in the face of counter-evidence of every imaginable kind.

And it is here that the actions of the leading characters need to be carefully integrated into the setting and structure of the play. The episodic material consists of three major kinds: events in the present that repeatedly reconfirm Willy's limitations; events in the past clarifying the status of the encounter in the Boston hotel room in establishing Willy as a fraud; and events in the past that promise another through-line for the play, one that validates Willy's aspiration to have lived a life that counts for something significant. The battle among the characters to establish which will be the defining moment in the narrative, Willy's firing (83), Willy and Biff's encounter in Boston (117) or Biff's performance at Ebbets Field (68), is a battle whose significance hinges surprisingly not on Willy's capacity to deceive himself, but on his inability to deceive himself enough. And this is one of the ways in which the play offers more than any of the characters ever manages to grasp.

The weight and variety of the negative evidence that Willy is unable to evade or ignore, in effect, lend cumulative stature to his unyielding determination to counter that evidence by transcending his constraining circumstances. The strength of this determination is reinforced rather than diminished by Willy's explicit recognition of the desperate strategies to which he resorts to keep the hope alive. Faced with the lowest point in his life and career, Willy acknowledges the strategies of deception and self-deception required to keep his mammoth aspirations alive for himself and his family, in spite of his limitations and theirs:

> *Willy:* I was fired today. . . . I was fired, and I'm looking for a little good news to tell your mother, because the woman has waited and the woman has suffered. The gist of it is that I haven't got a story left in my head, Biff. So don't give me a lecture about facts and aspects. I am not interested. Now what've you got to say to me? (107)

The direct appeal to Biff to provide him with an enabling story rather than with disabling facts is continuous with a disposition to live on the promise of future achievements—achievements that might ratify the family's strengths and minimize their moments of disillusionment. But the promising stories of future achievement are not themselves enough, either to satisfy Willy or to create so powerful a play.

If the encouraging stories Willy collects and invokes to ratify his preferred narrative line involved mere escapism and self-deception, this would be a less significant play. But there is a reality principle at issue here that is fundamental to the play and to Miller's work as a whole. Though it would be difficult to defend Willy against accusations of self-deception, the self-deception is as much strategic as self-indulgent. The solution Biff offers to their problems, self-knowledge based on external evaluation, is thus illuminatingly inadequate:

> *Biff:* What am I doing in an office, making a contemptuous, begging fool of myself, when all I want is out there, waiting for me the minute I say I know who I am. . . . I am not a leader of men, Willy, and neither are you. You were never anything but a hard-working drummer who landed in the ash can like all the rest of them! I'm one dollar an hour, Willy. I tried seven states and couldn't raise it. A buck an hour! Do you gather my meaning? I'm not bringing home any prizes any more, and you're going to stop waiting for me to bring them home! (132)

Biff's claim that in self-knowledge lies satisfaction is countered, of course, by the vehemence of Willy's "I am not a dime a dozen! I am Willy Loman, and you are Biff Loman!" (132), by the life he has lived to keep Biff's debilitating evaluation at bay, and by the death he deploys as a culminating effort to restart the cycle of success for himself and for Biff. And the trouble with Biff's version of self-knowledge is that it is based upon external evaluations that do not include internal values and personal aspirations, which have their own reality claims.

In a world in which everyone grows and changes, the challenge the play presents is one of requiring us to decide when aspirations are unrealistic and/or unworthy. Aspiration, after all, must often lead achievement into being, otherwise new achievements and new achievers would emerge only by chance. Lurking in the background of Biff's remark that Willy had the wrong dreams (138) and of Charley's remark that "a salesman has got to dream, boy" (138) is that characteristic notion of an American dream in which personal and social transformation is a widely shared expectation, an expectation ratified in a great many rags-to-riches stories of the kind exemplified by the career of Willy's brother, Ben. But if aspiration is an enabling aspect of achievement, who is to say when aspiration, necessarily at odds with current reality, is excessive? And the play's episodic structure and competing narrative lines suspend the question in the action along with others it invites the audience to consider.

It is in the play's epilogue that the overall function of the play's episodic structure becomes most clearly apparent, and it is very much one of challenging the audience to locate the appropriate means of measuring Willy's worth. It is evident enough in the play's action that Willy has many failings, is often self-deceived and self-deceiving, and is much misguided about what might constitute worthwhile success. But those limitations provide neither the measure of the man nor the measure of the play. What the epilogue provides to supplement the three stories that have obsessed Willy, one ratified by his firing, another by the event in Boston, and the other by the event at Ebbets Field, are the stories each of the other characters derives from the action and the values each locates in them. For Linda, Willy was a success after all, as he had paid off the mortgage; for Charley, the career of salesman was a destructive choice, and his raising of Bernard to be a bookworm and a within-the-system success exemplifies a set of values different from Willy's; for Happy, the way forward is beating the system by playing with rather than by the rules and doing so better than anyone else; and, as we have seen, for Biff it is a matter of reducing expectations to one aspect of self-knowledge. But the final speech is Linda's, as she both asserts and questions a mode of measuring Willy's value that has sustained her commitment to him, despite all his evident failings:

> *Linda:* Forgive me, dear. I can't cry. I don't know what it is, but I can't cry. I don't understand it. Why did you ever do that? . . . Why did you do it? I search and search and I search, and I can't understand it, Willy. I made the last payment on the house today. Today, dear. And there'll be nobody home. (*A sob rises in her throat.*) We're free and clear. (*Sobbing more fully, released.*) We're free. (*Biff comes slowly toward her.*) We're free. . . . We're free . . . (139)

And, at this point, "*the apartment buildings rise into sharp focus*" (139), reminding us at the end of the play, as they did at the beginning, of the sense of confinement and containment that the realistic aspects of the set provide to Linda's notions of freedom and success and to Willy's larger hopes and aspirations.

The action of the epilogue, however, takes place on the apron at the front of the stage, and the scene is not one circumscribed by the realism of the set: In "clothes of mourning" and accompanied by the beat of "a dead march," the characters "move toward the audience, through the wall-line of the kitchen" and out to "the limit of the apron" (136). And there, closest to the audience, and removed from the realistic set, the characters debate questions of sufficiency and excess:

> *Linda:* I can't understand it. At this time especially. First time in thirty-five years we were just about free and clear. He only needed a little salary. He was even finished with the dentist.
>
> *Charley:* No man only needs a little salary. (137)

Linda's domestic dreams seem impoverished when compared to Willy's implausible but more grandiose designs. Charley's remark, however, serves not only to raise the question of how much salary should suffice but also how much achievement, recognition, admiration, love, enduring impact and so on should suffice.

Willy's strength and weakness is his inability to locate a satisfactory measure of sufficient achievement, and he died, as he lived, fatally attracted to the notion that happiness consists of endless expectation of better things on the horizon. As Happy puts it: "Dad is never so happy as when he's looking forward to something!" (105). Willy's sense of containment and confinement is all-pervasive, and the "boxed in" neighborhood provides only an example and not a basic cause of his frustration. His preferred narrative line reaches beyond these constraints, and the play's structure and setting follow suit. When the play extends its episodic structure into a stage set whose partial transparency is designed to move the action beyond representational chronology to presentational rearrangement, it opens access to a world beyond the walls, a realm in which the possibilities of action, measurement and value extend beyond anything that the characters and their sociohistorical situation can encompass.

The play begins, as the stage direction puts it, with a melody, played upon a flute, that tells of "grass and trees and the horizon" (11). Much has been made of the grass and trees, but it is to the horizon that the episodic action of the play ultimately directs our attention. When Willy dies, there is no consensus on the stage about how we should measure his strengths and limitations or the ultimate value of the obsessive aspirations for which he is prepared to sacrifice his life. The conversation in the epilogue emerges from the realistic set of the play out onto the apron of the stage and ultimately out into the auditorium, where it will then be extended further. And looming ahead is a play of similarly episodic structure, that likewise seeks to entangle the audience in questions the play is better able to ask than answer; and in that play, too, questions about the appropriate limits of expectation, aspiration, responsibility and commitment play a central role. As Quentin puts it at a key point in the action: "If there's love, it should be limitless"—that play is, of course, *After the Fall.*[6]

Some of the issues that are central to the action of *Death of a Salesman* recur explicitly in *After the Fall.* Quentin asks himself a question that might well have been put to Biff: "Maybe it's not enough—to know yourself. Or maybe it's too much" (58). Too much, he suggests, because "the truth, after all, may merely be murderous. The truth killed Lou, destroyed Mickey" (61). But if the truth is not a reliable guide, what is the alternative? Which priorities should have precedence and how do we decide? As Quentin puts it in resigning from his law firm: "I couldn't concentrate on a case anymore. . . . I felt I was merely in the service of my own success" (2)—a self-criticism that Willy might well have contemplated at some point. And these thematic concerns, along with the episodic structures and fluid movements across time and place, link two otherwise radically contrasting plays. The two plays deal with significantly different aspects of human experience that turn out to be closely connected, the first play posing serious questions about the appropriate ceiling on belief and aspiration, the other about viable limits on doubt and despair.

For Quentin, as for Willy, a weight of evidence is cumulatively developed in an episodic structure from a variety of contexts and a range of examples. For Willy, the weight of evidence suggests that he is, indeed, a dime a dozen, and his manic/heroic response is to commit himself to a counter-narrative with his death as one of its central and enabling components. For Quentin, the weight of negative evidence raises a question of a different, but just as troubling kind, one that also requires of him an act of ratifying intervention.

Quentin's catalogue of exemplary instances includes the contemptuous criticism of his father by his mother, when, after many years of happy marriage, she calls him "an idiot" (20) for bungling the family finances; a complementary betrayal of the memory of the mother by the father when he registers and votes only two months after her death (10); Quentin's best friend's wife flirting provocatively with him (23); friends abandoning friends in the face of government investigations into un-American activities (33); Quentin's own "joy" when the suicide of his friend, Lou, relieves him of the obligation to defend him (59); the failure of his two marriages (42, 112); and his temporary abandonment as a small child by his parents (76). This selection of events seems so much skewed in the direction of pessimism and self-pity that it leaves the audience uncertain whether Quentin is deliberately seeking to ratify despair or struggling to come to terms with his own faults by focusing upon those of others. Willy, unlike Quentin, acknowledges both good and bad throughout, but Quentin seems obsessed with the bad. What restores the necessary balance to the play is Quentin's eventual question to himself: "Why is betrayal the only truth that sticks[?]" (76). And it is here, as was the case with *Death of a Salesman,* that it becomes essential to embed the actions of the characters in the context of the overall action of a play whose structure and setting play a central role.

The opening and closing scenes set the parameters of the inquiry Quentin is undertaking: "I have a bit of a decision to make," he announces at the outset to a "Listener" he has summoned to help him work it through (2). The decision involves whether or not to make a commitment to a new relationship with Holga when the weight of history, his own and other people's, seems to demonstrate that love between friends, siblings, spouses and other relatives promises more than it is ever able to deliver. His recurring bewilderment with "the death of love" (64) raises questions for Quentin not only about his own ability to love, but also about human bonds in general: "I don't know any more what people *are* to one another" (7), he asserts. "It's like some unseen web of connection between people is simply not there" (39). And it is in this context that the concentration camp tower that frames Holga's entry into the play (5) marks the ultimate extension of the collapse of human respect, responsibility, love and care that is exemplified in different ways in Quentin's catalogue of betrayals.

The answer to his question of why "betrayal is the only truth that sticks" emerges from his increasing awareness of the inappropriateness of the standards he invokes to establish the worth of personal commitments in general. Late in the play, the issue becomes both explicit in the dialogue and evident in the stage images:

> It's that if there is love, it must be limitless, a love not even of persons but blind, blind to insult, blind to the spear in the flesh, like justice blind, like . . . *Felice appears behind him. He has been raising up his arms. Father appears, slumped in chair.*
>
> Mother's voice, *off:* Idiot! (100).

The tableau and the voice register the accumulating dramatic evidence of a counterargument to Quentin's views on the necessity for limitless love, a counterargument that has been evolving throughout the play. As he argues for the necessity that love be limitless, his arms move once more toward the iconic figure of crucifixion that has recurred in the play. His mother's repeatedly recalled condemnation of his father suddenly critiques, in this context, both the father in the past and the son in the present. As it does so, another narrative line begins to take precedence, one that, as in *Death of a Salesman,* evolves through the network of images, episodes and questions, one whose point of departure early in the action suggests a different way of configuring the material, weighing the evidence and setting standards of value: "Why do I think of things falling apart?" he asks. "Were they ever whole?" (26).

It is in their capacity to have their unfolding events reconfigured into differing narratives that the episodic structures of *Death of a Salesman* and *After the Fall* invite comparison. In both cases Miller promotes and controls this reconfiguration by deploying not just a sequence of nonchronological events but also a series of redefined relationships among images, events and issues. If *Death of a Salesman* invites us to ponder in these terms the appropriate means of validating aspiration, *After the Fall* invites us to join Quentin in pondering the appropriate means of validating despair. But in both cases there is more in the plays than the characters finally grasp. Betrayal is the only truth that sticks in Quentin's initial narrative because his mode of measurement generates expectations that set up everyone, including himself, for failure. The other narrative he begins to construct, the one that incorporates his recognition of "the lie of limitless love" (107), is one that emerges gradually in the episodic action. It arises in opposition to the narrative of universal betrayal that leads Quentin directly from domestic disappointments to concentration camp catastrophes. The second narrative recovers for Quentin some faith in the strength of personal commitments, and it does so by adjusting the scale upon which worthwhile achievement is measured. But just as in *Death of a Salesman,* the opposing narratives coexist, along with the indication that others might also be contemplated. Neither play settles all the issues it raises. The answers provided are very much answers offered by the characters rather than the answers of the plays. And in the case of *After the Fall,* this has large consequences for the way in which we conceive of its structure and function.

One of the key challenges in performing *After the Fall* is to achieve an appropriate balance between the two voices of Quentin, who serves as both character and narrator, and between those voices and the other "voices" of the play, including that of the set and its dramatic images. The opening stage directions are specific enough: "The action takes place in the mind, thought, and memory of Quentin. . . . The effect . . . will be the surging, flitting, instantaneousness of a mind questing over its own surfaces and into its depths" (1). And it does so in the presence of a Listener who is invoked as a trusted friend and whose responses and advice will be taken seriously. Private concerns are being tested in a public context and, as the Listener is strategically located at the front of the auditorium, the theater audience is implicated in the role of trusted respondent. This, in turn, has its own effect on Quentin's role as stage narrator, enabling him to remain in character as a narrator addressing a Listener within the world of the play. The repeatedly signaled interrogative mode of narration is thus one that should result in shared inquiry into dramatized material, rather than one in which the narrator is presumed to know best. Indeed the very notion of "best" is rendered problematic by the evolving action.

Quentin's question, "Why is betrayal the only truth that sticks[?]" is thus only one of many questions and queries that are raised by Quentin in the action, by Quentin about the action, or by events and images in the action. For example, "I don't know what I'd be bringing to that girl [Holga]" (5); "I don't understand why that girl [Felice] sticks in my mind" (11); "I don't know why this [concentration camp] hit me so" (12); "Why can't I mourn her [his mother]" (16); "Why do I make such stupid statements" (4); and the key questions: "Why do I think of things falling apart? Were they ever whole?" (26).

What makes the structures of his life, of the narrative he develops and of the play as a whole so mutually problematic is the explicit search for a governing principle that will give life a sense of wholeness, character a sense of governing purpose and individuals a shared sense of responsibility. As Quentin puts it early in the play:

> I've lost the sense of some absolute necessity. Whether I open a book or think of marrying again, it's so damned clear I'm choosing what I do—and it cuts the strings between my hands and heaven. . . . And I keep looking back to when there seemed to be some duty in the sky. I had a dinner table and a wife . . . a child and the world so wonderfully threatened by injustices I was born to correct. It seemed so fine! Remember—when there were good people and bad people? And how easy it was to tell! The worst son of a bitch, if he loved Jews and hated Hitler, he was a buddy. (22)

The "choosing" that he now finds so repugnant seems to him like selecting options on the basis of personal preference and situational expediency rather than on the basis of more general principles. This sense of living a diminished life is set against an earlier experience, in the midst of world war, of a direct link between personal choice, human justice and moral consequence. The trouble with that nostalgia for a simpler world of simple moral choice is, of course, that it was never that simple, even though world war simplified some issues by pushing others temporarily to one side. The other trouble is that, by temporarily ratifying a world of simple moral choice, by reinforcing the claims of a moral world in which things were either fully good or fully bad, it helped establish for Quentin the narrative of universal standards and consequently of universal betrayal. In such a context, every failure of human relationship becomes, in effect, the same failure with the same ultimate consequence:

> *The tower lights.* Everything is one thing! You see—I don't know what we are to one another! . . . It's like some unseen web of connection between people is simply not there. And I always relied on it, somehow. (33 and 39)

The judgmental absolutism of a simple moral universe serves to link domestic betrayals directly to concentration camp atrocities, for the lack of total trust between human beings is readily convertible into its absolute absence.

This is the narrative that has led Quentin to the brink of despair, but it is important to recognize that it is a narrative in the play and not the narrative of the play. From the outset Quentin persistently questions it. Indeed, the invitation to the Listener to hear him out is evidently prompted by a desire to find a way of saying "yes" to Holga, thus committing himself to a third marriage after the failure of his first two. Those who question the juxtaposition of domestic squabbles and concentration camp atrocities are right to do so, but wrong to fault the play for unquestioningly doing so. For what the play ambitiously seeks to establish is not just a rationale for such linkage, but also a plausible alternative narrative that will enable Quentin to transcend the first one. Just as important, however, is the effort to provide an alternative way of asking questions about the issues raised that leaves the audience evaluating, and not just assenting to, Quentin's answers to his own questions.

Quentin's second narrative, painfully salvaged from the wreckage of the first, is that we accept our own evil and live, that the concentration camp provides the outer limit of human failure, but not its characteristic scale or its inevitable destination.

What burning cities taught her and the death of love taught me: that we are very dangerous! . . . To know, and even happily, that we meet unblessed: not in some garden of wax fruit and painted trees, that lie of Eden, but after, after the Fall, after many, many deaths. Is the knowing all? And the wish to kill is never killed, but with some gift of courage one may look into its face when it appears, and with a stroke of love—as to an idiot in the house—forgive it, again and again . . . forever? (113–14)

This is Quentin's culminating "vision" (113), but it is not that of the play. The lines conclude with a question mark and are immediately followed by a stage direction indicating a question from the Listener, to whom Quentin responds not with conviction, but with continuing doubt:

He is evidently interrupted by the Listener.
Quentin: No, it's not certainty, I don't feel that. But it does seem feasible not to be afraid. Perhaps it's all one has. I'll tell her that. . . . Yes, she will, she'll know what I mean. (114)

It is Holga, of course, who introduced the image of the idiot child (22) to the play, and their narrative alternative to the one with which Quentin began seems only to have swung the pendulum of expectation from the "lie of limitless love," of excessive expectation, to the "truth" of limitless capacity to hate. In the context of that murderous human capacity, any kind or degree of selfless commitment is enhanced in value. The achievement of limited goals in such a context suffices to encourage the belief that even if things are not ideal, they are nevertheless tolerable, acceptable and perhaps worthy of celebration. The play concludes with Quentin and Holga expressing their mutual commitment with a minimal gesture of mutual recognition, each saying "Hello" to the other, with the evident implication that their relationship will continue. In the context of the narrative they have generated together, even so small a commitment is a reassuring achievement.

Once "limitless love" has been recognized as an excessive expectation, what follows from it is not what Quentin initially made of it—that limited love and a capacity for murder are only inches apart—but that the expectation itself was seriously misleading. It is not a matter of accepting that human beings are not capable of this ideal of commitment, but that the notion of that as an ideal is itself a mistaken one. And much of the action of the play lends itself to a recurring review of its status and to a sustained search for a viable alternative. And that search is invited as Quentin's is conducted—through differing interpretations of and alignments among the play's evocative episodes.

The fact that Quentin's readiness to defend Lou is at odds with his desire to be released from this unwelcome responsibility is something that could as easily be invoked to enhance the value of his readiness to defend him nevertheless, as invoked to diminish it. Louise's desire not to be "a praise machine" in her marriage to Quentin but to remain somehow "a separate person" (41) is not a desire that is invalidated by the failure of the marriage. And Quentin's father's capacity to register and vote after the death of his wife can lead to other conclusions than that he lacked sufficient commitment to the relationship. Indeed, many of these images of qualified commitment invite comparison and contrast with an image of maternal love so absolute that Quentin is stunned to recognize it as somehow fraudulent, nevertheless.

> *Mother:* Darling, there is never a depression for great people! The first time I felt you move, I was standing on the beach at Rockaway. . . . And I saw a star, and it got bright, and brighter, and brighter! And suddenly it fell, like some great man had died, and you were being pulled out of me to take his place, and be a light, a light in the world!
>
> *Quentin, to Listener:* Why is there some . . . air of treachery in that? (66–67)

The "praise machine" mother loving her son into her version of greatness is, indeed, unexpectedly treacherous, not least because it speaks of her needs and interests before she has listened to his. And in Quentin's initial narrative the thread of treachery in unqualified admiration is traced from one relationship to another. In Quentin's mind Felice, too, admired him for all the wrong reasons ("I feel like a mirror in which she somehow saw herself as glorious" [6]). And his dismay that he finds himself unable to grieve for his dead mother is phrased in terms similar enough to weave the two relationships together.

> *Mother appears on upper platform, arms crossed as in death.*
>
> I still hear her voice in the street sometimes, loud and real, calling me. And yet she's under the ground. That whole cemetery—I saw it like a field of buried mirrors in which the living merely saw themselves. I don't seem to know how to grieve for her. (6).

And all of these questions about separateness and union in loving relationships focus finally on the relationship that raises most graphically for Quentin the question of locating appropriate standards and expectations.

The romance with Maggie emerges in the context of a failing marriage and the death of a mother whom he is finding difficult to mourn. And the play's images position Maggie at the pole opposite to his mother. Where the mother sought to love Quentin into an image that made her seem glorious, Maggie seeks to love Quentin in a glorious mold entirely of his own choosing:

> *Quentin:* You seem to think you owe people whatever they demand!
> *Maggie:* I know. (83)

The ironic consequence of such unqualified commitment is, however, provided by the false name Maggie proposes to adopt if she were to visit him in Washington:

> *Maggie:* I could register in the hotel as Miss None.
> *Quentin:* N-u-n?
> *Maggie:* No—"n-o-n-e"—like nothing. I made it up once 'cause I can never remember a fake name, so I just have to think of nothing and that's me! *She laughs with joy.* (77)

In both relationships, an ideal of love that goes back to the Bible, that of two people becoming one, is depicted in terms that reveal its potential limitations. Situated between the two extremes is Louise's insistence that even in a marriage she must remain "a separate person" (41). But this is a claim that initially enrages Quentin:

> *Quentin:* When you've finally become a separate person, what the hell is there?
> *Louise, with a certain unsteady pride:* Maturity.
> *Quentin:* I don't know what that means.
> *Louise:* It means that you know another person exists. (42)

Across this spectrum of separateness, connection and union, the action of the play positions its various episodes, with less than satisfactory results on all sides. But, as noted, personal satisfaction or even happiness is not the only thing at stake. The religious images and phrases that permeate both the play and its title focus repeatedly not just on what feels good, but on what is best, and best is a moral and not just an ethical and social context. And it is this recurring linkage of the personal and the moral that repeatedly escalates expectations of what a personal relationship should achieve and elevates the standards of measurement characters invoke.

What is at stake here for the play, as well as for Quentin, is the appropriate scale of consequence and implication for an individual life, a personal relationship and a species-wide sense of reciprocal responsibility. The word "moral" recurs repeatedly in the play, but most characteristically as a question whose accompanying assertion is rendered increasingly problematic:

> *Quentin:* What the hell is moral? And what am I, to even ask that question? A man ought to know—a decent man knows that like he knows his own face! (57)

The action of the play validates the first question more than the subsequent assertion. Brother Dan seemed to know exactly how right and wrong line up when he decided to devote his life to salvaging those of his parents, while Quentin moved away to build a life of his own. But whatever the virtues of Dan's choice, the action of the play suggests it is not the only good choice, though Quentin seems initially inclined to see it so. As he puts it in retrospect: "Yes, good men stay . . . although they die there" (68). For Quentin, as for us, questions arise in these complicated choices about the limits of obligations to others, limits that fuel Quentin's fear that our capacity for independence can degenerate rapidly into indifference, an indifference that reaches its culmination in concentration camp catastrophe: "In whose name do you ever turn your back—*he looks out at the audience*—but in your own? In Quentin's name. Always in your own blood-covered name you turn your back!" (112).

In the absence of a governing moral standard, a fixed and final set of principles, the action of the play begins to exemplify an alternative source of standards, with its evolving set of complex images each effectively critiquing each other. What follows upon the recurring demonstration in the action—that a vocabulary of right and wrong will not suffice to accommodate the complexities of the episodes—is not an argument that anything can be situationally justified. The recurring images of the concentration camp render that position untenable. What emerges from the various episodes is the necessity for judgment even in the absence of a governing standard of value. While we may not know what is best for all people on all occasions, we incur the obligation, nevertheless, to recognize what are better choices than others in a variety of different contexts.

Rather than providing a single mode of measuring or a unified narrative establishing a single principle of value, the action of the play provides a variety of exemplary instances in which each effectively measures the other, and these complex examples are not convertible into a governing precept. The characteristically interrogative tone of the play does not move from question to answer but from a variety of questions to multiple modes of generating answers.

What the play offers, however, is not simply the multiplicity of relativistic perspectives. Rather it is, as the structure and setting of the play exemplify, the multiplicity of coherent configurations of episodes that will guide us for a while, before the further complexity of human experience requires us to supplement them and reconfigure them one more time. Quentin's development of a narrative alternative to the one with which he began is not the achievement of a final narrative. Experience may not finally teach us what is always best, but, suitably contemplated and interrogated, it can help us make informed but not infallible decisions about what is likely to be better, as we compare current situations to others both like and unlike them. The play's complex structure is one of juxtaposed memories leading to a present-time decision, and it is no accident that Holga is described in this context as an "archeologist" (3). The set's governing image and the play's governing structure are thus those of evolving historical multiplicity. And it is in this context that character is situated, moral choice exercised and commitments made.

Between the God-self, who creates people in his own image, and the nonself, content to be created in someone else's terms, lies the separate person who forms variable connections with others, not on the basis of a single decision totally and forever, but on the basis of recurring decisions about whether to continue and extend unfolding relationships. The total and forever commitment ultimately emerges from the play not as an unachievable ideal but as a mistaken ideal. The strength of Quentin and Holga's evolving relationship lies in its repeated renewal by people independent enough to be able to walk away but bonded enough to want to stay. Giving, in any relationship, requires givers, separable people whose giving acquires part of its value from their capacity not to give. The final shape of the relationship, its unfolded narrative, is thus not given in the initial episode of commitment; the end is not written into the beginning of either the relationship or the play. For this reason the play concludes with an exchanged "Hello," which promises but does not guarantee further renewal of commitment. Certainty does not replace doubt, and regular reconsideration and renewal are an essential part of the relationship we have witnessed and of any narrative it will eventually generate.

The episodic structure of the play and the scenic images of ever-renewed inquiry thus lead Quentin's audience, as *Death of a Salesman* led Willy's, to a position outside of any of the narratives generated or posited by the characters. With Willy exploring the viability of unlimited aspiration and Quentin the validity of unlimited despair, the plays invite the audience to continue the inquiries beyond what the characters finally grasp, with episodic structures indicating that responsibilities, like causes, are never single or simple; those responsibilities remain unavoidable nevertheless. As Quentin puts it in characteristically interrogative fashion: "how else do you touch the world—except with a promise?" (61)—with a hypothetical narrative about what the future might hold. Such a narrative is informed by what the past has provided, but governed as much by a commitment to achieve more as by a readiness to settle for the less that has often been achieved in the past.

In the two plays neither Willy nor Quentin is able to locate an ultimately reliable mode of evaluating the claims of optimism and despair, but the plays provide, in their episodic structures and interacting images, the complexity of the experiential material we must draw upon and of the demands we make on it. In doing so they provide the word *moral,* in Miller's whole work, with a viability that enables his characters, though grounded in stage realism, to implicate and explore worlds that lie beyond what such realism can otherwise accommodate and contain. The complex structures and settings of these plays register and render characteristic concerns that arise in differing ways in many of Miller's plays: linking the social to the moral but relating morality to accountability rather than to predictability; positioning the linearity of narratives between episodic fragmentation and transformative reconfiguration; reconciling character reliability with personal aspiration and social change, achieved knowledge with continuing inquiry, barbarism with transcendence and realism with dimensions of experience it cannot readily accommodate. A creative interlocking of situation, set and structure gives the plays a power larger than character or conclusion can circumscribe, and audiences a role that continues after the curtain falls.

Notes

1. Albert Wertheim, "Arthur Miller: *After the Fall* and After," in *Essays on Contemporary American Drama,* ed. Hedwig Bock and Albert Wertheim (Munich: M. Hueber, 1981), 19.
2. Wertheim, "Arthur Miller," 20.

3. Wertheim, "Arthur Miller," 20.

4. C. K. Ogden, *Opposition: A Linguistic and Psychological Analysis* (Bloomington: Indiana University Press, 1967).

5. Arthur Miller, *Death of a Salesman* (New York: Viking Press, 1971). All page references are to this edition.

6. Arthur Miller, *After the Fall* (New York: Viking Press, 1973). All page references are to this edition.

Arnold Aronson

The Symbolist Scenography of Arthur Miller

Over the past few decades Arthur Miller's plays have often received a better reception abroad, particularly in London, than at home. There are many factors contributing to this situation, of course, but a significant—and largely overlooked—element is the design or scenography. The visual and spatial environment of a production, its physical texture, as it were, plays a profound if often subliminal role in theatrical reception. Miller's domestic productions, I would suggest, have frequently been hampered by the generally more literal and even prosaic American approach to design. Arthur Miller has created worlds of such vivid reality (and is thematically so closely tied to Ibsen) that he is often classed with nineteenth-century naturalists, but it quickly becomes apparent in reading his stage directions—and in listening to him rhapsodize about the magic of the theater—that as a playwright he is part of a different lineage. Resituating him within modern theater history—and locating the corresponding scenographic styles—may provide new insights into his work and suggest approaches to the scenography for his plays.

Anyone who has ever read essays by or interviews with Arthur Miller, or has had the pleasure of hearing him speak, knows that he is a superb raconteur. One of his most engaging stories regards the rehearsals for the initial production of *Death of a Salesman* and the way in which Lee J. Cobb, after nearly two weeks of listless line readings, stood up one day and brought Willy Loman to life. "And then, one afternoon, there on the stage of the New Amsterdam . . . Lee rose from his chair and looked at Milly Dunnock and there was a silence," Miller recalled in a 1955 essay. "And then he said, 'I was driving along, you understand, and then all of a sudden I'm going off the road. . . .' And the theater vanished."[1] What tends to be remembered about this now almost mythical anecdote is the powerful description of the transformation of an actor into a flesh-and-blood character, but Miller's account also emphasizes the transformation of the theater into a dramatic world and the consequent creation of space and time. It is, in other words, about the scenographic imagination. "The stage vanished," Miller continued, reemphasizing the alchemical transmutation effected upon a stage lit only by bare work lights and littered with the detritus of rehearsal.

> The chill of an age-old recognition shuddered my spine; a voice was sounding in the dimly lit air up front, a created spirit, an incarnation, a Godlike creation was taking place . . . made real by an act of will, by an artist's summoning up of all his memories and his intelligence. . . . A mere glance of his [Cobb's] eye created a window beside him, with the gentle touch of his hand on this empty stage a bed appeared, and when he glanced up at the emptiness above him a ceiling was there, and there was even a crack in it where his stare rested.[2]

For Miller, and for the others sitting in that rehearsal as well if Miller is to be believed, the stance of the body, the look in the eye, and the inflection of the voice combined to create—"Godlike" and out of thin air—a tangible space replete with the minutest of physical details. One is reminded of Marcel Collière's program notes for the 1891 symbolist production of Pierre Quillard's *The Girl with the Cut-Off Hands:* "We relied on speech to evoke the sets and to make them arise in the mind of spectators." Or as Quillard himself succinctly stated, "Language creates the scenery like everything else."[3] Miller's awestruck response to Lee J. Cobb is nothing less than an embracement of a central tenet of symbolism.

Why, then, is Miller, in the popular imagination at least, most often thought of as the quintessential realist of postwar American drama and not, as I believe, an artistic descendent of Chekhov? One answer, perhaps, can be found in the constant comparison with Tennessee Williams. Both playwrights erupted on the theatrical scene immediately after World War II, and together they seem to have reinvented and to sit astride the American theater of the period. Williams's plays were most often overtly poetic and symbolic and populated with nearly fantastical individuals, while Miller's characters were seemingly far more prosaic and situated in more pedestrian environs. Williams's characters, though psychologically compelling, were generally exotic to Broadway audiences, whereas Miller's characters seemed to have been drawn from the spectators' own lives. (A frequent response by spectators to Willy Loman—to the present day—is that he is, in many ways, just like their fathers.) Thus, given the critical tendency to create sharp Hegelian oppositions, Williams became the symbolist, Miller the realist. And once

Miller became identified with the tradition of Zola, Hauptmann, Ibsen and even Belasco, the illusionistic scenography associated with those late-nineteenth-century authors began to adhere to Miller as well. Although Miller's preoccupation with moral and social themes was certainly influenced by Ibsen, what Miller took from the Norwegian playwright was a worldview, not necessarily a dramatic structure, and certainly not a scenographic style. Ibsen, following the theories of the naturalists, needed to create fully realized environments onstage—the worlds that shaped the actions of his characters. For Miller, the real landscape was the one inside a character's—and by implication, the spectator's—mind.

There were essentially two major currents in Western scenography in the first half of the twentieth century. There was the naturalist branch, descended from the playwright Ibsen and the director André Antoine—and related to the minutely drawn descriptive passages of the Russian novelists—which stipulated a wealth of detail, creating a total environment in which the characters moved, and which left little to the chance associations of the spectators' imaginations. In this illusionistic style the so-called real world is replicated as closely as possible; objects come to represent themselves so that the symbolically signifying space of the stage is mistaken for that which is signified. The other branch belonged to the symbolists—inspired by the poet Baudelaire and reaching its consummate form in the works of Chekhov. Chekhov provided only the barest essentials of description in his stage directions, preferring instead to emphasize the world and the atmosphere that exist outside the windows and beyond the sightlines of the spectators—in other words, the milieu, not the room, in which the characters live. Miller—perhaps surprisingly—is similarly concerned with the world beyond the narrow confines of the stage. Both *Incident at Vichy* and *The Price,* for instance, begin with descriptions of translucent windows. "Across the back is a structure with two grimy window panes" read the directions for *Incident;* likewise the opening directions of *The Price* describe "two windows . . . at the back of the stage. Daylight filters through their sooty panes, which have been X'd out with fresh whitewash. . . . Now daylight seeps through a skylight in the ceiling, grayed by the grimy panes." A world exists beyond the view of both the characters and the spectators, a place separated from the onstage world by dirt, grime and soot, reducing the light to a faint promise of something—better?—beyond. A dialectic is created between inner and outer; between onstage and off. Virtually all theater, almost by definition, implies an offstage space, but many of Miller's works *begin* with the offstage world and provide some means, however minimal, for that offstage world to permeate the surroundings of the on-stage characters.

Similarly, this Chekhovian impulse may be seen at work in *The Crucible,* a play that most audiences would probably not associate with symbolist tendencies. After all, as Miller's most produced play—very often in high school and college productions—it is often thought of as a kind of historical pageant. The opening directions, however, describe

> A small upper bedroom . . . in the spring of the year 1692. There is a narrow window at the left. Through its leaded panes the morning sunlight streams. A candle still burns near the bed which is at the right. A chest, a chair, and a small table are the other furnishings. At the back a door opens on the landing of the stairway to the ground floor. The room gives off an air of clean spareness. The roof rafters are exposed, and the wood colors are raw and unmellowed.[4]

A few more details than Chekhov might have indicated, perhaps, but Miller still emphasizes mood, atmosphere and the world beyond the room—and the lone window through which the warmth of that world may filter. What is most astonishing for the reader (but unavailable—at least immediately—to the viewer) are the several pages of historical notes and moral philosophizing that follow these opening directions and appear elsewhere in the text as well. Miller is truly attempting to set the play in a larger context at once anchored in the historical accuracy of archaeology and at the same time floating in the boundless world of the stage and thus expanded to a larger worldview. Miller will not let the play remain within the walls of a colonial house or courtroom or even the village of Salem of 1692. His textual notes acknowledge a present-day viewer/reader, make reference to the American frontier and the Europe from which the colonists originated, and note the colonists' belief in Heaven and Hell as literal places. Miller is asking the viewer to perceive the play more or less as medieval citizens viewed the passion plays of their era, in which the prosaic realities of their own lives existed within the malleable space-time continuum of a divinely controlled universe. It is up to the director and designer, of course, to translate Miller's textual notes into comprehensible theatrical reality, but the implication is clear: the onstage world is merely one visible fragment of a larger environment, a cosmos, whose presence must clearly be felt.

In writings and interviews Miller constantly asserts that what he desires in the theater is "wonder." And very often this sense of wonder is generated by the miraculous ability of language and gesture to conjure up imaginary worlds that are not merely tangible to the spectator, but have the ability to feel more real than reality itself. At the same time, however, Miller is aware that such a reality cannot be created by vague generalizations or ethereal allusions. He is a realist, if by that one means that in his plays he creates a recognizable moral and emotional landscape; and there is no question that his plays must be anchored in a discernible universe. The question for Miller seems to be how to strike the delicate balance between a corporeal environment and a suggestive landscape of the imagination. He understands, perhaps intuitively, that he cannot present the audience with a fully executed setting—the spectators, too, have an obligation. Miller appreciates that the spectators will have a greater belief in the onstage world if they must do part of the job of completing it.

Reality, at least in Miller's world, is made up of an accumulation of details—such as the cracked ceiling conjured up by Cobb—what Miller calls "facts." Discussing his response to the failure of his first Broadway production, *The Man Who Had All the Luck,* Miller described how he turned to one of his great inspirations, the Russian novelist Fyodor Dostoyevsky.

> I went back to that great book of wonder, *The Brothers Karamazov,* and I found what suddenly I felt must be true of it: that if one reads its most colorful, breathtaking, wonderful pages, one finds the thickest concentration of hard facts. Facts about the biographies of the characters, about the kind of bark on the moonlit trees, the way a window is hinged, the exact position of Dmitri as he peers through the window at his father, the precise description of his father's dress.[5]

Dostoevsky, in other words, created a palpable world through the accumulation of scenographic details—textures, shapes, geometry and topography. But a novel, of course, is neither a painting nor a three-dimensional space—it is a collection of words that may evoke an image of a space so real that we feel it, but it requires an act of translation from the word to the image. Novelists have no tools other than words, and the nineteenth-century writers in particular often described settings and environments in exquisite detail that created tangible environments, some of which continue to live in our imaginations more than a century later. The mistake of many naturalist playwrights had been to adopt this novelistic approach in their dramas by writing long, explicit, descriptive stage directions. But the descriptive passages of novels were transformed into reality by the reader's imagination, whereas the precise delineations of the playwrights were transformed into a literal reality by the stage carpenter burdened by the quotidian limitations of the naturalist stage. The result, most often, was not wonder but the mundane.

But Miller does take an almost sensual pleasure in the details—the facts, if you will. In a 1953 *New York Times* article he described his research for *The Crucible.* One can sense a kind of eroticism as he describes sitting in the Salem courthouse holding the town records of 1692 in his hands.

> . . . the books, the faded fragments of paper that once meant Proctor must hang tomorrow, paper that came through the farmhouse door in the hand of a friend who had a half-determined, half-ashamed look in his eyes. The tourists pass the books, the exhibits, and no hint of danger reaches them from the quaint relics. . . .
>
> And a feeling of love at seeing Rebecca Nurse's house on its gentle knoll; the house she lay in, ill, when they came, shuffling their feet, ashamed to have to ask her to come to court because the children said she had sent her spirit out.
>
> And the great rock, standing mum over the bay, the splintered precipice on which the gibbet was built. The highway traffic endlessly, mindlessly humming at its foot, but up here the barrenness, the clinkers of broken stones, and the vast view of the bay; here hung Rebecca, John Proctor, George Jacobs—people more real to me than the living can ever be.[6]

By being able to touch the objects his historical characters had touched, by walking where they walked, by gazing at the remains of a lost world, modern-day Salem evaporated in Miller's mind and old Salem emerged, just as the prosaic theater had vanished in the intonations of Lee J. Cobb's voice. For Miller, the historical objects and images are "facts," and his task is to provide the audience with the theatrical equivalent of these facts so that they too may be transported as he was.

A similar impulse is seen in an anecdote regarding *The Price.* Although not, strictly speaking, autobiographical, the play nonetheless drew upon Miller's life and experiences for its characters and details. The vocal patterns of the character Gregory Solomon, the used-furniture dealer of the play, for instance, were, according to Miller, inspired by one of Miller's most constant collaborators, Russian-born set designer Boris Aronson, whose accented English and occasionally fractured syntax were well known in theatrical circles. The play, about two brothers reuniting to divide the belongings of their late father, is set in an attic filled with furniture. Aronson saw the furniture as an additional—and most important—

character.[7] He asked Miller to describe the furniture he had in mind, and Miller recalled the dining table from his youth, which, as it turned out, still belonged to his aunt. That very table which "had once been a center of life, where my brother sat and did his lessons and I learned to read while Mother sketched us in a silence warmer than blanket or fire,"[8] ultimately wound up onstage together with other furniture Aronson had gathered from secondhand shops. Aronson, however, understood that simply placing these items on the stage would create neither the theatricality nor the world of theater that was required. Instead of merely arranging the furniture onstage, he broke the individual items into pieces and recombined them—some larger than original, some smaller, and some even formed into sculptural creations.[9] As Miller later said, "You can't take [furniture] out of a showroom and use it. The furniture should not be real—but more than real."[10] Miller's plays are grounded in the reality of places, objects, people and experience, but the emotional reality that audiences feel in his works comes not from literalism but from a symbolic use—a theatricalization—of the source material.

Miller's scenographic combination of realistic detail with heightened theatricality makes him sound amazingly like Bertolt Brecht. Brecht, working with his great friend, the designer Caspar Neher, evolved a signature scenographic style of fragmentary scenic units sitting, island-like, in the midst of the stage. But even when the scenery was highly stylized, the props and costumes were done with the greatest care and attention to detail—"lovingly" was the word Brecht used. "If in big matters there is such a thing as a beautiful approximation," explained Brecht, talking about *Mother Courage,* "in small there is not. What counts in a realistic portrayal is carefully worked out details of costumes and props, for here the audience's imagination can add nothing."[11] Those items handled by actors and the costumes that cover their bodies need to be as real as the actors themselves—they are extensions of the individual. (There are exceptions, of course, such as the stylized costumes of Alexandra Exter for Tairov's productions at Moscow's Kamerny Theatre, or the designs by the Bauhaus artists for their mechanical ballets, but in such cases the human qualities of the performers were being intentionally subverted.)

It is worth noting that Miller and Williams both came of age in the 1930s, making them part of the first generation to grow up in a theater shaped by the New Stagecraft. Developed by designers such as Robert Edmond Jones, Lee Simonson and Norman Bel Geddes, this movement introduced new European scenographic styles, especially symbolism and expressionism, into the American design vocabulary. The primary result was the simplification of naturalism—a stripping away of extraneous and decorative elements, thereby reducing the stage picture to a suggestive essence of place. Freed from certain illusionistic restrictions, a play could move through time and space in ways unavailable to naturalistic drama. Given the increasing influence of Stanislavski-inspired acting methods at the same time, the theater that emerged was a strange amalgam of psychologically and emotionally realistic acting nestled within a semi-abstract visual environment. Miller's primary exposure to the new style came in the 1930s through attending the productions of the Group Theatre, whose work he idolized, and through their designers Mordecai Gorelik and Boris Aronson. Although several of the Group's designs, especially for the Clifford Odets plays, were strongly in the naturalistic tradition, Miller saw their symbolic quality as well. "Gorelik and Aronson used color interpretively, like painters," Miller observed, "for its subjective effects and not merely its realistic accuracy."[12]

Miller, like everyone of his generation, was, of course, also strongly shaped by the movies. On the one hand, movies were a logical culmination and extension of the naturalistic movement with their ability to re-create or, by going on location, even capture settings in scrupulous detail, and thereby transport the viewer to the actual site. But they could also do seamlessly what the stage could do imperfectly at best, which was to move fluidly through time and space—from scene to scene, moment to moment and even from present to past and back. Tennessee Williams quite consciously employed this relatively new cinematic style—*The Glass Menagerie* even calls for "fade outs" at the end of scenes—and Miller acknowledges the "cinematic" qualities of *Death of a Salesman,* but the effect of the movies went deeper than mere narrative strategies or theatrical gimmicks. Movies were transforming the consciousness of a generation, not unlike the way in which computer technology is altering our consciousness today. The world was no longer seen as a series of discrete moments placed in sequential order within a single frame—it now flowed, one moment dissolving into the next, creating rapid and sometimes startling juxtapositions. Aristotelian unity was forced to give way to the magic of the camera lens and the film editor. This new consciousness would seep into the work of Miller and others, even the most realistic of them.

But there was one other influence that is seldom discussed in relation to theater and it may have been the most significant in terms of scenography: *radio.* The 1930s gave birth to a society that was as much the radio generation as it was the film generation. Here was a world in which the entire visual and corporeal reality existed in sound and in the individual imagination. Miller, of course, grew up listening to radio and had even written for the radio as part of the WPA Writers Project, and continued to write for radio through the early 1940s. Through experience, but mostly through an imagination shaped by this wondrous medium, he understood the connection between the suggestive sound, the verbal image and the creation of a world. "We had twenty-eight and a half minutes to tell a whole story in a radio play," recalled Miller in a 1966 interview, "and you had to concentrate on the words because you couldn't see anything. . . . So the economy of words in a good radio play was everything."[13] In a certain way, radio's sound effects were the "facts" that delighted him in the works of Dostoyevsky.

In the spring of 1998, Miller read from his new play, *Mr. Peters' Connections,* to an enthralled audience of about six hundred at Columbia University. Sitting alone at a table on an empty stage, Miller, using nothing more than his words, his speech rhythms and his intonations, spun Harry Peters' world out of whole cloth—a world that encompassed the living and the dead in a place that was at once an abandoned nightclub as well as some version of Dante's Purgatory. The reading elicited laughter, created suspense and evoked the sense of wonder Miller so desired in the theater. For all intents and purposes, the audience that night was listening to radio. At the end of his reading—he did not read the entire piece—the audience vociferously demanded more, as they might of a rock star or jazz musician at the end of a concert. The actual production a few months later at the Signature Theatre in New York was disappointing to most critics and audiences alike. One could seek causes—the casting, perhaps, or the directing—but some of the responsibility lay in the literalness. The introduction to the published text says that "the set . . . should look like whatever the reader or producer imagines as a space where the living and the dead may meet, the gray or blue or blazing red terrain of the sleeping mind where imagination runs free."[14] But once a designer places a set upon the stage, the audience can no longer imagine it; the imagination is no longer free. The trick, of course, is to preserve as much of the wonder as possible. The actual stage directions (one wishes Miller had not provided them) are much more pedestrian: "A broken structure indicating an old abandoned nightclub in New York City. A small, dusty upright piano, some chairs, a couple of tables, a few upended. Three chairs set close to the piano with instruments propped up on them—a bass, trumpet, saxophone."[15] The "radio" performance at Columbia allowed the stage to vanish and gave birth to six hundred unique scenographic visions; the stage production—perhaps inevitably—was a victim of muddled naturalism.

Many of Miller's productions have been victims of the clash of his subtle poeticism with the naturalistic impulse of much American theater. This dichotomy may account for the relative lack of success of many of his plays in New York and their greater success in England and elsewhere around the world (though certainly the more substantial British interest in a sociopolitical drama is a contributing factor as well). *The Price* may serve as a case in point. Aronson's attempt to theatricalize the setting was ultimately defeated by director Ulu Grosbard, who pushed the production toward a more pedestrian realism by relegating most of Aronson's design to mere background while the action unfolded on a fairly conventional arrangement of furniture downstage center.[16] Something similar had occurred with the Broadway production of *The Crucible.* Aronson wanted to evoke the mystery he found in Salem. His original set, according to Miller, was "unstable, with an ambience of mystery and unexpectedness; you didn't know what the hell was going to come next."[17] But director Jed Harris desired something more conventional—to make Miller's text seem more like an old classic play. The production was not received well. Interestingly, in an attempt to save money and keep the production alive, the amount of scenery was reduced and replaced with black velours—making a more expressionistic setting—and the critics who returned gave it a more favorable review.[18]

Boris Aronson, with his background in Russian constructivism and the symbolic and fantastic worlds of Leon Bakst and Marc Chagall, was in many ways an ideal collaborator for Miller. In addition to *The Price* and *The Crucible,* he also designed the sets for the one-act version of *A View from the Bridge, A Memory of Two Mondays, Incident at Vichy,* and *The Creation of the World and Other Business.* But the more literal tendencies of producers, directors or other forces often led to compromises that undermined the productions—sometimes in subtle ways.

Curiously, the one production to employ a blatantly nonrealistic set, *After the Fall* in 1964, was in fact hampered by the set. The production by the fledgling Repertory Theatre of Lincoln Center (performing then at the ANTA Washington Square Theatre) employed some of the same team that had created *Death of a Salesman:* director Elia Kazan and designer Jo Mielziner. Mielziner had designed a rounded thrust stage for the ANTA (as he would for the Vivian Beaumont at Lincoln Center; Tyrone Guthrie had recently created similar stages for the Shakespearean Festival Theatre in Stratford, Ontario, and the Guthrie Theatre in Minneapolis). Such a stage, with its echoes of Greek and Elizabethan theaters, can allow for a greater intimacy between actor and audience, but its openness can also present challenges to the designer—for one thing, it is harder to create a sense of enclosure—and the psychological effect upon the audience is different from that of a proscenium stage. For *After the Fall* Mielziner designed a set of Adolphe Appia–like steps descending against a curtained back wall onto a stage of irregularly shaped platforms. While it could be argued that the locus of the play was abstract since it unfolded in the memory of the lead character, Quentin, it also occurred in a concrete space. Quentin's memories, however distorted, were nonetheless anchored within a tangible world. Mielziner's design left the actors marooned in an abstract setting that left the audience equally adrift. Symbolist, or at least Chekhovian, design does not mean featureless abstraction; if the actors are representing psychological and emotional reality, then the setting, too, must have links to the world of the characters. Mielziner's abstract set, in this case, presented another problem, as Miller noted, because there was no place to hide, no place suddenly to come into view: "What is supposed to 'appear' doesn't appear," he complained, "but lumbers on stage toward you."[19] Miller much preferred Franco Zeffirelli's Italian production composed of steel frames. Miller compared it to a "bellows camera."

> The sides of these steel frames were covered, just like a camera is, but the actors could enter through openings in these covers. They could appear or disappear on the stage at any depth. Furthermore, pneumatic lifts silently and invisibly raised the actors up, so that they could appear for ten seconds—then disappear. Or a table would be raised or a whole group of furniture, which the actors would then use. So that the whole image of all this happening inside a man's head was there from the first second, and remained right through the play.[20]

It was not that the abstract steps and platforms of the New York set were wrong in and of themselves; it was the vast openness of the stage that worked against the production. And herein lies another clue as to why Miller's plays often work better abroad than at home. The worlds that Miller creates are simultaneously confined—metaphorically as well as literally by walls, ceilings, encroaching urban growth, piles of furniture, sickbeds—and open. Once the stage vanishes, as it were, the characters, in a sense, are left helpless and alone in a void. The most successful productions of Miller's plays have tended to create islands of reality (both concrete and suggestive) framed within the larger construct of the stage. The classic example, of course, is Jo Mielziner's 1949 set for *Death of a Salesman.* The framework of the Loman house is set on a slightly raised platform in the midst of the stage, surrounded by scrims (unbleached muslin that could appear solid or transparent depending upon lighting) which transform back and forth from the idyllic backyard of Willy's memories to the harsh domination of modern apartment buildings. The hotel, office and restaurant scenes were created with utter simplicity in front of the house by the addition of a few pieces of furniture and a change of lights and projections. The hotel room, in fact, used no furniture, only the image of cheap, faded wallpaper projected onto the trellis at the side of the Loman house. "Both the house and the exterior trellis faded away," as Mielziner described the moment. "The audience saw the Salesman in that cheap hotel room with that woman. I stress the phrase 'in that room.' Actors should never play against a scenic background but within the setting."[21]

Naturalistic settings generally extend to the sides of the stage and imply that the illusionistic world seen on the stage continues into the wings and beyond. The audience is asked to believe that a character exiting through an upstage door, for example, will continue onto the street where he may get into an automobile and drive off to the next city and so forth. The proscenium arch in such a design is a kind of looking glass and if, like Alice, we were to go through it, we would find ourselves in a complete and total world. Such was the case with Mordecai Gorelik's design for *All My Sons* in 1944 (although Gorelik liked to create metaphoric sets and the symbolic element was always present amid the reality); believing that *All My Sons* was "a graveyard play," Gorelik designed a gravelike hump in the set's backyard.[22] The fragmentary and island-like setting, on the other hand, still implies another world—we may fully believe that Willy Loman, entering through the door, has just returned from an aborted trip to Boston—but by placing the set in the midst of a stage, we are also asked to focus on the theatricality that may also suggest a greater universality. Such a setting also, at least subconsciously, has a metaphoric value—a metaphor that is implied rather than made manifest as in Gorelik's sets. A character who may walk through a door into a complete world possesses a kind of freedom. The illusion has the effect of saying that the location we see on the stage is a mere fragment of the character's total world. He or she may go through that door at any time—to "another part of the forest"—abandoning us. But in an isolated setting, the character is trapped. We can see the limits of his or her world. This is something that many postwar European scenographers understood as a result of their own political situation. Much postwar European design, especially (and not surprisingly) that of Eastern Europe, utilized high walls that created an overwhelming sense of enclosure. By placing walled or enclosed spaces within the greater open space of the stage, the designers suggested a tantalizing freedom beyond the reach of the trapped characters. American design, by contrast—also not surprisingly—tended toward openness. While almost all of Miller's plays deal to some extent with the dialectic of enclosure and freedom, nowhere is this theme more dominant than in *Death of a Salesman,* in which Willy Loman dreams of the open road as urban confinement encroaches ineluctably upon his world. The play is suffused with references to the West, open spaces, and, as playwright Kenneth Bernard has pointed out, the "Territory."[23] Mielziner understood this well. Describing his own set, he notes that "the surroundings have cut off [Willy's] freedom and his hopes. Even the trees have had their limbs cut off, and cheap apartment houses hem him in on all sides."[24]

The theaters that were built or created in the United States after World War II, particularly those of off-Broadway and the regional theaters, abandoned the proscenium—and thus the box set—in favor of the thrust and arena. Actors were thus left at sea on these stages that blended with audience space, or on older proscenium stages now stripped of illusionistic decor and left open to the wings. The European and American approaches were simply subconscious reflections of the society that produced them. But many of Miller's plays seemed better served by the more clearly defined and confined space of much European scenography.

British scenographer William Dudley understood this social and aesthetic dialectic when he designed the 1990 National Theatre production of *The Crucible* in London for the vast stage of the Olivier Theatre. Whereas Aronson, in the original, had attempted to capture a mood, Dudley seemed to think more in terms of space. "In design terms we start with a bare stage, and then enclose it," explained Dudley:

> People may have gone to America to get away from enclosures, but they brought the enclosure mentality with them. So we try to pen the characters in. Walls and posts appear, and *we show a much bigger space outside, which is mysterious and full of potential, and possibly hidden dangers* [emphasis added], whether it's Indians or climate. We've put one small window in. I think it's the only window in the piece, and these small enclosures are a kind of reflection of what they haven't freed themselves from.[25]

It is the combination of enclosure and isolation working together that seems to achieve the greatest success. *A View from the Bridge* failed on Broadway in 1955 and succeeded in Peter Brook's London production in

1956. Once again there were many contributing factors, not the least of which was that Miller rewrote the script between the two productions, changing it from a one-act to two acts and eliminating the use of verse. But the set changed as well. Aronson's design for the original was striking—a fragmentary Brooklyn apartment framed with elements of classical architecture and almost floating against a backdrop of the sea. But despite the "real" elements within it, it was too blatantly symbolic. More important, perhaps, it was too open. The protagonist Eddie Carbone was trapped by the sea in this design (which was more evocative of neoclassicism than suggestive of the Brooklyn waterfront), not by the city. Brook's production, by contrast, provided more realistic details and anchored the action within an identifiable if still theatrical space. Folding wings depicted the brick exterior of the tenement, which, when opened, revealed a basement apartment. "Overhead and at the sides and across the back were stairways, fire escapes, passages, quite like a whole neighborhood constructed vertically," Miller described.[26] This setting, in combination with the greater number of extras, who created a sense of an active neighborhood, provided the "facts" that allowed the threatricality of the play to breathe. Miller's plays almost always need the details to support the symbolist imagination, and the sense of enclosure and entrapment to contrast with the openness of the surrounding world.

Death of a Salesman posed problems of how to move fluidly back and forth in time and through several locations. Most importantly, it moved from external reality to the interior world of Willy Loman's mind. Mielziner, working with Tennessee Williams, had confronted this problem to a degree in *The Glass Menagerie* a few years earlier, but Williams was more blatant about the movement into memory in that play—it was foregrounded as a theatrical device. In *Salesman* the movement needed to be as fluid as thought itself. Mielziner's solution remains one of the most stunning creations in American scenography. The skeletal framework of the house, sitting like an island on the stage, provided a structure that held the play together while emphasizing its theatricality. Mielziner's other tool, more tentatively employed in *The Glass Menagerie* set—and that would become Mielziner's trademark—was the use of scrim in conjunction with elaborate lighting. Under the direction of electrician Ed Kook, head of Century Lighting, the production employed more lights than did most musicals of the time. The combination of lights and scrim allowed walls seemingly to dissolve and gave the whole production a slightly ethereal quality. Although the script, of course, was substantially complete before Mielziner entered the process, it was his input, together with that of director Elia Kazan and producer Kermit Bloomgarden, that gave the play its final shape and especially its rhythm. Miller did not specify how to make the transitions from one scene to the next, other than emphasizing that they should be done without the usual blackouts. It was the designer and director who solved the problem. Thus, to this day, any attempt to stage the play must take into account the scenographic solutions arrived at by Mielziner.

The 1999 Broadway revival of *Salesman,* directed by Robert Falls and designed by Mark Wendland, is an example of the potential pitfalls when seeking new solutions to the scenographic requisites. It seemed to be based on Mielziner's concepts, yet fundamentally misunderstood the texture and rhythms of the original. The designer (and presumably the director) chose to keep a suggestive setting of a skeletal framework house. But their scaffold-like setting (the legacy of Mielziner disciple Ming Cho Lee) alone on a dark, cavernous stage seemed more a theatrical device than a representation of a house or other setting. The tangible realities, so necessary to anchor the memories and fantasies, never quite materialized. It was hard to find a reality to grasp onto. There was no sense of enclosure, no grounding in details (except, significantly, the richly detailed and historically accurate props, which, far more than the setting, I believe, drew the audience into the world of the play). More significantly, changes were effected not through lighting and the evanescence of the set, but by a double revolving stage (one inside the other) that launched scenic units into motion, creating the effect of a choreographed musical-theater transition. Every transition jolted the spectators back into an awareness of the mechanics of the theater. Perhaps this effect was intentional—a postmodern foregrounding of technology to counter the emotional impact of the text. But mostly it was distracting, fortunately ameliorated by the powerful performances of the actors and, of course, Miller's text.

This is not to suggest that only Mielziner's solution can work. There have, after all, been several successful productions that dealt with the contingencies of a particular space or reflected the changing sensibilities of the audience. One thinks in particular of the 1984 Broadway revival of *Salesman* with Dustin Hoffman, designed by Ben Edwards. But, it seems, the crucial dialectics of Miller's plays—the landscape of the mind versus the topography of the quotidian world, tangible reality versus ephemeral memory, the enclosure of urban spaces and domestic environments versus the openness of the sea or unexplored territories—must always be present and must always be made visible by the designer. At present, the American imagination, at least, seems bound by the overwhelming domination of television and film. The result is either a deadening literalism, or else an attempt at abstraction that lacks the range and subtlety required by Miller's symbolist worldview.

Notes

1. Arthur Miller, "The American Theater," in *The Theater Essays of Arthur Miller,* ed. Robert A. Martin and Steven R. Centola (New York: Da Capo Press, 1996), 49.
2. Ibid.
3. Frantisek Deak, *The Symbolist Theater: The Formation of an Avant-Garde* (Baltimore: Johns Hopkins University Press, 1993), 144.
4. Miller, "The Crucible," in *The Portable Arthur Miller,* ed. Harold Clurman (New York: Viking Press, 1977), 137.
5. Miller, "Introduction to the Collected Plays," in *Theater Essays,* 127.
6. In Miller, *Theater Essays,* 28–29.
7. Frank Rich with Lisa Aronson, *The Theatre Art of Boris Aronson* (New York: Alfred A. Knopf, 1987), 163.
8. Miller, *Timebends: A Life* (New York: Grove Press, 1987), 15.
9. Rich, *Boris Aronson,* 163.
10. Ibid.
11. Bertolt Brecht, *Brecht on Theatre,* ed. and trans. John Willett (New York: Hill and Wang, 1966), 219–20.
12. Miller, *Timebends,* 230.
13. Miller, *Theater Essays,* 277.
14. Miller, preface to *Mr. Peters' Connections* (New York: Penguin, 1999), viii.
15. Miller, *Mr. Peters' Connections,* 1.
16. Rich, *Boris Aronson.*
17. Ibid., 105.
18. Ibid.
19. Miller, *Theater Essays,* 289.
20. Ibid., 288.
21. Jo Mielziner, *Designing for the Theatre* (New York: Bramhall House, 1965), 47.
22. Miller, *Timebends,* 274–75.
23. See Philip C. Kolin, "*Death of a Salesman:* A Playwrights' Forum," *Michigan Quarterly Review* 37, no. 4 (1998): 596–600.
24. Mielziner, *Designing for the Theatre,* 145.
25. *Arthur Miller and Company: Arthur Miller Talks about His work in the Company of Actors, Designers, Directors, and Writers,* ed. Christopher Bigsby (London: Methuen, 1990), 94.
26. Miller, "Introduction to the Collected Plays," 167.

Andrew Sofer

From Technology to Trope
The Archbishop's Ceiling and Miller's Prismatic Drama

The Archbishop's Ceiling marks a significant departure in Arthur Miller's drama. Ever since his first Broadway success, *All My Sons* (1947), Miller has chronicled the American self under pressure, a pressure manifested as the past catching up with the present despite the self's attempt to deny that past. Yet in *The Archbishop's Ceiling* (1977), set not in the United States but in Eastern Europe, the fugitive self pursued by the external consequences of past acts of betrayal gives way to the self as a fiction: a maelstrom of conflicting forces that threaten to explode identity from within.

How then to express this internalized pressure within the framework of drama, in which conflict must somehow be externalized for an audience? Miller's revised notion of the self demanded a new dramaturgy, and one reason *The Archbishop's Ceiling* initially failed in performance is that its realistic production style obscured the fact that the play's true subject is not political repression, as most critics of the play suggest, but dramatic form itself.[1] Beneath a superficially conventional plot, which involves a dissident writer's choice between saving himself or his art, *The Archbishop's Ceiling* critiques the linear dramaturgy Miller inherited from Ibsen in order to embrace a prismatic, nonlinear dramatic structure. Miller's repudiation of a dramatic form he had earlier championed is signaled by the play's shift from stage technology to poetic trope: in other words, from theatrical devices that drive the plot forward, as in Ibsen, to a single metaphor, "the bugged ceiling of the mind," which transforms linear action into existential predicament.[2]

In drama, Miller writes, "It is necessary to employ the artificial in order to arrive at the real," and nowhere has this fact been more evident than in Miller's skillful use of theater technology.[3] I refer not just to computerized or electronic devices and effects, but to the concrete, theatrical means by which dramaturgical problems are solved on stage. In this sense, as Susan Bennett points out, "Technology has always been a part of theatre."[4] Every significant dramaturgy summons a technology adequate to it: the deus ex machina of the Greeks, the trap door to Hell of the Elizabethan playhouse, the groove-and-shutter scenery of the Restoration, the nineteenth-century black box, and so on. But the traffic between theater and technology moves in both directions. New theatrical technologies in turn open up new dramatic opportunities for playwrights able to seize them, as when the machinery concealed above the stage of the Blackfriars Theatre, which the King's Men acquired use of in 1608, inspired Shakespeare to grace his late romances with divine visitations. From the letter in *All My Sons* (1947) to the music in *Death of a Salesman* (1949) to the spotlight in *After the Fall* (1964) to the Brechtian projections in *Clara* (1986), Miller's increasingly sophisticated engagement with technology has had far-reaching implications for his dramaturgy. For if Miller's thematic quarry is what it means to be a responsible, morally accountable human being, modern electronic technology challenges the very existence of such a bedrock through its uncanny ability to double, fragment and disperse the subject.[5]

Not coincidentally, at the very point in Miller's drama at which technology threatens to dissolve the self's coherence, it is troped out of material existence on the stage. *The Archbishop's Ceiling* revolves around a listening device that may or may not be concealed in the ceiling of a former archbishop's residence, now frequented by local and foreign writers in an Eastern European police state. The soot-covered ceiling features a baroque painting of cherubim and the four winds; in Miller's ironic vision, the bug has displaced God as omniscient, inscrutable observer and judge of human behavior. Miller has described *The Archbishop's Ceiling* as "a dramatic meditation on the impact of immense state power upon human identity and the common concept of what is real and illusory in a group of writers living in a small European capital today."[6] Given his emphasis on the precariousness of human identity, Miller's decision to remove the onstage figure of the listener, Martin, from his revision of the play raises the ontological stakes considerably.[7] Is the bug there or not there? More disturbingly, does it finally matter whether or not the authorities are listening? "Do you think God sees me?" asks Gogo in *Waiting for Godot,* voicing the same existential uneasiness that afflicts Miller's performers in *The Archbishop's Ceiling.*[8]

The play's *esse est percipi* conceit, "to be is to be perceived," borrowed from Bishop Berkeley by way of Beckett, has wider political ramifications.[9] Although *The Archbishop's Ceiling* is set in Eastern Europe, it embodies Miller's frustrated response to the "indefinition" and "exhaustion" of radicalism in the United States of the seventies.[10] Miller's introduction to *The Archbishop's Ceiling,* a work of the 1970s, captures the sense of disillusionment within the American Left in the wake of the Kent State massacre: "Power everywhere seemed to have transformed itself from a forbidding line of troops into an ectoplasmic lump that simply swallowed up the righteous sword as it struck."[11] In the era of Watergate and Vietnam, the hidden listening device takes on an emblematic significance; the bug crystallizes Miller's conviction that "the visible motions of political life were too often merely distractions, while the reality was what was happening in the dark."[12] Still more disturbingly, in Miller's view authoritarian power has so saturated the self that to some extent we are all speaking to the bugged ceiling of the mind. Displaced from the United States onto an Eastern European stage, where power only *seems* to be more "sharply defined," *The Archbishop's Ceiling* is a political fable about how power undermines the "I" and turns resistance into performance (11).

Yet in addition to its political freight, *The Archbishop's Ceiling* contains a metatheatrical dimension. It is a play about how drama *itself* confronts the challenge posed by the postmodern disintegration of the self to a traditional dramaturgy built on the link between psychological motivation and individual behavior. Miller has acknowledged that he inherited this psychological dramaturgy from Ibsen, who himself adapted the structure of the nineteenth-century well-made play—along with its *raisonneurs,* reversals and denouements—for morally forensic ends. "What is precious in the Ibsen method is its insistence on valid causation, and this cannot be dismissed as a wooden notion," Miller insisted in the late 1950s.[13] In the linear, psychological drama championed by Ibsen, what one does is what one is—and what one is is nothing less than the sum of one's actions up to the present moment. In this drama of "valid causation," motivation *is* character, and vice versa. Mrs. Alving, Hedda Gabler, John Gabriel Borkman and the rest flee the consequences of their past failures of moral nerve only to be squeezed in the vise of the well-made plot. Richard Gilman tersely defines the well-made plot as "the unfolding of a 'story' through the concatenation of incidents that build logically to a climax."[14] Miller's own image of Ibsen's achievement is more vivid: "the marvelous spectacle of life forcing one event out of the jaws of the preceding one."[15]

Such moral accountability traps Joe Keller in Miller's early play *All My Sons.* As Hersh Zeifman writes, "The play's order stems from its relentless Ibsenite realism, a mimesis celebrating linearity, chronology, causality: the ghosts of the past—what Miller once termed 'the birds coming home to roost'—return to haunt the present and to shape its future."[16] With the implacability of an *Oedipus Rex,* the play brings Keller face to face with the fact that his shipment of faulty airplane parts during World War II, which resulted in the death of twenty-one pilots, is also responsible for the death of his pilot son Larry—who committed suicide on learning of his father's guilt. The very act Keller believed necessary to preserve the family business has destroyed his family, and this realization drives Keller to shoot himself.

Within the constraints of fourth-wall realism, Ibsen's challenge was to make the causal past tangible on stage without getting bogged down in interminable exposition. His solution was to borrow the fateful prop from the Scribean *pièce bien faite* in order to embody the past in "speaking" objects: Krogstad's letter in *A Doll's House,* Captain Alving's pipe in *Ghosts,* General Gabler's portrait and pistols in *Hedda Gabler.* In *All My Sons,* Miller makes similarly forensic use of the fateful prop. Causality is embodied in the letter *ex machina* from Joe's dead son, Larry, which appears just in time to explain his suicide and precipitate Joe's own. Like Captain Alving's pipe or General Gabler's portrait, Larry's letter is an indictment from beyond the grave. It is not a symbol, like the stunted tree that metaphorically represents Larry on the set of *All My Sons,* but a *medium of communication.* Miller seizes on the device of the letter—one of theater's most primitive technologies—to solve an ancient dramatic problem (a Greek messenger would have accomplished the same job still less elegantly).

Miller's next play, *Death of a Salesman,* demonstrates a quantum leap in Miller's mastery of theater technology even as it marks his attempt to break out of "a method one might call linear or eventual in that one fact or incident creates the necessity for the next."[17] As Enoch Brater has shown, the play modulates between Willy Loman's inner dream-life and his present-day reality thanks to Miller's fluid use of a transparent, highly symbolic set, expressionistic lighting and evocative flute music, as well as poetically expressive dialogue: "In *Salesman,* Miller's emblematic realism therefore holds the naturalistic and the symbolic in perfect equilibrium."[18]

Miller would push the expressionistic elements of his drama still further in *After the Fall* (1964), which Hersh Zeifman accurately calls an "expressionistic soulscape."[19] Entering middle-aged Quentin's tormented unconscious, we are plunged even further into "the inside of his head" (to borrow Miller's original title for *Death of a Salesman*). The set no longer pays lip service to a realistic environment: "The action takes place in the mind, thought, and memory of Quentin," and Miller calls for "a lavalike, supple geography in which, like pits and hollows found in lava, the scenes take place."[20] Here Miller's key technological device for modulating between inner and outer experience is not music but the spotlight that, as in Beckett's *Play,* acts the role of inquisitor. A "sharp light" isolates Quentin on the stage and choreographs the action as figures from Quentin's haunted past move in and out of its focus.[21] The lighting repeatedly directs Quentin's attention to key moments of betrayal, moments underscored for the audience by the lighting up of the concentration camp tower that looms at the rear of the set. Miller would not revisit such unabashed expressionism until his 1998 memory play, *Mr. Peters' Connections,* which also features a man seeking to draw the disconnected threads of his life together.

Miller is, above all, an anatomist of consciousness. He is fascinated with how individuals are seduced into ideologies that take the place of real, felt experience. Such anatomizing is at bottom optimistic, since it ultimately envisions what William W. Demastes calls "a (re)construction of a world more fully predicated on a sense of moral responsibility involving truly disinterested actions benefiting our fellows via a fully rounded sense of social commitment."[22] But by the time of *After the Fall,* the unitary self that would undergird such a project was already beginning to splinter, and Miller began to seek more sophisticated theatrical means to stage his unraveling conception of character. As bigamist Lyman Felt puts it in *The Ride Down Mt. Morgan* (1991):

> Look, we're all the same; a man is a fourteen-room house—in the bedroom he's asleep with his intelligent wife, in the living room he's rolling around with some bare-ass girl, in the library he's paying his taxes, in the yard he's raising tomatoes. And in the cellar he's making a bomb to blow it all up.[23]

In Miller's subsequent drama, the recurrent image of the split self represents an unintegrated identity that refuses to cohere into a morally accountable whole.

Miller stages this lack of coherence not through the video monitors beloved by theatrical postmodernists, but through machines cunningly introduced into the action.[24] At the climax of *The Price* (1968), exhausted furniture dealer Gregory Solomon, overwhelmed by the weight of the past, cannot resist joining in with the "Laughing Record" on a windup Victrola that plunges him into nostalgia for his younger days as a vaudeville artist. In *Clara* (1986)—a short play that, uncharacteristically for Miller, makes use of Brechtian projections on a screen to indicate the contents of consciousness—a disoriented man whose daughter has just been murdered reacts to his voice as a young soloist on a phonographic record with a weak "Good Lord."[25] Yet these instances are just that—fleeting moments that underscore the capacity of the self to experience itself as Other, as uncannily outside one's own body. This divided or split self is not the same as the *illusory* self anatomized in *The Archbishop's Ceiling*.[26] In such later plays as *The Ride Down Mt. Morgan* and *Broken Glass* (1994), Miller would return to the divided protagonist whose task is to integrate past and present into a coherent self; only in *The Archbishop's Ceiling* does the very self that underpins Miller's drama of moral accountability threaten to dissolve into an absurdist fiction. The existential threat posed by the bug unleashes a new dramaturgy based on a principle different from "valid causation": that of power.

The Archbishop's Ceiling, written thirty years after *All My Sons,* stages Miller's most insinuating technological device as a trope—the (invisible) bug—in order to pit the causal dramaturgy of motive against what one might call the *prismatic* dramaturgy of power. A prism, we recall, is a transparent solid (in this case a play) used to produce or analyze a continuous spectrum. Instead of a linear plot that dramatizes the protagonist's failed attempt to elude responsibility for his own actions—the pattern that tends to structure Miller's drama from *All My Sons* onwards—prismatic drama presents variations on a single theme. Within this "spatial" rather than linear dramaturgy, a play becomes a fugue of counterpointed melodies rather than an aria building to a crescendo.[27] There is little or no plot development to speak of; each character responds to a given situation in his or her own way, and that spectrum of responses *is* the action. No character is held responsible for his or her actions; there is no punishment or reward, as in melodrama, nor are we asked to judge who is behaving correctly or incorrectly, as in Ibsen's social drama. In prismatic drama, which dates back at least as far as Strindberg's *A Dream Play* (1901), there is no protagonist, no plot, no resolution—only variegated behavior in response to a common stimulus. Thus (to cite three exemplary instances) *Three Sisters* dramatizes the responses of a set of characters to unhappiness; *Waiting for Godot* to boredom; and *The Archbishop's Ceiling* to power.

The Archbishop's Ceiling hovers between the causal (in which *x* occurs) and the prismatic (in which *x* is refracted through mediums of different densities). Like an anamorphic painting, we can experience Miller's play from two competing perspectives. Depending on which perspective we take, the play's emphasis, and indeed its message, shifts. In the drama of causation, the play is a plea for personal responsibility in a world that has lost its moral bearings; in the drama of power, it is a wry acknowledgment of the impossibility of judging those whose actions no longer spring from coherent psychological motivation. Ingeniously, Miller dramatizes this clash not only through characterization, but by juxtaposing outmoded and emergent technologies. The causal and the prismatic principles are represented by two objects: the pistol, that most Ibsenite of fateful props, which (in part) drives the linear action; and the bug, whose "there/not there" ambiguity pitches the characters into existential crisis. Crudely put, in the drama of the pistol, actions have discernible origins and clear consequences; in the drama of the bug, they have neither. It is no coincidence that the first object is material, the second phantasmal.[28]

At the start of *The Archbishop's Ceiling* we meet Adrian, a famous American writer who has arrived in a nameless Eastern European capital (presumably Prague) to visit old writer friends. Adrian is fleeing a pompous symposium on the contemporary novel at the Sorbonne, and in a conversation with Maya, a local playwright turned host of an innocuous radio show, it becomes apparent that Adrian is in crisis. He suffers from writer's block, a condition brought on by the fact that a pill has magically lifted the depression of his lover, Ruth. Overnight, the pill has transformed Ruth into a happy and productive member of society: "It plugged her in to some . . . some power. And she lit up" (10). But if the self can be switched on and off like a lightbulb by chemical means, then the self cannot be held responsible for its own actions or even feelings. Adrian's psychologized brand of fiction has become pointless.

Adrian mistakenly believes that he can recover his moral bearings in a state whose repressive regime forces writers (as he thinks) either to take a firm stand against power or else connive with it: "You have no pills in this country, but power is very sharply defined here. The government makes it very clear that you must snuggle up to power or you will never be happy" (11). Adrian seeks to confirm a rumor spread by a fellow American: that Marcus and Maya, writers who enjoy a limited freedom denied their colleagues, invite fellow writers to orgies and tape the writers with young girls in order to compromise them with the government. That Adrian's quest for moral certainties is ultimately in bad faith is made clear by the fact that he not only wishes to interview Maya in the interests of his research, but to sleep with her as well—despite the fact that Maya is the lover of Adrian's absent host.

Miller depicts Adrian as a kind of vampire, a privileged outsider who seeks to revivify his voyeuristic art by exploiting the moral dilemmas of others; Adrian's situation thus mirrors Miller's own quandary in writing a play about his Czech colleagues. Adrian's crisis only intensifies in the course of the play, because his conception of the moral accountability of the "I" proves inadequate to the complexity of the situation. Under the archbishop's ceiling, the local writers must continually perform for an invisible audience who may or may not be paying attention. The play tracks Adrian's bewilderment, suspicion and anger at the fact that his friends seem largely unconcerned by their putative surveillance: "It's like some kind of continuous crime" (43). But performativity proves catching: the writers' condition soon infects Adrian, whose words sound increasingly hollow and self-serving.

Although Adrian is a novelist, he stands in for Miller the playwright, a man whose once firm faith in the moral accountability of the self has been shaken: "Here I'm laying out motives, characterizations, secret impulses—the whole psychological chess game—when the truth is I'm not sure anymore that I believe in psychology. That anything we think really determines what we're going to do. Or even what we feel" (9). What has shaken Adrian's faith is power, an intangible force-field that compels action even as it disconnects acts and their consequences from individual agency. Adrian travels to Eastern Europe in search of a place where the struggle between the individual conscience and power has not collapsed into cheap melodrama on the one hand or amoral chaos on the other. His quest is precisely the one that impels the playwright: "Whether it matters anymore, what anyone feels . . . about anything. Whether we're not just some sort of . . . filament that only lights up when it's plugged into whatever power there is" (83).

Marcus, Adrian's urbane and cosmopolitan host, personifies Adrian's predicament. To Adrian, Marcus is a man without definable qualities, "a total blank" (14). Adrian's question—is Marcus a government agent?—is naive, almost what one might call a category mistake. By turns anthropologist, American soldier, literary editor, imprisoned dissident writer and womanizing capitalist, the protean Marcus defies the principle and the poetics of accountability. Marcus is a series of acts without a self, a man whose every remark is at once overdetermined and obscure. (Disconcertingly, he alone besides Adrian speaks perfect English.) Marcus embodies the principle of adaptation to power, symbolized by his apparent indifference to the bug that may or may not lurk in the ceiling of his residence: "How can I know what is in this room? How ludicrous can you get?" (66).

Marcus returns unexpectedly from a trip abroad, one of the perks mysteriously allowed him by the authorities. He arrives at the door accompanied by a beautiful Danish woman, Irina, and by the country's greatest writer, Sigmund (whose name suggests Freud's Janus-faced legacy of psychological motivation on the one hand, and overdetermined behavior on the other). It turns out that Marcus's true motive is to convince his friend and rival Sigmund to emigrate. Marcus reports that in London he met a secret policeman who warned him that the flamboyantly dissident Sigmund faces arrest and imprisonment as retribution for publishing articles critical of the regime. Since exile to America would spell the end of his writing career—a kind of spiritual and artistic death—Sigmund must weigh the truth of Marcus's account, as well as Marcus's motivation, before making up his mind. Is Marcus driven by the urge to preserve political space for less openly confrontational writers, as he claims? Or is he spurred by jealousy over Sigmund's greater artistic powers and Sigmund's affair with Maya to invent the tale of the policeman? A brief exchange with Adrian underscores the ambiguity:

> *Adrian:* He's an agent.
> *Sigmund:* Is possible not.
> *Adrian:* Then what is he?
> *Sigmund:* Marcus is Marcus. (50)

In short, the inscrutable Marcus represents everything Adrian, the naive and insulated American, is unequipped to grasp.

From the perspective of psychological causality, the play is structured traditionally around the plot question: will Sigmund allow himself to be convinced to save himself by emigrating? As in *A Doll's House* or *Hedda Gabler,* objects propel the linear plot. First there is the manuscript of Sigmund's novel, an apparent masterpiece that is snatched from Sigmund's apartment at the beginning of the play and eventually (perhaps) returned as a demonstration of the regime's godlike mercy. Second, there is the pistol that Sigmund steals from Marcus's briefcase as insurance against arrest. If the offstage manuscript is a blatant device, a McGuffin to get the plot rolling, the pistol is a tried-and-true way to ratchet up the dramatic tension in a very talky play: at various points Maya, Marcus and Adrian each seek to retrieve the gun. But Miller's point here is metatheatrical: Sigmund steals the gun explicitly *as a prop.* If the authorities know he possesses it, they will be less likely to risk an international scandal by arresting him. Sigmund's recourse to the clunkiest of melodramatic devices is the logical response to his situation: "Is like some sort of theatre, no? Very bad theatre—our emotions have no connection with the event" (90). And as if to protest the fact, Sigmund stages a defiant piece of performance art for the benefit of his unseen audience by placing the cocked gun on the strings of Marcus's piano—that most egregious symptom of bourgeois realism—and playing a crashing chord that sets it off. The gesture is, quite literally, melodramatic.

The ending of *The Archbishop's Ceiling* observes the classical structure of reversal, revelation and resolution. Sigmund's return of the pistol to Marcus signals a turning point in the action; by conceding that he no longer fears arrest, Sigmund tacitly accuses Marcus of lying to him. This in turn leads to the revelation that Marcus and Maya have cut a deal: in exchange for keeping their privileges (Maya's radio program, Marcus's passport), the couple must "deliver" Sigmund's emigration to the authorities. At the play's climax, Sigmund refuses to trade the ability to speak truth to power at home for cushy exile in an American university, and *The Archbishop's Ceiling* ends with Sigmund's invocation of the names of great writers with whom he has corresponded. According to Miller's introduction, by bowing to the god of art, Sigmund transcends tyranny; but by setting up Sigmund as a martyr to the cause of art—albeit a flawed, narcissistic one—Miller buys a redemptive ending at the risk of replicating the very artifice he critiques.[29] It is as if Sigmund has become a character in Adrian's failed novel: "Funny how life imitates art; the melodrama kept flattening out my characterizations" (20).

To Miller's credit, the play sustains another reading, in which not Sigmund but Adrian is the protagonist. Seen from this perspective, the play is not an object lesson in authenticity but a study in the insidiousness of power, which is no longer a weapon (the pistol) but an environment ("the bugged ceiling of the mind"). In this much subtler drama, Adrian must absorb the Foucauldian lesson that power is a medium we move through rather than a tool wielded by the strong against the weak.[30] Every character, except for the two foreigners (Adrian and Irina, who seems not to realize that her femininity is itself an elaborate masquerade), already grasps this. The presumed bug in the ceiling only magnifies the conviction that one is always talking or behaving for an audience, a conviction that is at root existential.

Here Miller capitalizes on the phenomenology of theater itself. The audience is placed in the position of the bug: we are the invisible listeners (and observers) for whom the actors perform. The bug is at once a microphone and an amplifier that allows the characters to monitor their own inauthentic behavior. The truly disturbing thing about the bug—and the proof that in this play Miller transcends the drama's crudest devices, even as he trots them out—is that its actual presence is immaterial. Simply the belief that the bug *might* be there transforms life into "very bad theater," and this is no less true in Washington than in Prague. "It would seem that the 'I' must be singular, not plural, but the art of bureaucracy is to change the 'I' of its subjects to 'we' at every moment of conscious life."[31]

In the prismatic drama, then, each character embodies a different accommodation with power, a set of strategies that has congealed into a way of life. Irina, Marcus's girlfriend, represents sheer ignorance—unless she, too, is a plant; significantly, Irina's husband is said to work for the BBC, another invisible technological presence. Maya, whose name means "illusion" in Hindi, inevitably becomes a symbol of the country itself. Not coincidentally, she sleeps with all the men (even the American) in order to preserve what freedom of movement she has. Rather than use that freedom productively, she retreats into alcohol and the consumer-porn fantasies of *Vogue* magazine; her redemptive feature is that she recognizes Sigmund as the conscience of her nation, and her motive throughout is to protect him (it is interesting to speculate what would have happened to the play's sexual politics had Maya been the writer with the greatest talent).

Marcus, as we have seen, is an index of the fractured self that "ectoplasmic" power produces. It is impossible to determine whether or not Marcus is a government agent, hence guilty on Adrian's moral abacus, because his dance with power precludes a coherent subjectivity. Marcus's motivation is to survive, to maintain the freedom to continue performing. Since Sigmund's showy acts of rebellion threaten to force a crackdown by the authorities, he must be put safely out of the picture so that the dance can continue. As Marcus sourly notes, by playing power's game, he has carved out the very political space that allows Sigmund the luxury to accuse him of selling out.[32]

Thus Sigmund, who in the drama of accountability embodies a principled stand of which the other writers are incapable, stands revealed in the drama of power as a performer addicted to an outmoded dramaturgy of moral calculus. Such is Marcus's accusation:

> You are a moral blackmailer. We have all humored you, Sigmund, out of some misplaced sense of responsibility to our literature. Or maybe it's only our terror of vanishing altogether. . . . We have taken all the responsibility and left you all the freedom to call us morally bankrupt. But now you're free to go, so the responsibility moves to you. Now it's yours. All yours. We have done what is possible; now you will do what is necessary, or turn out our lights. (99)

No less addicted to performance than Marcus, Sigmund requires the persona of the dissident writer in order to sustain his oppositional art. His decision to stay (and, as it were, complete his performance) is as self-serving as Marcus's insistence that he leave. To Maya's plea for exculpation, "Is love not love because there is some profit in it? Who speaks only for his heart?" Sigmund responds, "I speak for Sigmund" (100–101). But Maya denies that "Sigmund" is any less a construct produced by power than the others: "They are your theme, your life, your partner in this dance that cannot stop or you will die of silence! They are in you, darling" (101). Beneath the hidden microphones, trapped on stage before a theater audience, Sigmund is less hero than poseur.

In the drama of accountability, Adrian is morally compromised beyond repair and merely provides a touchstone for Sigmund's principled stand. But in the drama of power, Adrian is a would-be *raisonneur* probing an alien dramaturgy: the first time we see him he is lifting couch cushions and peering into the piano, trying to uncover the rumored bug. Adrian arrives in Eastern Europe on a mission to regenerate his art, only to find his worst suspicions confirmed. Saturated by the technology of power, the self is a "strategic zone" rather than an agent, and psychological causality a myth rather than an explanation (65). More chorus than protagonist by the end, Adrian is left echoing the question with which he began: "Whether it matters anymore, what anyone feels . . . about anything. Whether we're not just some sort of whatever power there is" (73). Under the archbishop's ceiling, the self is not a clockwork orange programmed by the state but something more unnerving: Peer Gynt's onion, layers of performance without a core.

The Archbishop's Ceiling dramatizes not only the collision of American idealism with Eastern Europe realpolitik, but the clash between two competing notions of the self and the dramaturgies they summon. In a sense, the play's metatheatrical engagements are a response to its political ones, for *The Archbishop's Ceiling* reflects Miller's realization that the causal dramaturgy embodied in plays like *All My Sons* and *A View from the Bridge* is no longer adequate to the sociopolitical situation. Thus the play stages an outmoded dramaturgy that is critiqued theatrically by means of a trope. Just as the presence of the audience turns the onstage action into a piece of theater, so the invisible bug turns the pistol into a prop and the characters into mouthpieces. If the drama of causation cannot resist lionizing Sigmund as a symbol of artistic integrity (in contrast to the American selfishly seeking both artistic and sexual renewal), the drama of power reveals that we are all complicit with the bugged ceiling of the mind. In *The Archbishop's Ceiling,* Miller's subtlest piece of metatheater to date, theater itself becomes both master technology and master trope for exposing the incoherence of the subject, the performativity of behavior and the chimera of psychological unity.

Notes

1. See, for example, Dennis Welland, *Miller: The Playwright* (London: Methuen, 1985), 156–68; June Schlueter, "Power Play: Arthur Miller's *The Archbishop's Ceiling,*" *CEA Critic* 49 (Winter 1986–Summer 1987): 134–38; and William W. Demastes, "Miller's 1970s 'Power' Plays," in *The Cambridge Companion to Arthur Miller,* ed. Christopher Bigsby (Cambridge: Cambridge University Press, 1997), 139–51. Christopher Bigsby, *A Critical Introduction to Twentieth-Century American Drama,* vol. 2 (Cambridge: Cambridge University Press, 1984), views *The Archbishop's Ceiling* as a play about the nature of the real, in which "the social and psychological defer in some degree to the ontological" (236).

2. Arthur Miller, *Timebends: A Life* (New York: Grove Press, 1987), 573.

3. Arthur Miller, "On Broadway: Notes on the Past and Future of American Theater," *Harpers,* March 1999, 47.

4. Susan Bennett, "Comment," *Theatre Journal* 51 (1999): 358.

5. See Johannes Birringer, "Contemporary Performance/Technology," *Theatre Journal* 51 (1999): 361–81.

6. *New York Times,* May 3, 1977, cited by Welland, *Miller,* 139.

7. One might compare Samuel Beckett's decision to allow the Auditor to be omitted from the television production of *Not I,* which similarly raises the ontological stakes. For an account of Miller's revisions to *The Archbishop's Ceiling,* see Welland, *Miller,* 156–62.

8. Samuel Beckett, *Waiting for Godot,* in *The Collected Plays of Samuel Beckett* (London: Faber and Faber, 1986), 71.

9. Beckett's short play *Catastrophe,* written for Václav Havel, represents Beckett's own response to the predicament of Eastern European writers and provides a fascinating contrast to *The Archbishop's Ceiling.*

10. Arthur Miller, "Conditions of Freedom: Two Plays of the Seventies," *The Archbishop's Ceiling* and *The American Clock* (New York: Grove Press, 1989), vii. All subsequent citations from *The Archbishop's Ceiling* are cited parenthetically in the text.

11. Ibid.

12. Ibid., viii.

13. Arthur Miller, introduction to *Collected Plays,* vol. 1 (New York: Viking Press, 1957), 21.

14. Richard Gilman, *The Making of Modern Drama* (New York: Farrar, Straus and Giroux, 1974), 203.

15. Miller, introduction to *Collected Plays,* 22.

16. Hersh Zeifman, "All My Sons after the Fall: Arthur Miller and the Rage for Order," in *The Theatrical Gamut: Notes for a Post-Beckettian Stage,* ed. Enoch Brater (Ann Arbor: University of Michigan Press, 1995), 107–8. The Miller quotation is from *Arthur Miller and Company,* ed. Christopher Bigsby (London: Methuen, 1990), 49.

17. Miller, introduction to *Collected Plays,* 23.

18. Enoch Brater, "Miller's Realism and *Death of a Salesman,*" in *Arthur Miller: New Perspectives,* ed. Robert A. Martin (Englewood Cliffs, N.J.: Prentice Hall, 1982), 114. Brenda Murphy provides a useful account of *Salesman*'s "subjective realism" and of Miller's subsequent rejection of this technique in "Arthur Miller: Revisioning Realism," in *Realism and the American Dramatic Tradition,* ed. William W. Demastes (Tuscaloosa: University of Alabama Press, 1996), 189–202.

19. Zeifman, "All My Sons," 113.

20. Arthur Miller, *After the Fall,* in *Collected Plays,* vol. 2 (New York: Viking Press, 1981), 127.

21. Ibid., 128.

22. Demastes, "Miller's 1970s 'Power' Plays," 149.

23. Arthur Miller, *The Ride Down Mt. Morgan* (London: Penguin, 1991), 81.

24. An early use of such a device occurs in *Death of a Salesman,* when Howard's tape recorder uncannily jumps to life and terrifies Willy. However, the "self" on the tape is not Willy but Howard's small son. For Miller's careful use of objects as "pivots of human action and revelation," see Marianne Boruch, "Miller and Things," *Literary Review* 24 (1981): 548–61. For the postmodern use of technology to represent the fragmentation of the self, see Matthew Causey, "The Screen Test of the Double: The Uncanny Performer in the Space of Technology," *Theatre Journal* 51 (1999): 383–94.

25. Arthur Miller, *Clara,* in *Danger: Memory!* (New York: Grove Press, 1986), 65.

26. *The Ride Down Mt. Morgan* (1991) restages the divided self, but here the technology is much cruder. At various points in the play the actor playing Lyman—a paralyzed character confined to a hospital bed—steps out from behind his plaster cast, dressed in a hospital gown, and addresses the audience while a dummy "Lyman" remains in bed.

27. It should be noted that Miller, *Collected Plays,* vol. 1, 24, saw himself as jettisoning Ibsen's linear dramaturgy as early as *Death of a Salesman:* "What was wanted now was not a mounting line of tension, nor a gradually narrowing cone of intensifying suspense, but a bloc, a single chord presented as such at the outset, within which all the strains and melodies would already be contained." Yet *Salesman* retains a tragic line of action that reveals the betrayal at the heart of Biff and Willy's alienation (the woman in the hotel) and climaxes in Willy's realization of his son's love and Biff's rejection of the values that have destroyed his father. It is in *The Archbishop's Ceiling* that Miller's musical analogy is fulfilled, and "a single chord" quite literally sounded.

28. For a discussion of the anamorphic use of objects in early modern drama, see Andrew Sofer, *The Stage Life of Props* (Ann Arbor: University of Michigan Press, 2003), 89–115.

29. One can compare the sophistication of the bug as an emblem of amorphous power to Harold Pinter's eponymous dumbwaiter. Pinter's dumbwaiter, controlled by the mysterious offstage Wilson and used to torment the two ignorant, working-class hit men, is a much cruder symbol of political coercion. In *The Dumb Waiter* (1960), Pinter uses the device of the speaking tube to ventriloquize an oppressive offstage character—a possible nod to Strindberg's *Miss Julie* (1888).

30. Michel Foucault defines power as "the multiplicity of force relations" that produce subjects, in *The History of Sexuality,* vol. 1: *An Introduction,* trans. Robert Hurley (New York: Pantheon, 1979), 92. Foucault's analysis helps explain *The Archbishop's Ceiling*'s ambivalence toward Sigmund's final, heroic gesture: "These points of resistance [within power relationships] are present everywhere in the power network. Hence there is no single locus of great Refusal, no soul of revolt, source of all rebellions, or pure law of the revolutionary. Instead there is a plurality of resistances, each of them a special case. . . . by definition, they can only exist in the strategic field of power relations" (95).

31. Miller, "Conditions of Freedom," x.

32. If Miller takes Marcus's point, he betrays his greater sympathy with the rebellious Sigmund by artistically castrating his rival. As Marcus's ex-lover Maya confesses, "he can't write anymore; it left him . . . *(In anguish:)* It left him!" (85).

Laurence Goldstein

The Misfits and American Culture

Contexts

We are often told that the first task of the literary critic is not to overlook the obvious. In that spirit, I will begin by saying the most obvious thing possible about *The Misfits,* that it is a movie and not a play. This makes it *almost* unique in Arthur Miller's oeuvre of completed scripts—he authored another film, *Everybody Wins* (1990), and adapted *The Crucible* for the big screen in 1996. What I mean to indicate by opening on this elementary note is that unlike *Death of a Salesman* and *A View from the Bridge* and *The Ride Down Mt. Morgan* and other plays that will undergo intermittent reincarnations, fostering new interpretations because of choices made by a variety of producers, directors and actors, this performance vehicle filmed in 1960 and released by Seven Arts in 1961 will remain unchanged down through the ensuing decades and centuries. The chances of its being remade fall somewhere between unlikely and inconceivable, partly because its history of commercial and critical failure make it unappealing to the film industry, and partly because the cast and chemistry of the film's original creation repel any tampering with its legendary aura. If straightforward and successful films of the 1950s have failed in their remakes—*Psycho, Sabrina, Born Yesterday, Diabolique, Breathless*—what chance would there be for a film of such notorious backstories and period flavor to thrive in a market increasingly dominated by the shock of special effects and the aesthetics of postmodern cool?

The uniqueness of the film's identity links it not only with other classic films unlikely to receive another interpretation—imagine *Citizen Kane* being remade, or *Lawrence of Arabia*—but with novels and short stories, which can be adapted to other mediums but which have their primary and most enduring force in their original literary form. It is appropriate, then, that *The Misfits* should share its cinematic being with these other two modes of narrative. It began life as a short story, "The

Misfits," first published in *Esquire* in 1957 and reprinted in Miller's collection of 1967, *I Don't Need You Anymore.* And it has had an alternative existence since 1961 in the textual form of a novel, or rather what Miller calls in his introduction "neither novel, play, nor screenplay," but something like an immensely long treatment that preserves the dialogue and mise-en-scène of the film without reconceptualizing any of the dramatic materials. Indeed, the stubborn rootedness of *The Misfits* in all its forms in the soil of the late 1950s and early 1960s complicates our efforts to measure its continuing claims upon the public imagination in the early years of the twenty-first century.

The first thing we can say about the film, then, is that it is self-consciously a product of the Zeitgeist. That is, it attempts in complex ways to embody a historical moment and milieu. "The Imagination is always at the end of an era," Wallace Stevens reminds us, and this film imagines the termination of a hallowed American myth, the dying out of the old frontier and its values at the moment a "new frontier" was being proclaimed in Washington by a young president. Partly this impasse was a matter of real estate. Frederick Jackson Turner had noted at the end of the 1890s that "the frontier" officially closed in 1890 when the government's census report declared the abstraction no longer viable. The shock waves of that apocalyptic declaration resonated throughout the twentieth-century western movie, giving to its multitudinous range wars between homesteaders and cattlemen an elegiac cast that nourished the audience's sense of modernity. Numerous films, especially of the 1950s, had dwelt upon "the end of something," in Hemingway's poignant phrase. *The Misfits,* set in and around Reno, Nevada, is about the end of love (and also its renewal), about the end of a certain kind of wild natural life embodied in the doomed mustangs, and about the threatened end of a knightly role associated in American culture with the cowboy. That its leading actor, Clark Gable, known to generations of moviegoers as "The King," died shortly after filming, perhaps on account of his exertions while shooting scenes of the mustang hunt, sealed the mordant quality of the film. The death of Marilyn Monroe in 1962 provided the absolute closure of fatality the film seemed to summon from the depths of the American experience. Then a president was assassinated, the Gemini and Apollo missions explored the beckoning "high frontier" of outer space, the first "advisers" died in Vietnam and "The Sixties" began in earnest, a new frontier indeed, requiring radically innovative films, none of them westerns, to define its new culture.

It may be useful to consult another text of 1961 to position ourselves in relation to *The Misfits.* Daniel G. Hoffman's book of literary history, *Form and Fable in American Fiction,* became a leading guide, in classrooms and scholarly commentary, by crystallizing the main currents of American myth as it settled into a "communally determined, preserved, and transmitted" dogma handed down writer to writer from Washington Irving to Faulkner, Bellow and Ellison. Drawing on previous critics such as F. O. Matthiessen, Constance Rourke, and Richard Chase, Hoffman called attention to what he terms "the inherent danger of our unassuaged Prometheanism."[1] That is, he sees in American fiction and folklore a tendency to enlarge the frontiersman and the pioneer into national types of representative men, heroic to the degree that they enter into the enchanted woods of wilderness nature and conquer it by bold strength of violent deeds. Whether this transforming action is being deplored or applauded, or both at the same time, it tends when inscribed to establish an allegorical pattern in which the true knight, Paul Bunyan and Captain Ahab alike, beats down the alien world without and within. Such heroes have no need of the historical past, no need of families or social obligations; they live off the plenitude of their immediate environment, moving constantly from one abundant site to another, beneficiaries of an everlasting present that they constantly exhaust by their voracious "civilizing" appetites.

Any number of western movies manifest these archetypal patterns; indeed, structuralist critics feel more comfortable discerning and describing these epistemes in the western than in any other artistic genre. Hoffman is not a structuralist, but he does seek to categorize the variety of tricksters, confidence men, Horatio Alger go-getters, masqueraders and irrepressible native picaros who travel restlessly across the panorama of American literature in search of fortune. Such types, who occasionally swell into complex and even tragic figures, help to create the "radical forms of alienation, contradiction, and disorder" so clearly present in American literature, though Hoffman argues that in both comic and dramatic forms they can also engender "the possibilities of affiliation, resolution, and coherence."[2] In our best narratives, the ones we tend to canonize as illuminative of our deepest reality as Americans and as human beings, the positive and negative strands are so tightly interwoven that a lifetime of study is too little to understand them fully.

Hoffman's map to the territory can help us to identify *The Misfits* as a fable, nearly allegorical in structure, that draws upon the fundamental impulses of American fiction and film at a time just preceding a countercultural or postmodern turn in narrative itself during the middle and late 1960s. The title is our first clue. The main characters who affiliate in the course of the film are "misfits" of the kind Hoffman describes. The Oxford English Dictionary establishes the first use of the word *misfit* in the early eighteenth century, when it applied principally to clothing or to asymmetrical parts of the body. In a New World founded on counter-hegemonic principles of individualism and private enterprise, the word was an unlikely moniker for a person and his or her relation to society. Emerson had argued in his essay "Self-Reliance" that "Whoso would be a man must be a nonconformist." The idea of fitting the Yankee self into a prescribed and monolithic model was anathema except in the most generalized sense of suiting your behavior to a "code" or "ethic" shared by resourceful but also desperate and violent people on a frontier, at the boundary of society and history alike. In fact, the accusatory power of the term *misfits* has more to do with the anxieties of the 1950s than it does with the literary or historical tradition. Books like David Riesman's *The Lonely Crowd* (1950), William H. Whyte Jr.'s *The Organization Man* (1955), Erich Fromm's *The Sane Society* (1955) and Paul Goodman's *Growing Up Absurd* (1960) lay behind the term, books that surveyed the ways that corporate structures and what Whyte called "the Social Ethic" in the postwar era enforced an emasculating conformity upon people in the workforce. To be a misfit in a world dominated by the executive mentality as part of capitalism's war against alternative modes of social organization is to occupy a role that is both heroic and pathetic in the romance tradition of American life and letters.

In Miller's short story of 1957, the "misfits" he names Gay Langley, Guido Racanelli and Perce Howland congratulate themselves on living an outdoor life without a regular payroll. The life of an itinerant cowboy in the latter part of the twentieth century is something of an anachronism, but it's "better than wages," in their repeated phrase. They feel at home in a landscape that is ostentatiously retro, a visual and tactile recall of the mythic world of Edenic plenitude ebbing almost beyond reach or touch. That golden age is emblematized by the wild mustangs, which once ran through the West in the thousands but now have dwindled to the scattered family units of this story. The thematic complexity of the men's situation was shared by a number of cowboys in the western films of the 1950s, films that attracted an increasing number of first-level directors, actors and screenwriters. It is a commonplace now to note that westerns customarily were freighted with ideas about politics and community too hot to handle in dramas of contemporary America, thanks to the panopticon of the House and Senate committees on un-American activities. "One of the things the Western is always about is America rewriting and reinterpreting her own past," notes Philip French.[3] That was a provocative act in the 1950s if the critique of fundamental values seemed to cut too close to the bone. As an "adult Western" or what Miller jokingly called an "Eastern Western,"[4] daring to rethink radically the relation of Americans to their past, the land and to each other, *The Misfits* lacked the saving and salving ambiguity of classics like *High Noon* (1952), *Shane* (1953), *The Left Handed Gun* (1958), *Ride the High Country* (1962) and *The Man Who Shot Liberty Valence* (1962), in which the struggles of law and lawlessness, order and disorder, were pitched just far enough from the core debate over radical social reforms, and just close enough, to qualify as family entertainment.

Films in which misfits like Billy the Kid or Liberty Valence get killed by the upholders of community values are deeply satisfying to audiences, even or especially when they mix significant critiques of the triumphant good into their narratives. In *The Misfits* nobody is killed, nobody brandishes a weapon. The enemy is not some cattle baron or psychotic outlaw, but time itself, the aging of the West, the aging of the cowboys who have grown older and less vigorous hustling a living from the chapparal and scrub of desert milieux. In his wrinkled face revealed in close-ups, Clark Gable as Gay joined contemporaries like James Stewart, Gary Cooper, Randolph Scott and John Wayne as elder figures in a western landscape that belongs to the unrecoverable past. It's late for the cowpokes, but is it too late? Too late to save their manhood, too late for love, for renewal of the virile spirit that tamed the land and civilized it with Promethean energies? The crisis in so many westerns of the 1950s and early 1960s comes when the option of domestication beckons to the weary knight: the impulse to put down the gun finally, open a store, run for mayor. Here too the anxieties of the 1950s seep through the local color. We feel the ambivalence of the returning World War II and Korean War veterans, faced with the temptations of the modern organization—corporation, political machine, police force or armed forces, university, church—asking for either a small or significant amount of conformity in exchange for the wild unrestrained energy of the adolescent on the psychic frontier.

Miller had formed the idea for the story when he met some cowboys, the originals of Gay and Guido, while living in Nevada in 1956 waiting for a divorce from his first wife to clear the courts. Impressed with their resourcefulness and good humor, he also apprehended their plight as marginalized social creatures and let it germinate in his imagination until, on location in England for the filming of *The Prince and the Showgirl,* he felt moved to write about them in his short story. It has been a fundamental tenet of Miller's creed that the artist is a misfit whose vision of society is both caustic and healing. "The artist is the outcast," he remarked; "he always will be. He is an outcast in the sense that he is to one side of the stream of life and absorbs it, and is, in some part of himself, reserved from its implications."[5] Like the cowboys, the artist has to work with constant uncertainty, free from the orthodoxy that sustains most citizens who return to the same office every morning with more or less the same mind-set and the same tasks to perform. The sympathy he felt for the cowboys no doubt rose up in him from bitter memories of the Depression era, when artists felt a solidarity with fellow citizens who had no settled present or future, nor credible solutions to change their condition.

The director of the film, John Huston, remarked, "The movie is about a world in change. There was meaning in our lives, before World War II, but we have lost meaning now." Of Gay Langland, Huston comments, "He's the same man, but the world has changed. Then he was noble. Now he is ignoble."[6] The crisis of meaning that overtakes the characters is reminiscent of the crisis in most of Miller's plays, where the exhaustion or insufficiency of codes leads to the breaking of people's lives and spirits. Like Willy Loman losing his territory and his honorable status in the family, Gay Langland stands at a crossroads peering into a new kind of consumer society for which he is maladapted by training and disposition. "It . . . it just got changed around," he complains at the end of the film; "I'm doin' the same thing I ever did." (Clark Gable told Miller he wanted to play the role of Willy Loman.) Compelled to change or die out, Gay takes the first significant step toward reinventing himself when he cuts the rope that binds him to the hunted stallion as an antagonist, following the lead of his fellow misfits Roslyn and Perce who are (now, in another century) recognizably avatars of the radical new culture Miller hopefully observed in the making.

Roslyn

Here we confront the question of the role of women in western films, including this one. Women are usually "the voice of reason, speaking out against violence . . . and the idea that human affairs can be settled by force," remarks Philip French.[7] Roslyn in *The Misfits* is the perfect example, and I would like to consider first her role as the key to the film's unique claim upon our attention. In the short story version, Roslyn did not exist as an onstage character. Miller kept the focus entirely on the three men plying their trade in the Nevada wilderness. Although they pride themselves on their independence, in fact they are cogs in a giant industrial machine that provides cheap horseflesh as canned dog food. They think occasionally of Roslyn back in town, an eastern schoolteacher with whom Gay lives in a quasi-domestic arrangement. Roslyn disapproves of their occupation, and as they rope the horses for slaughter they hear her reproachful voice in their heads. "Roslyn's going to feel sorry for the colt," Gay says to Perce, "so might as well not mention it." Roslyn exerts a counterforce in the story against the brute masculine ethic of domination over nature.

The novel and film that Miller made of this short story features as its most significant change the foregrounding of Roslyn as a major character. The inspiration (or exigency) driving this change is clearly the entrance of Marilyn Monroe into the (re)production process, providing box-office dynamite for what would otherwise be an all-too-straightforward film narrative of futility and defeat. Monroe entered and captured the story, her first dramatic role, because she had first entered Miller's life, so that the film achieved a parabolic and intensely personal status from the first day it was announced. "I was constructing a gift for [Marilyn]," Miller explains in his autobiography, *Timebends.* "I would never have dreamed of writing a movie otherwise."[8] And with Monroe's screen persona comes a radical shift in the nature of Roslyn's character. In the short story we are led to believe that she is one of those "college graduated divorced women" from the East who rebound into Gay's arms after shedding their unsatisfactory mates Nevada style. In the long version Roslyn becomes an "interpretive dancer" who has dwindled to performing in strip joints. By making her less intellectual and more of a class match for Gay, Miller guarantees that their relationship will not be an uneven struggle in which each partner exerts an exploitive power over the other (her snob condescension, his sexual allure, the obverse of what the union of Miller and Monroe represented to the general public). What does not change from story to film is the deeper sensitivity that Roslyn displays about the fate of the hunted mustangs, and more generally her refusal to have love on terms degraded by her partner's habit of violence against living things.

The story begins in Reno, "Divorce Capital of the World" (a billboard informs us, in the script), where displaced people gamble and sin, hucksters ply their trades, and in venues thematically related to Reno, such as

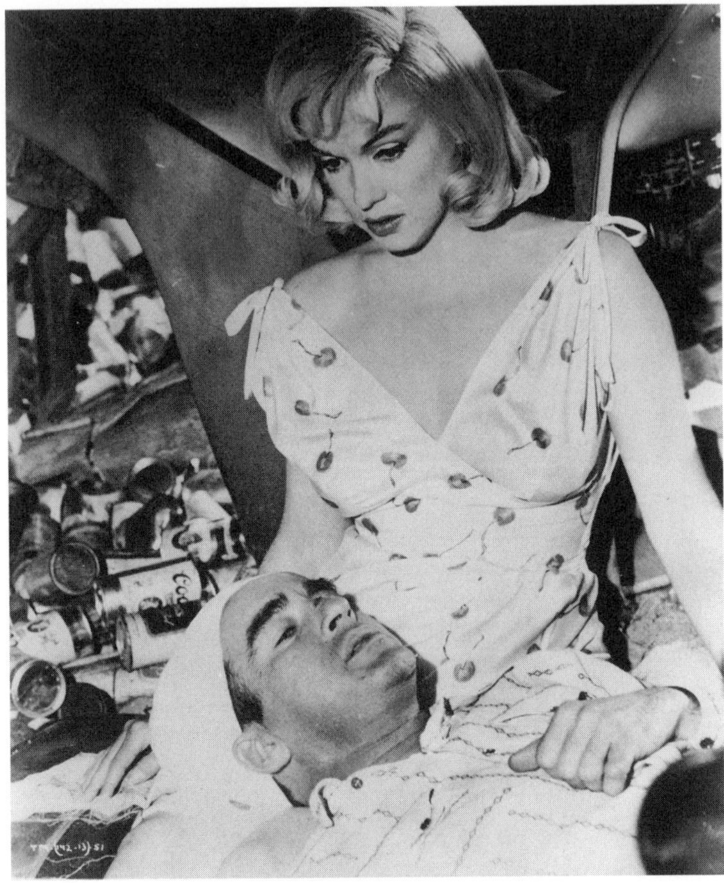

Roslyn (Marilyn Monroe) comforts Perce (Montgomery Clift) as he tells her about his earlier life. (Courtesy United Artists and *Michigan Quarterly Review*)

the rodeo town, a kind of barbaric lewdness erupts constantly into view. An older woman, Isabelle (Thelma Ritter) has befriended the insecure Roslyn, a high school dropout whom Isabelle compares to a little child and chaperones a short distance until Gay assumes the commanding role. Roslyn is all heart and no brain; she drinks "to Life—whatever that is," and Gay remarks to her, "I think that you're the saddest girl I ever met." But she does love life, and Guido tells her, "You have the gift of life." She wants to keep Gay from killing the rabbits desolating his lettuce garden; she loves the birds; she complains about the bucking strap on the rodeo horses. She is, in fact, a rather obvious allegorical trope for nature itself, an earth mother who in one scene embraces a tree in a wild dance. "Honey, when you smile it's like the sun coming up," Gay tells her.

As a figure for the life force she contains immense power to change other people by withholding sanction for their ruthless behavior, but she too must undergo change as a human being in a frontier community far from utopia. She must, for one thing, revise her rote sentiments about the holiness of life and understand Gay's need to capture the wild mustangs in ritual acts of domination and conquest. She must acquire a masculine vision of experience if she expects Gay to move a commensurate distance toward her nurturing piety toward nature. The captured colt is the critical figure in the evolving narrative that brings Gay and Roslyn together. The colt represents the child potentially possible between them, their future as a contracted couple. If Gay sacrifices it for the few dollars it would bring in meat (and the colt's mother another thirty dollars or so), he will forfeit the joyful life they might have together beyond the reach of a rapacious commercial system both he and Roslyn despise. The immense pathos of the short story, in which he does, unhappily, accede to financial necessity and his outworn code of professional pride, yields in the longer version to a happy ending in which he permits Roslyn and Perce to let the mustangs go, except for a stallion that he wrestles into submission and then frees to show that he is still in control. At the end of the film she mentions the child she believes they can conceive, and Gay remarks in the last scene, "I bless you, girl."

The Misfits is not sentimental about Roslyn; for one thing, she is too sentimental herself to attract the viewer's wholehearted sympathy. One gets tired of her fixed angelic nature, what Miller in *Timebends,* speaking of Marilyn, calls "a purely donative femininity," and also of the constant kvetching and sniffling and sobbing she carries on throughout the second half of the film. But the reader is snapped back to respect for her powerful feelings of moral probity when she lashes out at Guido, the veteran pilot, constantly evoking the memory of his dead wife as he hustles Roslyn. When Guido bragged earlier in the film about shooting eagles from his cockpit, Roslyn had winced but remained silent, but when he bargains with her to save the mustangs if she'll shack up with him, she explodes:

> "You! Sensitive fella? So full of feelings? So sad about your wife, and crying to me about the bombs you dropped and the people you killed. You have to get something to be human? You were never sad for anybody in your life, Guido! You only know the sad words! You could blow up the whole world, and all you'd ever feel is sorry for *yourself!*"

In speeches like this we hear the proleptic voice of the counterculture in America preparing its critique of the one-dimensional men who prosecuted the Vietnam War later in the 1960s. Roslyn emerges at the end of this narrative as a figure of resistance to the American leaders who justified the slaughter of millions of Asians by turning them into nothing but data. And in summoning the nuclear holocaust, Miller takes aim at the ultimate culmination of the genocidal impulse dramatized in his fabulist fictions, such as the short stories "Please Don't Kill Anything" and "Bees" and the antifascist novel *Focus* (1945). That Roslyn can embody such a range of moral imperatives—not, admittedly, without straining dramatic credibility—speaks well for the relevance of *The Misfits* in a feminist era.

Though Gay accedes to the civilizing force represented by Roslyn, there are undercurrents in the dramatic structure of *The Misfits* that complicate her symbolic role. One of these is Gay's comment when Roslyn offers to ransom the life of the mustangs by giving Gay the money she has won with her expertise at paddleball at the saloon back at the rodeo town. He says, "I sell to dealers only. 'Cause all they're lookin' to buy is the horse." Roslyn wants to buy his freedom and his manhood, he means. She wants to possess him by dispossessing him of his livelihood, in all the meanings of that word. Like the "witch" figure embedded in American folkore, she would strip him of authentic life and render him into one of the epicene male figures that haunted the arts of the 1950s, especially in Tenneessee Williams plays. In this sense, Roslyn can be seen as a predator as well, a latter-day Hedda Gabler who poses a torturous dilemma to male pride. If the film endorses her critique of the men's war against the mustangs, it also establishes a countercurrent in the allegorical narrative by casting suspicion on her self-righteousness and the absolutism of her ethical position. Arguably, in this role Marilyn Monroe played true to the legend that had grown around her during the 1950s: the sexpot-vampire that Miller himself would anatomize less sentimentally in *After the Fall* and that Joyce Carol Oates would envision as "the burning Princess, immortal" in her biographical novel *Blonde.*

Perce

John Huston said that "the essence of *The Misfits* really concerns the environment, what civilization does in the way of tarnishing the life around us and our souls."[9] As I've suggested, the allegorical nature of Miller's script draws into conjunction two distinct stories. One is the macronarrative: the Darwinian struggle in which human beings enter a wilderness and with their superior technology capture the creatures there for "civilized" purposes, wrenching the mustangs into the industrial process to meet a consumer demand. (The mustangs compete with cattle for forage, one reason for their diminishing numbers in the new West.) The second narrative is the romantic one, in which men occupying that liminal and masculine space at the frontier are magnetized by the sexual and domestic attractions of female space symbolized by the character Roslyn. Within the psyche and soul of each of the film's characters, then, we can see the process of "tarnishing" occur as civilization and its discontented antagonists chafe against each other in the quest for dominance and emotional gratification. The profundity of the script, as in Miller's most accomplished plays, lies in the irresolvable conflict between characters who define "civilization" in radically different terms, as, in fact, American society does in its canonical texts.

In this sense, Perce emerges as, perhaps, the most contemporary character of the film. If *The Misfits* were a more conventional western he might have ended up paired with the female lead, being closer in age and a seeming soulmate with the troubled Roslyn. Montgomery Clift was born in 1920, and Marilyn Monroe in 1926, and both had begun their film careers in 1948. Both had some training in method acting, in which psychological conditions are manifested and elaborated in highly individualized bodily movements, facial gestures and mannerisms of voice. (Clark Gable represented the older, classic Hollywood style of less inwardly motivated, less fastidiously articulated behavior and speech.) Clift's roles had made him a walking symbol of the conflicted psyche, both alienated from the orderly patterns of social organization and eager to find an opportune niche within them: the unruly son of *Red River* striking his father down, the hustler of *The Heiress* and *A Place in the Sun,* and later the helpless victim of depraved human nature in *From Here to Eternity, Lonelyhearts, Suddenly Last Summer* and *Judgment at Nuremberg.* If anyone needed to be rescued by a "donative femininity" associated with "civilization" it would seem to be the Clift persona. From his first big scene in the film, when he carries on an agitated phone call with his mother, Perce is typed as a vulnerable male in desperate need of some dignified emergence into a wholly mature self.

In a review of *The Misfits* Stanley Kauffmann manages to discuss the film at length without mentioning Perce until the last sentence: "Montgomery Clift, who was last seen as a Westerner (unconvincingly) in *Red River,* here brings life to Perce, the battered young exile, who has nothing to live on but his willingness to get thrown off bucking horses."

Perce (Montgomery Clift) competes in a rodeo while Gay (Clark Gable) looks on approvingly. (Courtesy United Artists and *Michigan Quarterly Review*)

When Kauffmann recalled *The Misfits* in a later review of *A View from the Bridge,* he referred to "the screenplay in which [Miller] tried to impose a *Götterdämmerung* on the doings of a mustang hunter and a stripteaser."[10] Kauffmann's assumption that Perce is beside the point, unworthy of significant notice, is echoed in many commentaries on the film. He is the most misfitted of all the characters, auxiliary to the main plot that brings Gay and Roslyn together in a redemptive love. "Perce, the rodeo rider, is just beginning," writes Sheila Huftel. "His life is not yet formed."[11]

If we return to the context of the 1950s, we can better appreciate the importance of what otherwise would seem to be the standard "sidekick" role occupied by Perce. In *The Lonely Crowd,* Riesman had defined the principal types of social character as tradition-directed, inner-directed and outer-directed. All of these types served the purposes of a highly mobilized and highly organized postwar society dominated by the irresistible forces of capitalist commerce and technological innovation. (Their native original, as Hoffman notes, is the resourceful Benjamin Franklin.) Occasionally in his lengthy study Riesman takes note of social types outside these mainstream personalities, namely those who enjoy "living at random" in the spirit of "inconceivable pure contingency." These existential types, these rolling stones unburdened by the "overidealized goals and grandiose dreams" of the high achievers, trouble the discourse of *The Lonely Crowd.*[12] These are figures who may or may not have jobs, but who value "play" more than "work," who recapitulate the dependent structures of childhood even as they proclaim themselves independent and autonomous. They survive, Riesman suggests, by the indulgence of the larger culture, thanks in large part to the mainstream society's nostalgia for less exacting models of behavior on the frontier.

Riesman calls these types "maladjusted," though he quickly adds that adjustment to the lonely crowd is not inherently virtuous. Indeed, "there are some cultures where I would place a higher value on the maladjusted or anomic than on the adjusted." (He doesn't name them, but any reader in the 1950s would recognize the reference to fascist and communist societies.) Perce's situation in life is clearly meant to echo Hamlet's, for Perce too has been dispossessed of a kingdom by his mother's remarriage, three months after his father's death, to a man who takes over the family ranch and offers Perce menial wages to work it. Like the melancholy prince, Perce loses his bearings once the scaffolding of patrimony is put in doubt by an oedipal contest. He withdraws from the struggle and goes on the road as an itinerant rodeo rider, sustaining constant physical pain in his low-paying gigs. He seems to be something of a masochist, punishing himself for the faults of a time that is out of joint. Miller does not give Perce a chance to revenge himself, however, or to die tragically while questing for a place in the sun. He is kept on in the film as a witness of the growing tensions among Guido, Roslyn and Gay. Miller, then, is no more certain what to do with Perce, and people like him, than Riesman is. Perce is *de trop,* superfluous to the society that others will constitute in the desert, neither protagonist nor antagonist. Paradoxically, this contingent role has made Perce more visible to generations of viewers who came of age during the countercultural period of the 1960s and afterward.

One example worth noting is Lynda Hull, whose poem on *The Misfits* is one of the more striking examples of film poetry in the latter part of the twentieth century. "Fortunate Traveller" appears in her posthumous collection, *The Only World* (1995). It tells how she viewed the film for the first time in Spain in the early 1990s, where it carried the title *Los Perdidos.* Halfway through the poem she focuses on the five-minute conversation between Roslyn and Perce, the longest dialogue scene Huston had ever filmed. The two characters gravitate to each other because of their shared histories and their shared philosophy that life is merely, in Roslyn's words, "the next thing that happens." Hull is aware that Monroe and Clift had shared alcohol and drugs freely on the set, and reads their dissolution into the film:

the chemistry fails to
ignite but for this love scene, tender and confused,
between Clift and Monroe. The alley outside the bar.
They'd kept forgetting their lines, passing between takes

a silver flask of vodka, washing down
barbituates until finally the shooting stopped
and that's why the scene's so lost. *Los Perdidos.*
Crimson Seconals, the Tuinals and canary-yellow

Nembutals, the stoked hues of leaves dervished in the parks'
dry fountains, sherried autumn air. Like trapdoors in time,
a yeasty breeze redolent as the breeze shaking
winged maples in the park by the railroad station,

the group of friends I had when I was young.

Hull then lapses, through the "trapdoor of time," into a nostalgic reminiscence of her own flaming youth in the late 1960s and 1970s, a time of bountiful experiments with drugs and sex. Though hardly an intention of Miller's script, Perce makes unexpected contact, then, with viewers like Hull who batten both on the need for love expressed in the words of the disadvantaged and scar-faced character, and on the backstory that links Clift and Monroe as *perdidos* who, like James Dean and many rock stars of the 1950s and 1960s period, survive as icons of glamour for the maladjusted in later decades.

The moment of communion in this "love scene" is repeated at the end of the film when Perce and Roslyn collaborate to free the mustangs. Perce is stung, as Gay and Guido are, by Roslyn's bitter shrieking at them when they begin to make plans to have the mustangs rounded up by dealers and sold for dogfood: "Liars! Killers! Murderers! Liars! You're only living when you can watch something die! Kill everything, that's all you want. . . . You know everything except what it feels like to be alive.

You're three dear, sweet dead men." Perce reacts first and most instinctively to her taunting and strikes a blow—against his fellow misfits—for liberation. (Gay will grudgingly follow him, while Guido remains defiant.) Like Hamlet, he is wrenched out of self-pity by the spectacle of unjust and untimely death: in Hamlet's case by Ophelia's grave and in Perce's by the imminent capture for slaughter of the horses. Now he has the possibility of a future; he has acquired a moral code that is elementary but at least provides some ground under his feet. He has escaped the worst consequences of the catastrophe that exiled him into the wilderness of Nevada from his Edenic ranch: he has ceased to pass along the cruelty to other innocent beings. Now he is no longer an isolated jigsaw piece, as in the cast titles for the film, but part of a growing composite—if not a community, then the beginnings of one. Lynda Hull, who died at age thirty-nine in a high-speed car crash, might have done well to consider Perce's implied fate rather than Marilyn Monroe's.

But what is Perce's implied fate? "A sensible awareness of the rules of the game can be a condition of individualism as well as a constraint upon it," remarks Whyte in *The Organization Man*.[13] Perce had joined Gay and Guido to form a workforce that parodies The Organization itself, depending on group dynamics for his well-being. The fissioning of that sense of purpose and his resistance to the task set before them by industrial needs, reorients him and makes him as an individual less susceptible to the blandishments of thinly disguised corporate demands. ("He must *fight* The Organization," Whyte says of the morally aroused citizen in the last paragraph of his seminal book.) Does Perce's newfound love for Roslyn and her ethic of liberation enhance his authenticity as a person in a rugged society that won't adapt to his refashioned identity? Is he fated to remain the transient "hand" surviving on odd jobs? "They grind up women out here . . . Don't let them grind you up," Perce tells Roslyn in their long scene together. But isn't it true that the rules of the game mandate his being ground up as well? He seems a candidate for the Beat Generation or, as Hull suggests, the punk generation full of runaways whose nihilist despair is mirrored in his character.

Perce recalls Biff Loman in *Death of a Salesman,* whose travels out west in emulation of the fabled Uncle Ben fall considerably short of the American dream. Clearly, by refusing to allow the mustangs to be ground up into dogfood Perce achieves enlightenment about the way his good nature can be co-opted by the system . . . and yet, isn't that understanding also a constraint upon his condition, the terminus of the very freedom or "floating around," as he calls it, that has defined his distance from an oppressive "civilization" back home? In *The Misfits* "home" is explicitly defined as the open road and its temporary shelters and sexual comforts. What destiny does the audience wish for Perce? These are damned-if-you-do-and-damned-if-you-don't conundrums that the script passes on to the generations of Americans who seek a life of Emersonian nonconformity in a culture of vanishing options.

Gay and Guido

We first meet Gay in the film on a railway platform; he is seeing off a divorcée with whom he has been having a fling. She is regretful and reminds him of "the second largest laundry in St. Louis" that would be his for the taking if he followed her east. "I wouldn't want to kid you, Susan. I ain't cut out for business," he tells her. If Perce seems to roam the West like a lone coyote, Gay seems to be the spirit of Reno, preying upon available women while dreaming of escape to the purifying open spaces. He eschews obligations, though we always sense in him a profound desire for attachments as powerful as his revulsion from them. (His joy at meeting his children at the Dayton Rodeo, for example.) Guido has stumbled upon Roslyn and Isabelle while working for an auto repair shop and seems willing to share Roslyn with Gay, showing her off and quickly losing her to the more attractive older man when they all meet at Harrah's Club. Immediately we are struck by the relation of these two men. They have an adolescent bond connected to womanizing, like so many buddies in western movies. But some ideological bond seems to inhere as well. Unlike Perce, who is all unrealized possibility, these misfits are connected thematically in the film through their identity as hunters, sharing their tasks and prizes alike.

Barbara Leaming claims in her biography of Marilyn Monroe that Guido is a recognizable figure for Elia Kazan, who had had an affair with Monroe before Miller rescued her from Kazan's more exploitive and selfish claims. No doubt this interpretation is based in part on the rivalry between the two men embedded in *After the Fall* and *Timebends,* as well as Kazan's autobiography, *A Life.* Once the notion settles in the viewer's mind, it's difficult not to watch the film with some sense of a biographical purpose being played out. ("I've always felt a misfit," Miller told an interviewer; "I've always identified with those fellows, even down in the middle of New York.")[14] Leaming attributes the failure of the film's script to Miller's unwillingness to follow through on the biographical subtext. Monroe came to the film, Leaming claims, expecting that the script would dramatize Miller's forgiveness for her depraved life. Roslyn's anger at the men for sacrificing the horses would be rooted in her identification with the mustangs' suffering at the hands of brutal, self-serving men. But Miller would not forgive, in Leaming's account; instead he sentimentalized the story, attributing Roslyn's bitter denunciations of the men to her soft-hearted attachment to animals. This scenario permitted the enlightened and liberated Miller to welcome Monroe into his (Gay's) arms while pushing away Kazan (Guido) as an unredeemable predator who leaves the screen screaming about new conquests, new mustangs to capture.

Whatever the crosscurrents of their relations—and it is virtually impossible to keep personalities out of a discussion of this film—Miller is certainly dedicated to drawing some contrasts between the two men, as well as similarities. The key scenes between them occur at Guido's ranch house, which he had been building as a love nest for himself and his wife and left unfinished at the time of her unexpected death. Nowhere is the film's allegorical structure more apparent than in this symbolic halfway house between the Babylon of Reno (and its thematic partner, the Dayton Rodeo) and the desolate primordial lake bed of the final scenes. Reno has been depicted in the film as a place of troubling collisions, beginning with the actual collision that brings Guido into the opening scenes to inspect Roslyn's damaged car. Roslyn runs into her soon-to-be ex-husband (Kevin McCarthy), and they have a conflicted exchange. She is distraught in the scenes at Harrah's Club, but soothed gradually by Gay and his dog, Tom Dooley, and persuaded to drive out to Guido's house, which he offers to Roslyn as a temporary refuge—hoping that he'll eventually be invited into her bed.

As the four of them drive further from Reno, the landscape becomes increasingly visible through the windows. "Gee, it goes on forever," Roslyn says, and claims the scent of sagebrush is "like perfume." Yet viewers are not so likely to look fondly on the desert vista rushing by the car. The black-and-white photography flattens the land into a grainy backdrop, not unlike the alkali flats of later scenes. The camera does not leave the point of view of the passengers to pan or focus close up on the landscape. (In fact, the landscape scenes were prefilmed and back-projected behind the actors in postlocation shooting in the MGM studio.) In Technicolor westerns the landscape sports green cacti and yellow blossoms and a variety of attractive tints in the rockfaces. Here the landscape is forbidding, blank, not pastoral or pictorial.[15] Guido's house and the garden Gay places near it shine as ideal reconciliations of the wilderness and the

Gay (Clark Gable) and Roslyn (Marilyn Monroe) are the charismatic central couple who share feelings of love and suspicion toward one another. (Courtesy United Artists and *Michigan Quarterly Review*)

urban, a fugitive domestic space that becomes entirely feminized by Roslyn's presence. It is here that we get scenes of dancing, slow and fast, between Roslyn and the two men—scenes that are visually contrasted to the paddleball scenes at the Dayton Rodeo, where her movements are lewd and raucous and the camera (following the eyes of the men in the saloon) dwells on her swinging backside. The two-shot compositions of Roslyn and Gay are tender, even luminous: her pale skin and hair tone (a platinum wig, we know from other sources), her black dress and shoes. A scene where Gay leans over to kiss her awake while she dozes in bed, nuzzling and gazing at her, is the quintessence of movie romance. The constant drinking of the foursome at the ranch, mostly whiskey, has an ambiguous place in the narrative. Drinking is part of the hard life on the frontier, a source of emotional release, even joy, but also leads to flashpoints of conflict, especially as Guido and Gay come on to Roslyn in more and more uninhibited ways. (At the Dayton Rodeo, Gay will fall off a car while drunk, no longer charming but pathetic.) Likewise, when Perce is jazzed up on painkillers, he exudes an artificial gaiety that is part of his unstable lifestyle.

Eli Wallach, who plays Guido, was born in 1915; Clark Gable was born in 1901. They relate to each other in the film as peers. When Perce and Roslyn dance, Guido says, "Nothing like being young" as a way of distinguishing the vital couple from themselves. Yet it's obvious in his body language that Guido is younger than Gay; he struts and swaggers and postures and dances in swing rhythms, in the spirit of mating behavior before an available female. When Gay remarks that his daughter wears a size 12 dress, just like Roslyn, we get a whiff of incest to deepen the age theme, as when he says to her, "Didn't your papa ever spank you?" as if he wants to put himself in her papa's place. On one level these are routine acknowledgments that a generation separates the romantic couple, a convention of the 1950s when pairings like Gary Cooper (born 1901) and Audrey Hepburn (born 1929) or James Stewart (born 1908) and Kim Novak (born 1933) raised few eyebrows. But in *The Misfits* the motifs of mutability and mortality are so powerful that the intergenerational Gable-Monroe relationship has a special frisson. Part of Monroe's scandal biography is that she suspected Clark Gable of being the father she never knew; her mother worked as a film-cutter at the studios and kept Gable's framed photograph on her bureau. In her novel of 2000, *Blonde,* Joyce Carol Oates imagines that the secret mainspring of Monroe's career is her insatiable need for the absent father figure she fantasizes as Clark Gable and calls the Dark Prince:

> *Long ago in the darkened theater. I was a child, I adored you. The Dark Prince* She had only to shut her eyes & it was that long-ago time in the movie house to which she would go after school on Highland Avenue & pay for her solitary ticket & [her mother] Gladys would have warned her *Don't sit by any man! Don't speak to any man!* & she lifted her eyes excited to the screen to see the Dark Prince who was this very man who kissed her now & whom she kissed with such hunger. . . ; this handsome dark man with the thin-trimmed

> mustache now in his sixties, now with lined face & thinning hair & the unmistakable eyes of mortality. *Once, I believed you were my father. Oh tell me, tell me you are my father!*[16]

Thus does the oedipal theme—not the brother-sister incest examined in such depth by Faulkner in his novels but the more fundamental taboo enforced on Western culture by the Greek tragedies—stamp itself on the modern imagination via the star biographies and re-created fictions of major American writers.

If Gay is held spellbound by the erotic fascination of the younger generation, and then lashed into fury by its claim upon his manhood and his way of life, Guido's sentiment, both for his dead wife and for Roslyn, is revealed to be meretricious, a stage effect. Miller remarked that "because Guido could never give himself to anything, he could not give himself to Roslyn. Gay gave himself entirely to his concept of freedom, so he could give himself to her."[17] Guido cannot be reconciled to letting the mustangs escape. He might say to Gay what Gay says to Perce in an earlier scene, "I'm beginnin' to smell wages all over you, boy." Guido assumes the role forfeited by Gay when Gay joins Roslyn and Perce in surrendering the mustangs. Guido is intransigent, the victim of a reactionary mind-set immune to the changes in his fellow misfits, who now gravitate toward each other as elective affinities in the puzzle of life. At the end of the film, when the romantic couple ride off into the night, they cling to each other, a tentative victory for Eros, leaving behind the landscape Perce had compared to the chaste and uninhabitable moon.

To appreciate how far this film does go in its moral structures, we might compare it briefly to a John Ford film featuring Clark Gable, *Mogambo* (1953), scripted by John Lee Mahin. Gable plays a "white hunter" in Kenya who guides tourists on safari through the jungles. His relation to the animals he locates and captures for zoos or, in this case, displays for an anthropologist and his wife who want to record the sounds of gorillas in the wild, is ambiguous. Clearly he kills them from time to time, as he does a rare black leopard in order to save the life of the wife (Grace Kelly) who has foolishly wandered into the wild and fallen into a trap set for the leopard. These animals are not being used for dogfood; nevertheless, the hunter's guilt at transporting so many creatures from their native home is a visible subtext. At the climax of the film he confronts the tribe of gorillas (pushing Grace Kelly to the ground when she interferes just as he does Marilyn Monroe in the later film), kills the male leader, and sends the academic couple packing. Clearly he is going to stay on happily in his occupation, with Ava Gardner, a fancy-free chanteuese and courtesan thematically linked to Roslyn in the later film. This is quintessentially a Hollywood plot—the film, in fact, is a remake of the popular film of 1932, *Red Dust,* also starring Gable.

Miller insists on giving symbolic weight to the hunted animals, making them figurative doubles of the human misfits who prey on them. (The mustangs are referred to as "misfits" also.) If there is a thematic connection between the bull gorilla in *Mogambo* and the hunter with his harem of two gorgeous actresses, the connection is a joking one. In no sense are we made to feel that Gable has slaughtered some inner self when he pulls the trigger. But in *The Misfits* there is more at stake than adventure and romance in an exotic setting. Gable now has to wrestle with inner demons and with a historical crisis, like "a Hemingway character," as Huston rightly notes.[18] So long as he catches horses, he is not free; he achieves meaningful freedom when he disengages from the market-driven forces that have taken control of his work. Miller identified Guido as "the liberal in society, the man who can go just so far into the clinches and then just isn't there,"[19] an odd labeling that may derive from Lionel Trilling's critique in *The Liberal Imagination* (1951) of the instrumentalist or progressive mentality that art is constantly trying to subvert in the name of more fundamental human values. In fact, Guido is an unlikely figure for the liberal in society, with his ranting and totalistic rejection of obligation and compassion. Gay might be a better figure for the liberal, riding the postwar trend toward greater tolerance despite the constraints a commercial culture has enforced on his way of life. There are traces of the triumphalist Guido in the white hunter in *Mogambo,* insisting on love and work on his terms, but not in the resigned and converted Gay who drives off with Roslyn, following a star.

Conclusions

When *The Misfits* began filming, there was an air of excitement about the project that carried it to completion through immense difficulties. The producer described it as "the ultimate motion picture" featuring "the first original screenplay by a major American writer."[20] All of the actors joined Huston in the belief that the film would make an impressive showing at the various award ceremonies. Yet the film received no awards, was roundly condemned by the press and lost money at the box office. Much of the blame for this failure was laid at Miller's door. Stanley Kauffmann called the screenplay of *The Misfits* "in idea and much of its execution, several universes above most Amerian films" but "unsuccessful both in its treatment of its subject and as a use of the film form."[21] Leonard Moss in the Twayne book on Miller remarks that the film is "undoubtedly, the poorest product of the dramatist's mature years."[22] Barbara Leaming calls it "a mediocre screenplay."[23] Henry Popkin in his review in *Commentary* complained that "the language in which these events are embodied is incredible. The dialogue of the film is wooden, hollow, reeking of portent."[24] Such negative judgments could be multiplied—indeed, they seem to batten upon each other and repeat the same reproaches, especially about the unsuitably high-toned or poetic language Miller put into his thinly educated characters' mouths and the sheer quantity of words that spill out from a film whose genre had always cherished the laconic and understated.

On the question of dialogue, there is no disputing taste. In this essay I have quoted lines that are sententious in the way Miller's speeches often are, such as Linda Loman's in *Death of a Salesman* insisting, "Attention must be paid" or the ruminations of John Proctor in *The Crucible.* When we hear "speeches" in film, we're tempted to stigmatize the dialogue as "theatrical" or "literary." I think it's fair to say that audiences probably have a greater tolerance for "literary" speech than many critics give them credit for, and not just in Eric Rohmer films or adapted literary works like those by Jane Austen and Henry James. Whether cowboys have a right to speak eloquently, or with the pitch of eloquence preferred by Miller, is another matter. Critics who have taken pleasure in the verbosity of *Johnny Guitar* (1954) and the language-rich *Hud* (1963) need to define better their uneasiness with Miller's script. Miller likes to punctuate his action with "memorable speech," to cite W. H. Auden's definition of poetry. Often it is expressionist in mode, epigrammatic and full of rhetorical surprise over and above its function as mere communication. It can be peculiar, off-key, as well as perfectly apt and haunting in its phrasing. On screen in close-up exchanges, such language can compete with the action as well as forward it, and moviegoers accustomed to hundreds of westerns may find the dialogue too ostentatiously written against genre as an experiment. The "Eastern Western" may in performance be as nonviable as the pastoral poem or the minstrel show.

On the set Miller had to struggle night and day with the need to find new language, and less language, in order to realize the narrative. James Goode asked him, tongue in cheek, "Is it possible to make a movie in which people talk to each other?" Miller answered, "I used to think so, but I changed my mind. There's a basic conflict between the word and the image. The greatest impact will come from the image."[25] Though Huston and Miller cooperated amiably, the film shows an obvious tension between word and image rather than the perfect reconciliation we expect from the greatest films. Yet, in an era that has canonized the films of Robert Altman, Quentin Tarantino and David Lynch, this tension will inevitably sound different than in 1961, when films were routinely hammered by reviewers for wandering too far from the popular formulas.

On the larger matter of the film's allegorical shape, which includes its moralistic viewpoint, taste may differ as well across generations. At the beginning of the twenty-first century, a time when phrases like "the end of history," "the end of nature," and, thanks to the appearance of new trends in robotics and virtual reality, "the end of humanity," have the specificity and credibility to alarm large publics, the mythic substructure of *The Misfits* and its hopeful, if tentative, assertions about the power of love may seem less strained and less banal. The characters may rise in our memory as nourishing archetypes when we strive to understand determining factors in the evolution of the national character. Especially pertinent is the issue identified by Hoffman in *Form and Fable in American Fiction:* how to reconcile the egoistic drive of Promethean individuals with the privileges and rights of nature and the community. As Hoffman points out, that question had one answer when the land provided abundantly for all of America's appetites. But in our time the ecological facts of life have rendered many of yesterday's solutions and texts useless and rhetorically suspect. By plotting a course from the extravagance of Reno to the desolation of the primitive lake bed and its pathetic group of endangered horses, *The Misfits* sounded an early trumpet call about conditions that have moved to the very center of national and global life, implicating humans as well as animals. Like other talky and moralistic films of the early 1960s—*To Kill a Mockingbird; Judgment at Nuremberg; Hiroshima, Mon Amour; The Miracle Worker*—*The Misfits* can be condescended to or repressed because of its didactic form, but thanks to that form it may return upon us when serious debate begins on issues of national policy and destiny.

There is one more thing to say about the contemporaneity of *The Misfits.* Since 1961 spectators have become increasingly aware of the self-regarding quality of artworks, even when the works themselves have been seemingly unaware of their self-referentiality. In our time, to speak of *The Misfits* as a film about the industrial civilization and its discontents is to acknowledge how this film, too, became in its shooting and in its exhibition a part of the colonization of reality. According to Goode's fascinating chronicle, *The Making of* "The Misfits" (1963), the descent of the film crew upon Reno and the Nevada countryside jolted the citizens of the area into a media consciousness that must have diminished their "reality" significantly, making them into the shadow people the film deplored. The crew noticed immediately that the landscape itself was insufficiently real; it struck them as, their word, "hyper-reality" because it simulated so completely the images propagated in western movies. The art director, Steve Grimes, remarked that "Dayton looks like a movie backlot itself. All of the television western sets are based on towns like Dayton."[26] Nevertheless, Dayton was made mediagenic to conform to the conventional visual properties of a western film. At the same time a publicity factory was established at the center of the film set and at all the urban peripheries to satisfy consumer demand for images and reportage about the personalities and dynamics of the much-awaited film. Fifteen items were written every day for distribution to journalistic outlets and time taken from filming to arrange photo-ops and interviews with the national and international press. The irony of a film about the resistance to commercial exploitation being merchandised in this frantic way need not be underscored. Irony this corrosive gives the film, in retrospect, a visible patina of the postmodern.

Miller himself would dwell on this aspect of the film in his autobiography. He begins by noting how the cowboys he met in Nevada in 1956 looked to Hollywood films as models for their own behavior, remarking sardonically, "The movie cowboy was the real one, they the imitations. The final triumph of art . . . was to make a man feel less reality in himself than in an image."[27] As the filming commences and continues, he feels increasingly estranged from the fictions he is concocting to deceive the public into thinking that life has a more satisfying dramatic shape. "The whole make-believe business seemed detestable now, a destroyer of people," he notes, and finally makes the connection to the entirety of American culture: "The whole country seemed to be devolving into a mania for the distraction it called entertainment, a day-and-night mimicry of art that menaced nothing, redeemed nothing, and meant nothing but forgetfulness."[28] The film had become a crisis in his own life, hateful and false, despite the truth, or half-truth, enacted within its rhetorical structure.

It is no accident that the corruption of American society in Miller's novel *Focus* is represented by a job in the film studios. For any playwright the lure of the movies is substantial and often irresistible. *The Misfits* was Miller's significant effort to transfer his creative powers to what he called "the single great cultural invention of this civilization."[29] Miller worked on this film with a zeal and devotion that cannot be faulted. When the film failed, and his marriage to its star with it, he retreated to the theater that had sustained and rewarded him, ready to write new plays under his full control and extend the line of remarkable works that continue to engage audiences in revivals on stages around the world. If *The Misfits* is a sport, off the line of his great tradition, it nevertheless continues to fascinate us, in some ways more powerfully than ever, as a record of the road not taken, the frontier he closed behind him as another dead-end of the American dream.

Notes

1. Daniel G. Hoffman, *Form and Fable in American Fiction* (New York: Oxford University Press, 1961), x, xiv.

2. Ibid., 15.

3. Philip French, *Westerns: Aspects of a Movie Genre* (New York: Viking Press, 1974), 24.

4. Arthur Miller, *Timebends: A Life* (New York: Grove Press, 1987), 462.

5. Interview with Phillip Gels, "Morality and Modern Drama," in *The Theatre Essays of Arthur Miller,* ed. Robert A. Martin and Steven R. Centola (New York: Da Capo Press, 1996), 205.

6. Quoted in James Goode, *The Making of* "The Misfits" (1963; New York: Limelight Edition, 1986), 44–45.

7. French, *Westerns,* 68.

8. Miller, *Timebends,* 459–60.

9. Quoted in Lesley Brill, *John Huston's Filmmaking* (Cambridge: Cambridge University Press, 1997), 77.

10. Stanley Kauffmann, *A World on Film* (New York: Harper and Row, 1966), 102, 104.

11. Sheila Huftel, *Arthur Miller: The Burning Glass* (London: W. H. Allen, 1965), 175.

12. David Riesman, *The Lonely Crowd* (New Haven: Yale University Press, 1950), 287–91.

13. William H. Whyte Jr., *The Organization Man* (New York: Simon and Schuster, 1956), 11.

14. Christopher Bigsby, "Arthur Miller: An Interview," *Theatre Essays,* 508.

15. Miller has complained in several places that Huston neglected the cinematic possibilities of the landscape in favor of close-up shots of the actors. In 2000, in an interview preceding a portfolio of photographs chronicling the making of the film, he remarked, "I felt [Huston] stayed too close to the actors all the time and we weren't getting that atmosphere of people living on the moon. We were losing their surroundings too often." And later in the interview, "[T]here are no wide shots [of Pyramid Lake] in the film, except a medium one where Marilyn steps out of the

water. . . . There's an irony between those people loving each other against that death, but we did not get that presence of death." See *The Misfits: Story of a Shoot,* a collaboration of Miller, Serge Toubiana and the photographers of the Magnum company (London: Phaidon Press, 2000), 13, 32.

16. Joyce Carol Oates, *Blonde* (New York: Ecco Press, 2000), 656.
17. Huftel, *The Burning Glass,* 170.
18. Goode, *Making,* 74.
19. Ibid., 215.
20. Ibid., 17.
21. Kauffmann, *A World on Film,* 100.
22. Leonard Moss, *Arthur Miller* (New York: Twayne, 1967), 75.
23. Barbara Leaming, *Marilyn Monroe* (New York: Crown, 1998), 375.
24. Henry Popkin, "Arthur Miller Out West," *Commentary* 31 (May 1961): 435.
25. Goode, *Making,* 261.
26. Ibid., 62.
27. Miller, *Timebends,* 477.
28. Ibid.
29. Janet Balakian, "A Conversation with Arthur Miller," *Theatre Essays,* 487.

Jonathan Freedman

Miller, Monroe and the Remaking of Jewish Masculinity

What does it mean to be a man—a father, a son, a husband, a lover? These questions are central to the work of Arthur Miller, who has over the course of his career explored the contradictory penumbras of meaning surrounding each of these with a persistence and an intensity that often—quite literally—reduced audiences to tears. One such access of sentiment was particularly significant. As Miller recalls in his autobiography, *Timebends,* when *All My Sons* opened in Boston,

> I was surprised to see [his salesman uncle] Manny among the last of the matinee audience to leave. He had a nice gray overcoat on his arm and his pearl gray hat on his head, and his little shoes were brightly shined, and he had been weeping. It was almost a decade since I had last laid eyes on him. Despite my name on the marquee he had clearly not expected to see me here.
>
> "Manny! How are you? It's great seeing you here."
>
> I could see his grim hotel room behind him, the long trip up from New York in his little car, the hopeless hope of the day's business. Without so much as acknowledging my greeting, he said, "Buddy [Miller's cousin] is doing very well."[1]

Manny's gratuitous mention of his son sparked a reflux of Miller's resentment of his lower-middle-class, uninhibited relative—"my boyhood need of his recognition, my resentment at his disparagements, my envy of his and his sons' freed sexuality, and my contempt for it too" (*Timebends,* 131). But it also sparked, he claims, his most famous achievement. This was when, Miller later claimed, the method (and, it would seem, much of the matter) of *Death of a Salesman* was born. The playwright said that the image of the appropriately named Manny's "hopeless hope of the day's business," combined with his empathic vision of his uncle's life gave the impetus to the work with which he was to be associated for the rest of his career.

If this is a crucial moment in the history of American theater, it is also a crucial moment in another, equally theatrical, history: that of Jewish-American masculinity. The relation between Manny's family and Miller's experience represents a divergence between an ideal of maleness that conjoins business success with sexual potency and one associated with more refined sentiments—with cultural attainments and cosmopolitan amplitudes. The anecdote I have begun with suggests the triumph of this form of masculinity over Manny's, for (not to be *too* Nietzschean about the matter) to empathize with someone who once frightened or appalled us is also to stage a victory over him—a victory that confirms the very values Miller opposes to those of his uncle, those of art and imagination itself. It is a double triumph as well. The quite worldly success of that play brought with it fame, fortune and the love of a movie star—an undeniable achievement in Manny's world as well as in Miller's.

The playwright's double triumph has cultural as well as personal ramifications, for it accompanies, and perhaps even accomplishes, the creation of an entirely new ideal-type of Jewish masculinity: the persona of the pipe-smoking Jewish intellectual as star-marrying studmuffin—a persona that, later on in the decades, Woody Allen and Philip Roth also came to represent in the publicity-mad public sphere, to their delight and chagrin. It is the construction and ramifications of this new social type that I will be studying here. I should stress, especially to the reader of this volume, that despite my deep respect for Arthur Miller the man and playwright, he is subsidiary to my interest in "Arthur Miller" the cultural phenomenon. (His marriage to Marilyn, Miller told an interviewer in 1983, "is not part of my life now . . . except when some stupid jerk says something about it";[2] it is my hope in what follows to be as little a jerk as possible.) To be sure, there are points of overlap between the two, particularly as Miller commented on or attempted to come to terms with "Arthur Miller" in works like *Timebends* or *After the Fall*. But it seems to me that, like so many figures caught up in the publicity machine of American popular culture (like, for example, Norma Jean Baker/Marilyn Monroe) it is precisely the gap between the self-understanding of the historical subject and that figure's reflections in the media that is significant. Such a gap is even more germane when the making of that reflection is part of a thoroughly imaginary process—albeit one that had real consequences in real lives: the contradictory process by which Jewish masculinity has been defined in the cultures of the diaspora West for the past two hundred years.

In these pages (part of a larger study on the relations between Marilyn Monroe and three distinct styles of American assimilation as represented by Joe DiMaggio and John Kennedy as well as Miller—by sports and politics as well as the entertainment industry), I want to argue that the Miller-Monroe conjunction represents an important and neglected stage in the Americanizing process. It emblematizes both the desires of assimilating Jewish men to break out of the spaces in which they had been contained and the ways in which new organs of entertainment and publicity constructed new boxes in which to confine them. In this sense, the creation of "Arthur Miller," like that of, say, "Woody Allen," is a sign of the cultural transformations that either bring to an end the centuries-long process of constructing Jewish masculinity in problematically double terms—or a sign that that process has shifted into a new, and not necessarily more expansive, key.

To understand Miller's situation, his transformation into "Arthur Miller," and the ramifications of that metamorphosis, we need to understand something about the changing shape of Jewish masculinity, first in Europe, then in America. For, as a number of critics have reminded us, from at least the eighteenth century forward, the Jewish man has been persistently defined in double terms. On the one hand—like his companions, the working-class man, the swarthy southern European, or the colonial subject—the Jewish man was seen as primitive, more fully sexual, impulsive and hyperphallic. On the other, the Jewish man (unlike these other figures) was also seen as unmanly, weak, effeminate or otherwise outside the norm of properly assertive masculinity. Thus in the anti-Semitic literature that flooded to the surface in late-nineteenth-century Europe—much of which had its origins far earlier, in the anti-Jewish polemics of the medieval period—Jewish men were either seen as debased lechers yearning for Christian girls (preferably virgins) or as men-women—this is the famous allegation of Otto Weininger's *Sex and Character* (1903), which artists as various as Marcel Proust and James Joyce were to play with in the early decades of the twentieth century. As these works begin to suggest, the cultural contradiction was ameliorated when the two merged into a new character type: the Jewish pervert, a figure who conjoined the will-to-power of the hyperaggressive Jewish male with the sexual nonnormativity of the feminized Jewish man.[3]

At once more and less of a man than Gentile men: this was the odd position in which Jews were placed in early-twentieth-century America and to which they were forced to respond as they sought to assimilate into that culture. But to tell this story only one way—as being about Gentile constructions—is to miss its full complexity, for it is also a narrative about changing models of masculinity within an assimilating Jewish community. Within traditional Jewish culture, for example, conventional ideals of Western manhood were contravened by an ideal that stresses study, passivity, physical inactivity, which places ideal men in the *cheder,* the traditional school, rather than the battlefield or the marketplace, loci of, respectively, the residual chivalric and the emergent bourgeois ideals of masculinity. The result is a strikingly different notion of what constitutes ideal maleness than is the norm in Euro-American culture. As Daniel Boyarin writes,

> In direct contrast to the firm handshake approved (for men and businessmen) in our culture, a *Yeshiva-Bokhur* [traditional scholar of the Talmud in Orthodox Jewish culture], until this day, extends the right hand with a limp wrist for a mere touch of the other's hand. . . . The very handshake of the ideal male Jew encoded him as femminized [*sic*] in the eyes of European heterosexual culture, but that handshake constituted as well a mode of resistance to the models of manliness of the dominant fiction.[4]

To a certain degree, in other words, what Gentile culture read as Jewish male effeminacy was a different order of masculine value, one that indeed merits Boyarin's term "resistance." But from the Jewish side of the equation, "resistance" was yet more complicated: assimilating Jewish men had to differentiate themselves from traditional models of masculinity even as they were distancing themselves from anti-Semitic ones. These dynamics became even more sharply complicated when Eastern European Jews emigrated in enormous numbers to the United States. For what they found in America was an entirely different social order—one in which the traditional models of Jewish masculinity, already under attack, were found at best irrelevant, at worst dysfunctional. In his ethnography of the Lower East Side, *The Spirit of the Ghetto,* Hutchins Hapgood eloquently summarized how Jewish boys rebelled against their foreign parents by vigorously adopting the most aggressively American of guises, thereby establishing a dynamic that was to play itself out for the rest of the century:

> The boys not only talk together of picnics, of the crimes of which they read in the English newspapers, of prize-fights, of budding business propositions, but they gradually quit going to the synagogue, give up "chaider" promptly when they are ten years old, seek the up-town places of amusement, dress in the latest American fashion, and have a keen eye for the right thing in neckties. . . . Then, indeed, is the sway of the old people broken.[5]

What's important to notice here is not only that the younger generation secularized and assimilated in self-conscious revolt against their parents—this is a familiar dynamic in American Jewish life—but rather that they did so through their participation in American mass culture: in the world of amusements, prizefights and advertisements spread in large measure, in the later years of the nineteenth century and early years of the twentieth, by the proliferation of new media like penny newspapers, mass-market magazines, nickelodeons and the motion picture industry. But as they came into increasing dialogue with American constructions of masculinity, they faced a persistent question: namely, which of the various models of American masculinity were they to assimilate to?

Amid the welter of possibilities, two distinct models emerged in the 1920s—and were to find their reflection in Miller's family. On the one hand stood ideals of bourgeois but disembodied respectability ("If you can't beat 'em, join 'em"); on the other, a more rambunctious but embodied assertiveness ("If you can't join 'em, beat 'em up"). To be sure, the first of these patterns predominated, as Jews marched into small businesses or the professions starting in the 1900s and continuing well into the 1920s and beyond—indeed, so much into the latter that law schools and medical schools as well as Ivy League universities started closing their doors to them. Although, as we shall see in more detail below, the power of this ideal type was to be challenged by the Depression, its greatest salience to Miller's own life was doubtless one of its offshoots, the high-culture intellectual.

But even as the *yeshiva-bukher* metamorphosed into the high-culture intellectual, another, more bodily model of Jewish masculinity started to appear alongside it. Valorizations of assertive, embodied Jewish masculinity were always present alongside the middle-class and intellectual ones I have mentioned above. These became all the more important as the second generation of Jewish youth rebelled against the seemingly uptight strictures of their parents, particularly as the Depression made their parents' faith in success through bourgeois restraint seem risible, and raised the specter of ineffectuality or even emasculation as businesses failed and professional careers withered or were blocked. Their model of Jewish masculinity met anti-Semitic constructions of feminized Jews and Jewish constructions of the *yeshivah-bukher* head on, affirming the Jew's toughness, worldliness, power. Its cultural embodiments took the form of boxers, athletes and proletarianized workers; but by the late twenties its main cynosures were the gangsters, pimps, and hangers-on who defined the Jewish mob in large cities like New York, Philadelphia and Detroit. The entertainment industries, then and now, were particularly shaped by the image of the tough-guy Jew—it was a significant element in the persona of such figures as Harry Cohn or Louis Mayer, not to mention such actors as Emanuel Goldenberg (aka Edward G. Robinson), Muni Weisenfreund (aka Paul Muni, Howard Hawks's Scarface), Julius Garfinkle (aka John Garfield), and, in a later decade, Issur Danielovich (aka Isadore Demsky, aka Kirk Douglas) or Bernard Schwartz (aka Tony Curtis).[6]

It is against this background, with its welter of sharply contrasting, if not contradictory, models for Jewish manhood being offered from outside the Jewish community and within, that we are to understand Miller and, more to the point, "Arthur Miller." As far as the former—the real live Arthur Miller—is concerned, the relation between Arthur and Isidore Miller on the one hand and Arthur and his cousins on the other suggests (as it did for so many of his generation of Jewish men) the inadequacy of both the businessman and the tough-guy models—and indeed of the Jewish ones entirely. The business failure of Miller père—one enhanced and ratified, according to Miller, not only by his wife but also by his own mother, who refused him a loan as his business failed—played off against the relative success and rambunctious sexuality of his uncle and cousins in ways that are virtual paradigms of each model of manliness. And both were plainly not viable for Arthur, for whom—as for Jewish sons from at least 1900 onward—a different form of manliness needed to be found.

At least for the Arthur Miller of the 1940s and early 1950s, that model followed the tradition I have sketched above of finding in the mechanisms of high culture a form of superiority to both his own family origins and that of a decreasingly, but still palpably anti-Semitic culture. Like many of his peers, Miller rejected available models in his neighborhood and followed the assimilation-by-high-culture trail, asserting an identity for himself as the ethnicity-transcending artist, writing plays despite the opposition of his father, who urged upon him a more conventional career. And as it did for many of his fellow travelers on the assimilation-by-high-culture path, such a choice also meant rejecting an identity for himself in terms of the Jewish family itself, rejecting his parents' expectations by marrying Mary Slattery, a woman of Irish Catholic background, albeit one who, like Miller himself, was self-alienated from her own ethnicity, seeking to identify with "mankind, rather than one small tribal fraction of it" (*Timebends,* 70).

But despite his efforts to escape or evade the "tribal" aspects of his Jewish origins, Miller's personal commitments and, perhaps more importantly, the representations of him in the public sphere were powerfully linked to the double constructions of Jewish masculinity I have been outlining above. Or, to be more precise, Miller's rise to fame was in large measure a response to the more invidious of those constructions, as American society in general started to overcome its aversion to Jews. Miller came to public attention in the period after World War II, at a moment when opposition to Hitler, knowledge of the death camps and a general opening up of an insular America to the world at large forced underground the anti-Semitism that had flourished in the early years of the twentieth century, and had been given new impetus during the Depression by figures like Henry Ford and Father Coughlin. At that moment, Jewish artists and writers were entering the cultural mainstream, not as marginalized figures but as full participants in middlebrow production; the 1950s were not only the time of writers like Miller attracting a new audience to Broadway, but one when writers like Herman Wouk and Leon Uris were extending both the subject matter and the reach of mass fiction. As Jewish writers moved into the previously WASP-dominated cultural and literary spheres, however, new inscriptions of Jewish identity needed to be written. And the representation of Miller, who emerged in this welter of new talent as its most towering figure, was an integral part of this process. For the popular press constructed Miller in terms that united the dualities of Jewish male identity, positioning him as someone straddling the lines between mental and manual labor, body and intellect, high and mass culture, art and business—and even normativity and perversion.

Consider, as a prime example of this process, the following, a *Saturday Evening Post* profile of Miller just after *Death of a Salesman* opened on Broadway:

> "A man who can't handle tools is not a man" says Willy Loman in the title role of *Death of a Salesman*. Willy speaks for his creator. Before "Salesman" was written, Miller built a house in which to write it. He owns some country property in Roxbury, Connecticut and a year ago he dug a cellar, poured a concrete foundation, built a one-room shack with windows and a door, installed workable plumbing and finally got the roof up. The roof gave him some trouble, working alone, but he devised a way to fit the rafters on the ground, get them on top of the house upside down, and flip the rafter joints over and in place.
>
> Then Miller sat down in front of a thirteen-year-old secondhand portable typewriter . . . and started to write "Death of a Salesman." Six weeks later the play was completed. Produced with only the most minute changes, it may

> become the most profitable six weeks' work ever undertaken in the history of show business.[7]

Note here how this figure—the first glimmerings of what I am calling "Arthur Miller"—unites the antitheses between which Jewish male identity had been divided in such a way as to modify or normalize their extreme aspects. The negative side of the Gentile construction of Jewish masculinity—Jews as ineffectual, intellectual sissies, if not queers—and the negative side of the Jewish counter-response—Jews as working-class, manly, tough guys—both get ameliorated as they are mainstreamed. Indeed, the mainstreaming of this "Brooklyn Boy" who "Makes Good" (as the title of the profile has it) casts that "goodness" in the most traditional of American terms, terms in which his identity as a Jew or even an intellectual are effaced in favor of values more finely homespun, if resolutely un-Jewish:

> The man responsible for his solid milestone in theatrical history . . . until recently insisted there was no truth to his friends' belief that he resembled a beardless Abraham Lincoln. Not long ago, his wife showed Jane Ellen Miller, age four and a half, a shiny new Lincoln penny. "Daddy on money," she said knowingly. Daddy sighed and accepted the inevitable.

This is, not to put too fine a point on it, what we mean by assimilation: Miller is admitted into the ranks of the normatively American, but the price of that admission is an extinction of his own ethnic difference, the collapse of it into a sanitized version of one of America's most canonical heroes and then the placement of that image on the most thoroughly American of objects, a piece of money. In terms of the unfolding of American political life, this image was to have striking consequences; but in terms of the unfolding of structures of assimilated Jewish masculinity, it was to exert a powerful synthesizing effect as well, uniting the insider and outsider, the mental and the manual, the Jew and the average Joe into one complex—and Americanized—amalgamation.

Yet less than a decade later, "Daddy on Money" was to launch first an affair, then a marriage, with the most sought-after woman in America, the actress cum sex-bomb Marilyn Monroe—and it was in this guise that his transformation from Miller into "Arthur Miller," or at least the "Arthur Miller" that was to do such powerful cultural work, was wrought. To be sure, such a process would seem to involve some of the more insidious stereotypes of Jewish masculinity, that of the showbiz variant of the tough-guy Jew. And indeed, this is the precedent set by the numerous liaisons between Jewish men and Gentile women throughout the 1930s and 1940s, perhaps the most salient of which being that between Miller's precursor Clifford Odets (to whom some of the most powerfully ambivalent pages in *Timebends* are devoted) and Frances Farmer, a beautiful free spirit who was to go mad and be, infamously, lobotomized. As no less an authority than Philip Roth's Alexander Portnoy observes, such liaisons became all too common: Eddie Fisher and Debbie Reynolds, Phil Harris and Alice Faye, even Elizabeth Taylor and Mike Todd—and "you know what Mike Todd was—a cheap facsimile of my Uncle Hymie upstairs!"[8]

The liaison between Monroe and Miller makes Portnoy's list, too, about which more below. But it is important to note that, especially in comparison with these other liaisons, matters between these two were far more complicated. For one thing, it was not as a tough Jew like Harry Cohn (who used Monroe as a concubine early in her career while her image was being molded, then dropped her from his studio), or a business Jew like Mike Todd, but rather as an intellectual Jew—and hence an exception to the Hollywood norm—that Miller wrought the Monroe marriage. To be sure, part of Miller's appeal to Monroe was his gentlemanliness: when the two first encountered each other in 1950, they spent a long time talking at a party during which Miller, coyly but chastely, sat holding her toe. As such, he was at distinct odds not only with the wolves who Marilyn had been afflicted by in her early career as Hollywood party girl, but also his own friend Elia Kazan, who was conducting an affair with Marilyn at the time of Miller's first trip to Hollywood. As a man of sensitivity and tact, as a New York playwright, as an intellectual, Miller stood apart from the prevailing ethos of the male-dominated Hollywood entertainment industry, an industry that, as we have seen, served both as the lure for and the validation of Jewish men of Miller's generation.

But, interestingly, the actress's response to the playwright was very much like his own daughter's, and the *Post*'s—and the playwright, infatuated, was not above using it to his own advantage. For, after their first meeting, "Miller wrote Marilyn within days," according to one unauthorized biographer, "with a reading proposal":

> "If you want someone to admire, why not Abraham Lincoln?" Marilyn, as the world could hardly fail to know, admired Lincoln already. Her idolatry had started, she said, in junior high school, when her essay on Lincoln was judged the best in the class. By happy coincidence, Arthur Miller had attended

> Abraham Lincoln High School. Five years later, before her marriage to Miller, Monroe would enthuse to Joshua Logan, director of *Bus Stop*, "Doesn't Arthur look wonderfully like Abraham Lincoln? I'm mad for him."[9]

The anecdote suggests how fraught and charged were the issues involved in the transformation of Miller's persona. For especially in Monroe's and Miller's circles (and as opposed to those of the *Saturday Evening Post*), to be identified with Lincoln was not an innocent conjunction. The Great Emancipator was a favorite icon of the Popular Front—it was not for nothing that the anti-Fascist, racially integrated Abraham Lincoln Brigade identified with *that* particular president; and he was even more frequently evoked by less radical leftists like Carl Sandburg, whose hagiographic biography of Lincoln was completed in 1939, or Aaron Copland, whose *Fanfare for the Common Man* was first sounded in 1944, with Sandburg as narrator. And Marilyn was a passionate Hollywood liberal, particularly with respect to civil rights: although she had no involvement at all in the Communist Party, she nevertheless attracted the attention of J. Edgar Hoover long before her dalliances with the Kennedys filled his file. Miller and Monroe, considering the possibility of a relationship, thus concocted first a private, then a public image of Miller that was distinct from the normative one of his family or the popular press. Yet that image was made out of many of the same materials—especially the Lincoln-like artist, here constructed as the man of political integrity and progressive sentiments. When Miller and Monroe were married, the then liberal *New York Post* reported on their nuptials with the following banner headline: *Our Man Kissed the Bride!*—referring not only to Miller's New York origins, but also to the legitimacy of the Jewish liberal Left that Miller, like that newspaper at that time, represented in the culture at large.

To remind ourselves of the leftist spin that Miller and Monroe gave their union is also to observe the difficulties it faced—difficulties that helped cement the transformation of Miller into "Arthur Miller." For there is no doubt but that Miller's relationship with Marilyn brought him to his greatest test, and the one that remade his persona for a third time: his appearance before the House Un-American Activities Committee in 1956. It does not seem to be the case, as Miller later claimed, that his affair with her was the sole reason he was called as witness. Nevertheless, the committee did indeed make as much of the publicity that attended from Miller's engagement to Monroe and his desire to leave the country with his new wife during her filming of *The Prince and the Showgirl* in London. (Indeed, Miller reportedly was offered the opportunity to get out of his obligation to testify if the chair of the committee could pose for photographs with Marilyn.) But Miller himself was not above using his relationship with Monroe to help him ease his political difficulties; he mentioned her as frequently as he possibly could (as, to be sure, did the press, for whom the word *Miller* was conjoined as frequently to *Monroe* as it was to *testimony*.) Monroe, for her part, stood by her man, demurely standing behind Arthur when he spoke to the press even as she participated in his private war-councils, urging a resolute stand. Because of her celebrity, she served an invaluable purpose. One of Monroe's most sympathetic biographers, Barbara Leaming, describes the scene outside the HUAC hearings, after an uninspired performance by Miller, as follows:

> Finally, Marilyn Monroe and Arthur Miller emerged hand-in-hand from the apartment-house lobby. She looked adorable, yet properly subdued for the occasion. . . .
>
> "I've never been happier in my life," said Marilyn, nuzzling Miller for the cameras. He looked sweaty in a dark suit and tie.
>
> As the couple stepped out onto the sidewalk, Marilyn leaned very hard on Arthur as if to emphasize that she depended on his protection, though in fact it was very much she who was going to protect him today. It wasn't enough to give a brilliant performance; she had to be a director, too. . . . She had to show people an Arthur Miller they had never seen before. "You better stop that," Miller whispered to Marilyn. "If you lean too hard, I'm going to fall over."
>
> Marilyn, all smiles and giggles, responded by closing her eyes and kissing Arthur's wrinkled cheek.
>
> "Do it again, Marilyn," the photographers cheered.
>
> She did—numerous times.
>
> "It's a good thing we'll only be getting married once," Miller remarked to reporters. "That's all I can tell you."
>
> Marilyn whispered something in Arthur's ear that caused him to hold her very tightly, burrowing his nose in her forehead. He was the image of a man deeply in love, of a man who certainly deserved to be permitted to go on honeymoon.[10]

Leaming's gossipy account of the scene seems partial, in every sense of the word. Miller was thirty-nine when he married Monroe, and she was ten years younger, which is to say that he was hardly the *senex amans* that Leaming sketches any more than Monroe was the blushing young bride that she played. But her sketch does capture something important about the Miller-Monroe dynamic, at least as it was represented in the public sphere. For, as in their initial dalliance with each other, it seems as if these two are collaborating to create a collective fiction; but here, the fiction is meant to be public rather than personal, an improvised performance rather than an erotic *pas de deux*. Indeed, the drama they created is essentially a transformation story—an American Pygmalion, or perhaps, more appositely, a real-life version of the smash hit musical and film *Born Yesterday*.[11] Like Judy Holliday in that work, Monroe plays the innocent but sexy guttersnipe redeemed by the love of a decent, if awkward man, the naïf sex-bomb tamed by the power of high culture. For his part Miller is cast and (to a certain extent) casts himself in the other part in the drama: the ugly duckling redeemed by the love of a beautiful woman, the powerful, severe intellectual whose austerity is overcome by his swinging, sexy beloved—but one whose chief role remains that of the savior.

It is *this* mutual transformation story—one that only partially catches the complexity of the relation between these two—that initiates the most significant act of metamorphosis in the Miller saga. What is crucial about it is not just that he is the man who succeeded with the woman whom Joe DiMaggio and countless other American men (virtually all of the heterosexual ones) wished to win; he succeeds *because* of his status as an awkward, press-shy, sensitive man. This moment, and the transformation story it witnesses, is one, in short, in which the stereotypical Jewish male firmly gets remade into the cynosure of heterosexual potency and success not by becoming something different—Abe Lincoln, "daddy on money," and so on—but merely by being himself. And more: Miller was transformed into a figure of such potency in the very media—the very entertainment industry—to which Jewish men turned for their models of American masculinity on the non-Jewish plane. Just as Marilyn was (literally) converted to Judaism through her encounter with Miller, so Miller was transformed, not so much into a Gentile or a goy—this was the point of previous incarnations—but into a celebrity in his own right. Whatever else one can say about it, none of the subsequent events of the marriage—its inevitable breakdown in mutual mistrust and the inability to conceive a child, Marilyn's suicide, Miller's grief and guilt—would or could change the cultural importance of this development.

I want to be clear here: I am not writing about this moment in a spirit of cheap cynicism, nor am I suggesting (as does Leaming, or, in a different form, David Savran) that Miller was deploying his wife in a tactical manner.[12] The couple at this moment experienced enormous strain: pressures from the press, from the HUAC, from their lawyers, from their own needs and desires. Nevertheless, considered in cultural terms, the moment is absolutely crucial. For the construction of "Arthur Miller" and the cultural work that circulated in his wake initiated a new style of Jewish masculinity among the subsequent generation of Jewish writers and intellectuals, one in which the kind of notoriety that Miller found, the kind of celebrity he achieved, became an explicit goal rather than (as I think it was with Miller) the by-product of a series of life choices. And more: not only do a number of Jewish intellectuals who came to maturity during the 1950s and early 1960s play out the Miller pattern—I have mentioned already the two most prominent, Woody Allen and Philip Roth, but one needs to include the envious Norman Mailer in this list as well—and many make explicit reference to him as they do so. For Miller—or rather "Miller"—served as something of a Bloomian influence figure for these writers: a figure, that is, who had to be overcome by mechanisms of imitation for them to claim masculine literary authority for themselves.

Some explicitly staged this relation as an Oedipal battle—this would seem to be Mailer's path, for example: what is his *Marilyn* but a long attempt to claim Monroe's body for himself, and implicitly wrest it away from Miller? With others, the relation seemed to be more mediated; Allen's liaisons with Diane Keaton and Mia Farrow, for example, often remind one of the notoriety of the Miller-Monroe liaison without acknowledging its consequences, until those consequences reached up and bit him. But the clearest example of the salience of Miller's example to Jewish-American intellectuals is Philip Roth, who not only followed the great-American-writer-marries-a-Hollywood-star-and-lives-to-regret-it pattern, but has written about Miller and Monroe in at least two contexts. One of them—which I will not be writing about here—is his novel *I Married a Communist,* which turns back to the days of the Hollywood blacklist and imagines a marriage between a movie star and a Jewish radical radio personality in which she betrays her husband and ruins his career by penning a novel with the same name as the book's title. (That the novel was published just after Roth's former wife, the actress Claire Bloom, published a tell-all biography about him is part of the story, too.) But I want in conclusion to focus briefly on the Millerism of Roth's most famous novel, *Portnoy's Complaint,* because it suggests just how enduring the cultural forces called into being by the Miller-Monroe conflation turned out to be—and just how enduring are the patterns of Jewish masculine definition that Miller's career seemed to transcend.

At least two points of contact between "Arthur Miller" and Alexander Portnoy are woven into the novel. The first, and to my mind most systematically underappreciated, is the way the novel stages an important aspect of its revision of modes of Jewish masculinity on the back of Miller and his most famous cultural production, *Death of a Salesman.* For the character who is most systematically forgotten in critical accounts of the novel, but who dominates its second section (the memorably entitled "Whacking Off"), is Alexander Portnoy's father, who is by profession an insurance salesman. And like Willy Loman, he is a figure who has bought into the American dream with ironic results, although, of course, Roth plays these for comedy, not tragedy. Although like Isidore Miller, Arthur's father, Jack Portnoy is eclipsed by "the potent man in the family—successful in business, tyrannical at home," his older brother Hymie—he is most notably a driven Lomanesque salesman; he "work[s] the longest day of any insurance agent in history" (117), in his case vending insurance policies to poor, vulnerable African-Americans in the worst sections of Newark and pouncing on them to collect their small payments on weekends. This occupation is doubtless galling to his rebellious son, but even he understands that, although Jack is clearly an exploiter, he is treated with the same indifference that Willy Loman experiences from his employer. More importantly, perhaps, he is like Willy in another way: Alexander thinks he is cheating on his wife with someone from the front office. In this case, the party in question is not called "the Woman" but rather a shiksa named Anne McCafferey—a new cashier, Jack Portnoy tells Sophie, who wants to come home for a real Jewish meal. Her arrival in the home precipitates a most un-Loman-like battle between Jack and Sophie Portnoy; but it also provides the psychogenesis of Alexander Portnoy's own form of sexual expression. Whether or not Jack is (as Alex puts it) *schtupping* Anne McCafferey, Sophie seems to think he is; and when she confronts her husband, she turns and hugs Alex's sister Hannah to her breast, consigning the two Jewish men in the family to what Alex perceives, years later, to be a commonality of guilt that becomes "the most prevalent form of degradation in erotic life"—Alex's need for exogamous relationships with Gentile women, as if to do openly what his father could only do covertly.

I want to suggest, then, two things: that the impress of Miller's literary example is felt on the character of Jack Portnoy, who is an ethnic version of Willy Loman, a Willy Loman who is definitively a Jew and whose treatment by his insurance company is tinged with systemic anti-Semitism—but also a Willy Loman without any tragic or transcendent dimension. I am also suggesting that the force of Miller's personal example is felt here as well, and that Jack Portnoy brings into the novel the thematics of Jewish-Gentile sexual attraction that get played out in the experience of Alexander Portnoy with direct allusion to the Miller-Monroe relationship. As with Roth's rewriting of Willy as Jack, his reinscription of Miller and Monroe takes a powerful comic form: he rewrites it as Alex's affair with the character he knows as "the Monkey"—a model and actress whose name literally echoes that of Norma Jean Baker: Sally Jane Reed. Like Norma Jean/Marilyn Monroe, Sally Jane/"the Monkey" is born into a "dirt poor" white-trash family, in her case Appalachian rather than the descendents of Appalachians who emigrated to California (as was the case with Monroe). Like Norma Jean/Marilyn, Sally Jane/"the Monkey" enters the entertainment industry (here the fashion industry) via her spectacular beauty, but is also taken up by a string of rich men who use her sexually and then discard her. Like Norma Jean/Marilyn, Sally Jane/"the Monkey" enters into a protracted analysis with an orthodox Freudian shrink, one of the results of which is her attraction to a seemingly stable Jewish man—Alexander Portnoy—at the same age and with many of the same motives that Marilyn seems to have entered into her relationship with Miller. Alex's role in this drama is to be exactly that which Miller portrayed in his *public* relation with Marilyn: to be the stable family man who grants her her wishes, the intellectual who helps elevate her tastes (on one of their most idyllic weekends, he reads her "Leda and the Swan," for which she rewards him a particularly inspired bit of oral sex). And finally, "the Monkey" has, at the end of the novel, attempted (in the Marilyn fashion) to force Alex's hand by attempting suicide—causing Alex to retreat into a state of guilt-induced impotence. No wonder Roth concludes his first description of Alex's relation with Sally Jane Reed with an explicit invocation of the Miller–Monroe relationship:

> What was I supposed to be but *her* Jewish saviour? The Knight on the Big White Steed . . .[who] turns out to be none other than a brainy, balding, beaky Jew with a strong social conscience and black hair on his balls, who neither drinks nor gambles nor keeps show girls on the side; a man guaranteed to give them kiddies to rear and Kafka to read—a regular domestic Messiah! . . . What we have before us, ladies and gentlemen, direct from his long record-breaking engagement with his own family, is a Jewish boy just dying in his every cell to be Good, Responsible, & Dutiful, to a family of his

> own. The same people who brought you Harry Golden's *For 2c Plain* bring you now—the Alexander Portnoy show! If you liked Arthur Miller as a savior of *shikses,* you'll just love Alex! (154)

To be sure, in the context I have been discussing in this essay, this is a deeply suggestive passage; but it is also a troubling one. It is insightful in its recognition that the Miller-Monroe duet sets the stage for subsequent Jewish-Gentile relations and, more particularly, that such a coupling is quite literally a "show"—a spectacle, a TV sitcom or variety special in which Jewish men are granted their full masculinity, yet are made to play a domesticated role as family men, educators, saviors of "shikses." Indeed, as that last phrase implies, as Jews they are asked to assimilate into a thoroughly Christian pattern, one in which their job, in other words, is not only to sleep with Gentiles but also to redeem them from their own transgressions. And, even more problematic, Alex-as-Miller fits himself into the Gentile imaginary in other ways as well. Here he stands in the midst of the not-enough/too-much of a man pattern we have seen in the image of Jewish men in America: either he is a kind of ravening beast filled with transgressive desires (the larger context of this passage, and his entire relation with "the Monkey," is her reproaches to him for initiating a sexual threesome with a prostitute from Rome) or he is to be the very model of the good Jewish boy that Portnoy found to be confining at best, emasculating at worst. Indeed, at the very end of the novel, Portnoy is quite literally caught in this double bind: he finds himself afflicted with guilt at Sally Jane Reed's suicide attempt and thoroughly impotent even—or especially—when he attempts to force himself on a sabra soldier he has picked up in Israel.

Roth's hope here is clearly for a new beginning to Alex Portnoy's narratives of Jewish masculinity. But this is not what his hero finds—indeed, to the contrary. As Alex both explores his own sexuality over the course of the novel and revolts against it in the comic conclusion, he clearly reinscribes himself as an all-too-familiar character type: the Jewish pervert. There is now the added intensity that this vision of himself comes not only from Gentile and Jewish culture, each of which condemns normative Jewish sexuality, but from his own guilt-inducing superego, which continually reproaches him for his transgressive desires. This is the fate of the new beginning of Jewish masculinity represented by the construction of "Arthur Miller" as well. Although Miller's transformation into "Miller" in many ways registered the amelioration of the most invidious forms of Jewish masculinity, it also suggested that such an amelioration came with a heavy price. Not only could Jewish men not be Jews, but they weren't allowed to be human, fallible, governed by the same desires as their Gentile peers; rather, they had to display exquisite ethical sensitivity, perform acts of earnest self-sacrifice, display strenuous intellectualism. If they failed in that task, Jewish men had to inscribe themselves and see themselves as degenerates, perverts—as the very figures that this ethical imperative was intended to relieve them from embodying.

One response to that dilemma, of course, is Roth's and Woody Allen's—to revel in the role of the Jewish pervert, to play it to the hilt and to subject the mechanisms of amelioration to comic scrutiny and hence critique. But as I have been implying with respect to Portnoy, this solution is no solution at all, merely a different version of the familiar situation in which Jewish men can sometimes find themselves. And that may indeed be the final lesson posed to us by the cultural work done in, around and through Arthur Miller and Jewish men of his generation: that while cultural prejudices may fade, they leave in their stead double binds and impossible demands that persist despite the best attempts of people to make their way out of them. These double binds are not only imposed from the outside, but are lived from the inside, even as—or precisely because—people struggle so hard against them. That cultural construct "Arthur Miller" made out of the materials of his own life before and during his relationship with Marilyn Monroe was ineluctably linked to him despite his best wishes to avoid its double logic of Jewish masculinity. His very efforts to get out from under that logic only reinforced its power—not just in his own experience but in that of the Jewish men who followed him and found that they, too, were subject to its dual imperatives—in large measure because they were imitating his patterns of responding to them. Perhaps now, fifty years after these events—and some thirty years after *Portnoy*—we are in a position to imagine what an alternative Jewish masculinity might look like: it might prove more playful than any of the ones I have been conjuring with here, or less angst-ridden and self-immolating, at the very least. But whatever way it develops, it seems to me it will need to take into account the manifold forces unleashed through the rich experience of Arthur Miller—and expressed by Miller the writer as well as represented by "Arthur Miller" the invidious, inescapable construction of a deeply conflicted American culture.

Notes

1. Miller, *Timebends: A Life* (New York: Penguin, 1995), 130–31.

2. Jennifer Allen, "Miller's Tale," *New York Magazine,* January 24, 1983, 37.

3. See George L. Mosse, *Nationalism and Sexuality: Middle-Class Morality and Sexual Norms in Modern Europe* (Madison: University of Wisconsin Press, 1985), and inter alia, Sander L. Gilman, *The Case of Sigmund Freud: Medicine and Identity at the Fin de Siècle* (Baltimore: Johns Hopkins University Press, 1993).

4. Daniel Boyarin, *Unheroic Conduct: The Rise of Heterosexuality and the Invention of the Jewish Man* (Berkeley and Los Angeles: University of California Press, 1997), 151.

5. Hutchins Hapgood, *The Spirit of the Ghetto* (Cambridge: Harvard University Press, 1967), 27.

6. For these developments, see inter alia, Albert Fried, *The Rise and Fall of the Jewish Gangster in America* (New York: Holt, Rinehart, and Winston, 1980), Jenna Weisman Joselit, *Our Gang: Jewish Crime and the New York Jewish Community, 1900–1940* (Bloomington: Indiana University Press, 1983), and Michael Alexander, "Jazz Age Jews: Arnold Rothstein, Felix Frankfurter, Al Jolson, and the Jewish Imagination," Ph.D. diss., Yale University, 1999. For a contrasting view, see Enoch Brater, "Ethics and Ethnicity in the Plays of Arthur Miller" in Sarah Cohen, ed., *From Hester Street to Hollywood: The Jewish-American Stage and Screen* (Bloomington: Indiana University Press, 1983), 123–36.

7. Robert Sylvester, "Brooklyn Boy Makes Good," *Saturday Evening Post,* July 16, 1949, 26.

8. Philip Roth, *Portnoy's Complaint* (New York: Random House, 1969), 152. Further citations in the text refer to this edition.

9. Anthony Summers, *Goddess: The Secret Lives of Marilyn Monroe* (New York: Macmillan, 1985), 65.

10. Barbara Leaming, *Marilyn Monroe* (New York: Three Rivers Press, 1998), 243.

11. It may be appropriate to note, in this context, that this 1951 film presented a blonde mistress of a Washington politician educated by—and in turn educating—an intellectual snob. The film's blonde bombshell—Judy Holliday née Julie Tumin—was not only groomed by the studios to be the next Marilyn Monroe but was the daughter of Upper West Side socialist intellectuals. To complete the chain of ironic associations here, she testified before the House Un-American Activities Committee in 1952 and was cleared by that body.

12. See David Savran, *Communists, Cowboys, and Queers: The Politics of Masculinity in the Work of Arthur Miller and Tennessee Williams* (Minneapolis: University of Minnesota Press, 1992).

Peter W. Ferran

The American Clock
"Epic Vaudeville"

There is nothing quite like *The American Clock* among Arthur Miller's plays. Some of the earlier ones approach its presentational directness, others share its documentary impulse, a few make some use of music; but no other Miller play exploits all these features to make such a distinctive *theatrical* definition. And all the plays that follow are *theatrically* illuminated by it, to a markedly greater degree than by anything preceding this remarkable work. The reason has to do with the author's formal intentions.

In a 1980 interview soon after the play's mounting at the Spoleto Festival, Miller told Studs Terkel: "I have experimented with formal problems since the time I started writing. There's an attempt here to do two things at the same time, which is the nature of a mural. . . . When you look close at any face, it may turn out to be a real person's. When you step away, you see a whole pattern, the grand movement. It's fundamentally a picture of many people interacting with each other and with the heavens. . . . That's the form I'm trying to create: a picture of people interacting with each other and with a significant historical event, the Depression."[1] This formal aim, nascent in the Charleston tryout but thwarted in the Broadway premiere later in 1980, was only realized by Britain's National Theatre in 1986; under Peter Wood's direction, Miller's original wielding of two dramaturgical elements—*narration* and *vaudeville*—finally received appropriate theatrical expression. This landmark production finally stamped the play's generic character as "epic," the term Miller pointedly uses in his introduction to the published final version of the text.[2] Underpinning these performance components is a correspondingly "epic" substance—story and thought—which is drawn both from Miller's personal experience of the Great Depression and from Studs Terkel's oral history, *Hard Times.*[3]

The formal "epic" elements of *The American Clock* challenge its producing theater artists to create a particular playhouse experience for audiences. To appreciate this challenge theoretically, we have to entertain questions about what happens in a theater when the play is performed—affective questions such as these: How does the audience respond to actors who serve intermittently as narrators of the action they are also performing? How does an episodic structure of some thirty scenes, and the resultant performance rhythm, affect the audience's reception of the ideas informing the various experiences being dramatized? How is this rhythm and its cumulative effect defined by a design scheme that calls for eleven lighting "fadeouts" and an abstract-theatricalist scenic decor? What is the possible range of feeling incited by juxtaposing such disparate scenes as—for example—a routine by a comedy team, a twenties-style melodramatic scene in a speakeasy, and a Black jazz vocalist's performance of a tune identified with Billie Holiday?

Actors, directors and scenic designers must also manage the practical demands arising from the two formal features of the play that stamp it as uniquely unconventional among Miller's works: narration and vaudeville. The artists have to discover how each instance of narration differs from the others, as well as how each suits its individually developing character. A crucial question is how to define the relationship with the audience that an act of direct address always assumes. These concerns determine the fundamental task for actor and director, which is to find the actor's intention or objective for every instance of addressing the audience. A glance at the play's text shows how variable this is. Obviously, no single objective will govern all instances of the play's narrative activity; the whole dramatic context must be considered. From it emerge two telling facts: first, there are several narrating characters, all having different interpretive "objectives"; second, the play is labeled "A Vaudeville."

The Narrators

The first words of the play are spoken, in turn, by Rose, Lee, Moe and the company. They use the past tense.

> *Rose:* By the summer of 1929 . . .
> *Lee:* I think it's fair to say that nearly every American . . .
> *Moe:* Firmly believed that he was going to get . . .
> *Company:* Richer and richer . . .
> *Moe:* Every year.

Then Robertson: "The country knelt to a golden calf in a blanket of red, white, and blue."

Arthur Robertson is the most prominent of the several narrating personae. Compared to him, Lee and Rose engage in substantially less narrative activity, although theirs can be said to be more personally involving. Then there is Banks, the black former hobo, chain gang prisoner and armed forces veteran who does not interact dramatically with other characters, but who sings and addresses the audience with poetic testimony on behalf of all neglected minority Americans. There are others who also speak to us, far less frequently than do the major personae and certainly for different reasons: Diana Morgan, Irene, Mrs. Taylor and, uniquely, Ted Quinn. We must also include those isolated narrative comments delivered by individuals "from the choral area."

All the narrators share a common functional objective, which is "by talking directly to the audience, to keep the mode of this dramatic presentation basically documentary." As a group, the narrators remind us that this is a reported story. But each narrating persona also has an individual point of view. In the rehearsal process, it must be determined what stance the actors will adopt in each instance of narration. The theoretical question here is this: Is it possible for an actor simply to tell the audience something, without also conveying what he or she thinks about it, what stance or position he or she takes? In the practical work of acting, it is not. This, then, becomes a concrete consideration in the performers' interpreting of the play.

In a university production staged in 2000 under my direction,[4] the actor playing Robertson realized early that he was going to have to establish, and then maintain, a strong narrative authority over the whole presentation in order to reassure the audience that they could indeed accept a "documentarizing" mode of theater. We asked: How much "personal" distance should this enigmatic persona exercise throughout the performance? Although he conducts himself with a certain aloofness, discernible in his discursive invention and style, he will at the same time have to command the audience's trust, which he cannot do by patronizing them in any way. Robertson is neither an uncritical devotee of the stock-investing craze nor an amorally greedy partaker. Nevertheless, he emerges as a rueful observer of its unchecked influences on the general population; at the same time he remains a staunch proponent of capitalism. He must present himself as a sort of prophetic witness to large-scale human folly, who also wonders at it. In the final determination, he is at one and the same time the chief reporter of this epic adventure and a complex, intriguing individual. His "character" is basically that of Studs Terkel's oral historian Arthur Robertson from *Hard Times.*

Perhaps Robertson's most telling moment is his first one in the play, where he sets up a demonstrative scene with Clarence, a bootblack who is playing the national game of stock-investing along with everyone else. In warning this cash-poor fellow to sell his one hundred thousand dollars' worth of stock, Robertson ostensibly dispenses helpful advice. Actors could try playing sincerely—the respectful shoeshine guy and the expansive upper-class advice-giver—as in a realistic vignette out of an earlier, more likable America. In my production's rehearsal, this attempt proved as boring as a scene from a "straight" 1930s film. We thought: If Robertson imitates a minstrelsy-derived comedian, and Clarence his slow-witted "Negro" partner, the audience will experience a stock variety routine from early vaudeville—the Black-on-White two-man repartee. Could a production in the year 2000 take a chance on such a "politically incorrect" presentation?

We found our necessary conviction in Miller's dramaturgy. The audience's very first experience is of a crowd of actors filling up the stage, singing. And then, "All form in positions onstage." After the opening line is delivered piecemeal by the actors playing Rose, Lee, Moe and company, they will all watch the Robertson-Clarence scene. Only after they witness this emblematic scene do they retire to the choral area. This opening action, in fact, sets the stylistic temper for the entire play, establishing the deliberate showiness of everything to ensue.

In Rose Baum's narrative contributions, we must be impressed by a persona who combines the stock Jewish mother character with a Depression-era matron, hovering authoritarian and a refined urban individual struggling to maintain spiritual values against their grinding down by the catastrophic economic reality. When Rose talks to the audience, it is usually to induce an affirmation of the worth of her values in that monumental struggle taking place in the Baums' domestic drama. The hazard for an actress creating this role is allowing it to descend into sentimentality. But this danger is offset by the play's dramaturgy, which has her playing piano and singing musical comedy tunes, teasing her relatives, appreciating literature and the theater, suppressing her disappointment with husband Moe, using humor to keep her spirits up, and eventually succumbing to the debilitating anxiety of the era. Rose is a plausible, sympathetic, deeply conceived character who is fully realized in the script, despite the apparent limitations imposed by its episodic plot structure. She is also a character to quiet complaints about Miller's alleged failure to write parts for women that are fully dramatic. And she is also a finely comic creation. Miller has her speaking the most sophisticated ironies, including the best gag line in the play: "But how can he become a sportswriter if he's a Communist?"

In Lee's case, a more complex point of view operates from the start, when he is just fourteen years old. It is a perspective that is essentially characterizing, devised by Miller carefully in the familiar manner of his early dramatis personae. As Lee grows older in the story, his personal outlook finds more varied articulation, grows increasingly self-conscious and adapts to a shifting reality. In building this role, the actor can find many suggestive details in Miller's autobiography, as well as in the 1955 essay "A Boy Grows in Brooklyn."[5] Lee is not Miller, of course—and not merely because a sportswriter is different from a playwright. We see that the author so fashioned his lead character's maturation that it would be definitively compromised by the time of the recapitulative, epilogue-like last scene. Lee, in order to become a professional sportswriter, has sacrificed his earlier idealistic convictions for the sake of personal ambition. It is, therefore, not wholly comforting for the audience to watch him conversing diffidently with his grown-up cousin Sidney, whom Miller has depicted from the start as the perfect realization of a superficial American. By this comparison, as a person Lee comes off only slightly better.

But here we remark the affective force of a character who also narrates. Lee, unlike Sidney, transcends his realistic character (in a manner of speaking) in order to function as a narrator one last time. In his final speech to the audience, which is impelled by his mother's memory, his demeanor and voice can strike readers of the text as too lofty, nostalgically sentimental or self-indulgent. But the actor who has created the whole role knows that Lee, narrating himself, is both ambivalent and sincere as he buries his compromised life under the immediacy of commenting on a particularly emotional aspect of his own personal history.

Narration is a defining trait of a presentational style of performance. These narrative performances, which are both characterizing and repertorial, constitute an aggregate "distancing" device for the audience's overall experience of the play. We are not invited with any consistency into a "real world" inhabited by these personae; instead, we are kept aware of the story's fabricated nature by these figures' presentational activity.

The American Clock's story is a dramatic fiction employing multiple perspectives. What makes this work forceful in the theater is the concrete fact that the actors, presenting the "past" lives of fictional characters, visibly occupy the theatrical here-and-now—waiting onstage to play their scenes, witnessing other scenes being played, occasionally commenting on them. Thus they strike the theater audience as existing at both an aesthetic and historical remove from the events as they unfold. This adds up to something more significant than "metatheatrical": the undisguised fact of actors' *acting,* of showing the audience that this is a performance, emphasizes their attitudes toward both the dramatic matter and the fact of their acting. Not only must they think about what they are portraying, but they must also show a particular attitude about performing itself.

"A Vaudeville"

In *Timebends* Miller explains that the play's structural basis is that of America's most popular form of variety entertainment in the first three decades of the twentieth century: "In acting terms, the play should have the swift panache of vaudeville, a smiling and extroverted style, in itself an irony when the thematic question was whether America, like all civilizations, had a clock running on it, an approaching time of weakening and death" (588). In the introduction to the published edition of the play, he says: "When Peter Wood [director of the 1986 National Theatre production] asked for my feeling about the style, I could call the play a vaudeville with an assurance born of over a decade of experimentation. He took the hint and ran with it, tossing up the last shreds of a realistic approach, announcing from the opening image that the performance was to be epic and declarative."[6] About the 1988 Williamstown Theatre revival, directed by Austin Pendleton, he told an interviewer: "It's found its form. . . . Onstage, it's a kind of vaudeville. In vaudeville people get up and tell you what they're doing; it's a presentational piece of work. It just took a long time to find its production form, in terms of design, the way the actors act, the speed, the use of music and the interpretation of themes."[7]

The directions for *The American Clock*'s initial moments of performance make it clear how Miller's subtitle, "A Vaudeville," informs the play's structure. As the stage lights come up on the set ("a flexible space for actors, giving an impression of a surrounding vastness"), the jazz band plays "Million-Dollar Baby" ("I Found a Million-Dollar Baby in a Five-and-Ten-Cent Store!"). Momentarily, "a baseball pitcher enters, tossing a ball from hand to glove," and from the balcony the actor playing Quinn whistles the song, then begins to sing, as the rest of the company joins in and slowly enters the stage. By the end of the song's verse, the audience will see the assembled company arranged "in positions onstage." Then come the opening lines: "By the summer of 1929 . . ." Thus, as Miller said of the London production, "the sheer festivity of the occasion is already established."[8]

The audience will not receive from this play the same kind of dramatic continuity and coherence they expect from a realistic-domestic ("social") drama. Instead they will have a disjunctive experience of large-and-small, serious-and-light, dynamic-and-contemplative scenes, arranged not in a logical sequence but in an episodic, time-leaping concatenation—these being "epic" features, too. Some spectators will recognize the vaudevillean features, which include extended performances by single actors; comedy routines for duos and groups; choral song-and-dance numbers; stump speeches and formal recitations; solo song renderings and poetic monologues; interlocutors' announcements; and short, vignette-like dramatic presentations, which make use of stock characters and situations. And throughout, the jazz band performs.

A comedic impulse accompanies a natural musical inclination in the early domestic scenes set in the Baums' affluent, pre-Crash home. Besides enjoying the predictable situation of the father-in-law's reluctant transfer to the slow-witted sister's place in Brooklyn, accompanied by running wisecracks from the self-possessed head of the better-off household, the audience should feel the healthy high spirits of a family that sings together. When the Depression's effects begin to encroach, the Baums' humor and lightheartedness turns to grim irony. When Lee's bicycle is stolen, the atmosphere is primed for the disturbing scene of Iowa farmers protecting their homesteads against legal foreclosure—an "epic" episode recalling the *Living Newspaper* experiments of the Federal Theatre Project.

This juxtaposing of scenes that generate contradictory moods well illustrates Miller's incorporation of vaudeville, where "the contiguity of sublime and ridiculous is perfectly acceptable."[9] Miller maintains this dynamic structure of contrasting mood throughout. He concludes act 1 by contrasting an affecting mother-son scene between Rose and Lee with the loud and funny altercation between the other mother, Fanny, and her would-be songwriter son, Sidney, concerning the economic necessity of his marrying the landlady's daughter, Doris. Then follows Robertson's "thematic" monologue, in which his description of the Hoovervilles along Riverside Drive gives rise to the ideas of Americans maintaining their humor while also blaming themselves for adversity, and of America as a society with "a clock running on it." This sets up the almost sentimental act-closing scene in which Lee loans his father a quarter to get to work; the sentimentality is forestalled when Lee then talks to the audience about the sudden disappearance of the would-be American dream.

Act 2 continues the dramaturgical pattern: alternating scenes of light and grave spirit; the jazz band providing linking continuity; the Baum family drama progressing in episodic fragments intercut with other acts from the Miller "mural." Between two comic "love" scenes Miller deftly structures the second solo appearance of Banks, singing and summarizing his hoboing fortunes, followed by another fadeout (the third of six in this act), then the spotlit interlude of Rose as her piano is taken away (capped by her powerful line, "Lee, wherever you are—believe in something"). Then comes a direct segue into the Louisiana encounter between the white sheriff whose salary has stopped and the black fried-chicken proprietor, Isaac, with Lee the writer observing how Depression circumstances have inverted the usual roles in the social hierarchy of the South. This scene contains an "epic" device that might have come straight from Piscator or Brecht: the sheriff's bartered radio suddenly produces the voice of FDR in midspeech, and as we listen we also watch three different reactions to its message of governmental responsibility and human fortitude. Lee is acutely attentive; Isaac is "absorbed"; the sheriff pays it no mind. The lights fade on this part of the stage, along with Roosevelt's voice: "We cannot afford to accumulate a deficit in the books of human fortitude." And into their own opposing light come Sidney and Doris, already playing their lovers' quarrel fast and loud. The pair sings the reconciliatory lyrics of "Sittin' Around." Larded with the innocuous lines of a typical Tin Pan Alley love ballad ("I want to hear the words of love, I want to feel your lips on mine"), this is a trademark Sidney tune (presumably composed by Arthur Miller). Its gooeyness is deliberate: their duet stimulates the mood for the second act's "crowd scene," set in the Relief Office, comparable in action and scale to the farm auction of act 1. In conceiving this scene, which attempts to exhibit America's multiculturalism, Miller seems to have been influenced by the format of both the minstrel show and the *Living Newspaper,* as well as by standard comic vaudeville routines. He has also injected it with most of the play's explicitly American themes: self-determination, reluctance to admit personal need, suspicion of communism, father-son uneasiness and inconsonant versions of citizenship. The "star" of the scene is Irene, who enacts the combined roles of variety-show emcee, vaudeville headliner and minstrelsy interlocutor.

Set in the Baums' airless Brooklyn living room, the last episode of the family's Depression-era fortunes is almost pure Chekhov, via Clifford Odets, but mediated by both vaudevillean and epic ingredients. It is of course "obligatory" that the plot show us Rose crumbling psychologically under the cumulative pressure of the thirties' tribulations and the looming threat of dispossession. Women in houserobes gather to beguile the long hours with card-playing and idle talk; Rose fortifies herself against the dread coming of the mortgage man; a muddled Grandpa reads his paper and remembers Europe—these are the scene's Odets-ian marks. Chekhovian is the deeply sensed humor of such mismatched personalities confined together in mutual need. Into the pressured mix of Grandpa, Fanny, Doris and Lucille, as well as the solitary pathos of Rose, Miller also injects the manic energy of the desperate former ship's steward, Stanislaus, easily the most bizarre of all the play's vaudevilleans.

What keeps it this side of farcical cataclysm is the epic device of narration. Twice Rose distances her character from the action. To start, she sets the scene by figuratively suggesting an "endless Brooklyn July" in the "baking house" with its ominous smell "as dry and dusty as an owl." Several minutes later, on the edge of nervous collapse, she isolates herself from the slow-witted females at cards to tell us just how poorly her generation was prepared for this national debacle. "When I went to school we had to sit like soldiers, with backs straight and our hands clasped on the desk; things were supposed to be upright." Offsetting this moment of "epic" objectivity is the inspired comic misapprehension concerning Gray's "Elegy Written in a Country Churchyard," which bubbles underneath Rose's consternation about her fortune-telling cards, Stanislaus's increasingly zany serving business, and Grandpa's daft notion that Lee should go to Russia and "open up a nice chain of clothing stores." All this nonsense peaks in Rose's visually arresting, silent "staring ahead in an agony of despair." A moment later she "bursts into tears." Then the scene plunges into its intense and protracted climax as a man's voice calls from the choral area: "Hello?" Rose almost collapses—it's the mortgage man! No, it's only Moe.

Miller's technique is forceful. The false climax soon gives way to the actual one: at the height of Rose and Moe's husband-wife confrontation about "being a man," with Rose "screaming and weeping," the doorbell rings again. And the scene ends in a way that identifies it as quintessentially Miller: the doorbell becomes a persistent, heavy knocking. The lights fade slowly as the harrowing sound continues into the darkness. The parallel with Nazis banging on doors of Jewish homes in the 1930s in the middle of the night is blood-curdling. This is indeed something like the dark night of the American spirit.

This certainly seems like the rhythmical pinnacle of the whole performance. Indeed, a twentieth-century *pièce bien faite* might well end here.

But *The American Clock* is not finished. The play's overall affective rhythm originates in its entwined formal features, which include episodes of both domestic and social drama, narrative interventions and the performance of vaudeville "acts." This formal mixture emanates from Miller's "epic" impulse to present a historical picture of something already familiar, clearly and entertainingly, and with the object of making it seem *un*familiar. Here is the precisely Brechtian influence. Do we Americans really comprehend the abiding effect of the Depression on our national-cultural identity? *The American Clock* obliges us to "see again, think again."

The Instructive Epic Theater Mode

Miller told Studs Terkel: "I don't care for a theater that is absolutely personal and has no resonance beyond that."[10] Although the content of *The American Clock* is alluring to scholars and students of Miller's biography, it is important to recognize how that material's formal use contributes to the play's performative energy. It was valuable for students in my production to discover the correspondences (as well as the discrepancies) between the Baum family's story and Miller's life. They were able to connect certain historical references to particular character impulses, and they also gained a particular feeling for the realities of life in that distant Depression era. But it was more illuminating for the whole company to see that the "epic" qualities of the play modify its autobiographical substance and place a deeper resonance in the experience of the audience. Besides the varied kinds of narration and the quilt of vaudevillean presentation, another "epic" impetus influences the theatrical dynamic of *The American Clock:* Studs Terkel's oral history of the Depression, *Hard Times.* The material of this book counts as modern legend, its dramatic use by Arthur Miller as historical testimony.

An audience for the play may not know that characters like Arthur Robertson, Ted Quinn, Doctor Rosman, Jesse Livermore, William Durant, Diana Morgan, Judge Bradley, Banks, Joe, Isabel and Edie the "Superman" writer are drawn from annals of historical memory. Nor will an audience necessarily be aware that Lee, Rose, and Moe Baum have personalities and histories that resemble those of Miller's own family—or that Fanny, Sidney, Grandpa, Lucille and Doris are all based on his relatives. The ostensibly autobiographical "story" of the Baum/Miller family has been dramatically reimagined within the legendary context of the Depression and filled with a richness of American characters supplied by Terkel's *Hard Times.*

Miller closed his interview with Terkel by saying: "I've attempted a play of about more than just a family, of forces bigger than simply overheard voices in the dark."[11] With his "epic vaudeville" *The American Clock,* Miller has written a dramatically mythopoeic chapter of America's own biography. Its performance gathers his audience into communion with this act, which may well impress them as "autobiography"—but one about their historicized country. By experiencing *The American Clock* in the song-and-danced, mythicizing mode of twentieth-century "epic" theater, they participate in this wondrous "story of the United States talking to itself."

Notes

1. Studs Terkel, *The Spectator* (New York: New Press, 1999), 81–82.
2. *The Archbishop's Ceiling and The American Clock* (New York: Grove Press, 1989); *The American Clock* (New York: Dramatists Play Service, 1992). All quotations are from the 1992 edition.
3. Studs Terkel, *Hard Times: An Oral History of the Great Depression* (New York: Pantheon Books, 1970; 1986).
4. "RIT Players," Rochester Institute of Technology, Rochester, N.Y., January 27–February 6, 2000.
5. Reprinted in Arthur Miller, *Echos Down the Corridor,* ed. Steven R. Centola (New York: Viking, 2000).
6. *Timebends: A Life* (New York: Grove Press, 1987); introduction to *The American Clock,* 6.
7. Leslie Bennetts, "Miller Revives 'American Clock' Amid Resonances of 30's," *New York Times,* July 14, 1988, C23.
8. Miller, introduction, 6.
9. Ibid.
10. Terkel, *The Spectator,* 82.
11. Ibid., 83.

Toby Zinman

"Vaudeville at the Edge of the Cliff"

From the beginning, Arthur Miller has been writing memory plays; his interest has always been in how the weight of the past shapes the present. The past, for Miller, is not merely the events that alter subsequent events—the easy causality of chronology—but the way his characters remember, how they interpret those past events: memory, with its entourage of regret and nostalgia and denial, and with its vivid and inevitable social context, is his great subject. And how to stage memory has been Miller's theatrical task from *Death of a Salesman* to *After the Fall* to *The Ride Down Mt. Morgan* and *Mr. Peters' Connections.* The "subject" continues in *Resurrection Blues* and *Finishing the Picture.*

But there has been a significant shift in the *way* memory is made manifest on stage in his later plays. As the past inevitably gets both longer and further away, the moral certainty of the preacher, the *engagé* stridency that some feel mars Miller's earlier work, has given way to an acknowledgment of the human mystery, the muddle memory makes of the illogic of life. It strikes me that Miller has finally discovered the Absurd.

Miller strugged with *The American Clock* for more than a decade,[1] a play very much about his oldest themes: the betrayal of the American public by the American dream, the relation between a society and a family. It was not until 1986, during the British National Theatre's production, that he found the solution: "The secret was vaudeville" (xv). As a theatrical mode, it suggests everything that might be useful to Miller: nonelitist entertainment, delivered in fragments, with wild mood shifts between melodrama and farce. That vaudeville is no longer a living theatrical form furthers the usefulness, in that it creates the crucial aura of the long-gone. Miller has enlisted this form and this spirit not only to re-express his vision, but to re-create it. In so many of the later plays, including *The American Clock, The Last Yankee, I Can't Remember Anything, The Ride Down Mt. Morgan* and *Mr. Peters' Connections,* there is vaudevillian "business"—singing, dancing, pratfalls, sexy burlesque, piano playing—and all of it with the Beckettian tone of "laughing wild amid severest woe." It is memory—what you remember, what you can't remember, what you won't remember—that finally strikes Miller as the hilarious, terrible joke of mortality.

In *I Can't Remember Anything,* one of the two plays of *Danger: Memory!* two old friends have this disagreement about reading newspapers:

> *Leo:* Well, I like to know what's happening.
> *Leonora:* But nothing is "happening"! Excepting that it keeps getting worse and more brutal and more vile. . . .
> *Leo:* What the hell are you getting so angry about if I read a newspaper? . . . Listen, I'm depressed too . . .
> *Leonora:* No, you are not depressed, you just try to *sound* depressed. But in the back of your mind you are still secretly expecting heaven-knows-what incredible improvement over the horizon. . . . This country is being ruined by greed and mendacity and narrow-minded ignorance, and you go right on thinking there is hope somewhere. And yet you really don't, do you?—but you refuse to admit that you have lost your hope. That's exactly right, yes—it's this goddamned hopefulness when there is no hope—that is why you are so frustrating to sit with![2]

Given the similarity of their names, Leo and Leonora may well be two sides of the same person, making it likely that we are listening to Miller arguing with himself. This philosophic debate is fundamental to the deep change in Miller's drama.

Eros and Thanatos: the catastrophic vaudeville act. In the battle Freud defined in *The Ego and the Id*[3] between the force of life manifested in the sexual impulse, and the force of death, Miller has always been on the side of Eros; but in the early and middle plays, life is worth living only if it is lived with moral conviction. But, as he has shown us in play after play, such living is difficult and painful and full of sacrifices most people are not willing to make. As *Mt. Morgan*'s protagonist, Lyman Felt, says, "Maybe it's simply that if you try to live according to your real desires, you have to end up looking like a shit" (31).[4] As he does. Later in the play he redefines the struggle: "A man can be faithful to himself or to other people—but not to both" (75). That self-interest and the common good are not identical is the bitter pill Miller has been swallowing since *All My Sons.*

The Ride Down Mt. Morgan opens in a hospital room: Lyman Felt in a full body cast, his two wives in the room outside, bigamy waiting in the wings. Lyman's brash vigor suggests a familiar contemporary American impulse to renovate the personality, remake identity, carpe diem and go for the gold: "I'm going to wrestle down one fear at a time till I've dumped them all and I am a free man" (24), he tells his young second wife, Leah, when he announces his astonishing decision to learn to pilot a plane. The idea of equating freedom with fearlessness is a curious and, it strikes me, adolescent assumption, unchallenged in or by the play, and leading to a preposterous confrontation with a lion on safari. This hilarious faux-Hemingway posturing is not just Lyman's; it is one thing to create a character with such delusions of grandeur, but it is unclear whether the playwright shares them, whether Miller mocks Lyman's memory as he revels in it. The play presents a central problem of tone: does it laugh *at* Lyman or with him?

This testosterone-driven male fantasy includes such startling declarations as Lyman's telling his lawyer, Tom, "I love your view. That red river of taillights gliding down Park Avenue on a winter's night—and all those silky white thighs crossing inside those heated limousines . . . Christ, can there be a sexier vision in the world?" (31). It is difficult to take this seriously—not only is it puerile in its view of female allure, but its sleazy linking of money and sexiness is a TV commercials cliché. Lyman's relishing of the vision of silky thighs in heated limousines suggests that the self-made man of humble origins adopts society's standards about what to value; it further demonstrates that the American dream governs his sexual excitement, which runs counter to the play's assertion that Lyman Felt is an original, a wild rebel, a daring charmer, and sounds rather more like Willy Loman in that hotel room, proffering those nylon stockings. Lyman's commitment to Eros is evident in everything he does, although it is most blatantly expressed in his declaration to Theo, his wife of thirty-two years, that "I never had taste, we both know that. But I won't lie to you, Theo—taste to me is what's left of life after people can't screw anymore" (82).

Miller, often considered America's theatrical conscience, has given us many suicides, usually as an expression of the character's recognition of his culpability. But in Lyman Felt, Miller has created a character whose social conscience is clear: "Here I start from nothing, create forty two hundred jobs for people and raise over sixty ghetto blacks to office positions when that was not easy to do—I should be proud of myself, son of a bitch! I am! I am!" (30). This desperate-sounding, self-justifying liberalism springs from the same man who tells his black nurse (Miller requires her to be an African-American apparently to create occasions to reveal Lyman's attitudes) that back in the day when Lyman was still a writer, "Jimmy Baldwin used to say, 'Lyman, you're a nigger underneath.'" This pride is embarrassing—not to mention dated and bourgeois; Lyman seems unaware that many black writers in the 1960s and 1970s (which is when this would have been said) thought James Baldwin was "white underneath"; remember the famous sneer that Amiri Baraka (then LeRoi Jones) was "the black James Baldwin."

Despite the play's apparent intention to condemn the man who has broken faith with fidelity, Miller seems to be arguing the question out of both sides of his mouth, creating a far more intense portrait of male sexuality than he ever has before. In the scene where Lyman leaves Leah in the Carlyle Hotel and dashes around the corner to his apartment to make love to Theo, he says, in full-throated goatishness: "has there ever been a god who was guilty? . . . It feels like the moon's in my belly and the sun's in my mouth and I'm shining down on the world" (114). This after he confesses to his nurse, "I'm very attracted to women who smell like fruit; Leah smelled like a pink, ripe cantaloupe. . . . And of course slipping into her pink cathedral" (73). And Miller seems to endorse this erotic energy when he has Leah tell Tom,

> Well, it's just he wants so much; like a kid at a fair; a jelly apple here, a cotton candy there and then a ride on a loop-the-loop . . . and it never lets up in him; it's what's so attractive about him—to women, I mean—Lyman's mind is up your skirt but it's such a rare thing to be wanted like that—indifference is what most men feel now—I mean they have an appetite but not hunger—and here is such a splendidly hungry man and it's simply . . . well . . . precious once you're past twenty five. (37)

The dramatic device that has served Miller well for half a century works again in *Mt. Morgan:* the central character's fantasies or memories or dreams are made visible for the audience; most of the play happens only inside Lyman Felt's mind as he lies in his hospital bed, and the only scenes that seem to be happening in "reality" are those with the nurse. The wives' scenes are imagined by Lyman, making him the surrogate playwright within the play and linking him to Miller, his creator.[5] These female characters and their dialogue are his concoctions; thus Leah's and Theo's views of Lyman are his desires made manifest. It is tempting to see the play as a dream before dying, but that notion is defeated by the play's last scene, which takes place in "reality" and suggests hope for Lyman's recovery both physically and spiritually.

Lyman has driven his Porsche down Mt. Morgan on an icy dark

night, having deliberately decided against the safety of a hotel room during the winter storm and having even more deliberately moved the barriers to get his car onto the dangerous road. The central ambiguity of the play is whether his accident was a guilt-inspired suicide attempt, or hubristic over-confidence, or the wish to precipitate the crisis and thus escape from the fraud he has made of his life. There is much in the text to support each reading, especially since each of these motives has driven other Miller characters to their deaths. When I asked Patrick Stewart, who played the role of Lyman Felt twice, first at the Public Theatre in New York in 1998 and then on Broadway in 2000, about this ambiguity and how he understood his character's motive in the event that triggers the play, he replied with this illuminating comment:

> The ride down Mt. Morgan, the actual car ride is done in a desperate attempt to reconnect with life. He says very clearly at the end, "What I really thought—silly as it sounds now—was that if I walk in two, three in the morning, out of a roaring blizzard like that, you might believe how desperately I needed you . . . and *I would believe it too!* I would believe in my love, Leah, and life will come back to me again."[6]

It seems significant—and odd—to me that neither woman knows that Lyman has fallen into such a desperate state of existential doubt; doubt always gives death the advantage. Miller's understanding of the play's conclusion is, according to Stewart, a clarity that emerged from rehearsals of the Broadway production; the director, Miller and Stewart were working on what they called "the Mt. Morgan speech" when

> Arthur said, "I've got it: he's at the foot of the right mountain." I asked him what he meant. And he said, "All his life Lyman has been climbing a mountain. He was climbing the wrong mountain. Now he's at the foot of the right mountain."

It is significant that Miller, exercising the playwright's prerogative to tip the balance of the Eros/Thanatos debate, revised the play in a particularly meaningful way.[7] In the script that was produced in London in 1991, the version published by Penguin in 1992, there was another character: the small, crucial role of the ghost of Lyman Felt's father, a stage image strong enough to be a real sacrifice for a dramatist. In his three appearances the ghost abuses his son, mocks him, tells him what a disappointment he is, tries to kiss him, threatens him with a cane and twice tries to cover him with a shroud before disappearing into the darkness. If this father is the figure of death, Lyman eludes him each time, finally triumphing totally when Miller deletes the ghost of the father from the play. All that remains in the revised version are Lyman's occasional remarks about his father.

It is interesting to see how *Mr. Peters' Connections*[8] continues many of Miller's concerns in *Mt. Morgan. Mr. Peters,* a surprisingly abstract play, seems to spring from another of Lyman's remarks about his father:

> I keep thinking of my father—how connected he was to his life; couldn't wait to open the store every morning and happily count the pickles, rearrange the olive barrels. People like that knew the main thing. Which is what? What is the main thing, do you know? (31)

This philosophic aporia, this lack of clarity and lack of focus, is the thematic—and stylistic—motif of *Mr. Peters' Connections.* Harry Peters asks, "What is the subject?" in a variety of ways fifteen times in the course of the short play, sometimes meaning, "What are you talking about?" or "What are we talking about?" or "What is anybody talking about?" This is often funny, sometimes desperate, frequently exasperated, occasionally despairing. His brother Calvin, in response, disavows meaning, declaring that he is "just talking." This is exactly the problem: "There is no subject anymore! Turn on the radio, turn on the television, what is it—just talking!" (21).[9]

In order to convey dramatically the gridlocked forces of life and death in a struggle for possession of a character, Miller often uses a physical metaphor, some form of paralysis that makes both the moral and the existential stalemate visible.[10] In an interview in London on the occasion of the opening of *The Ride Down Mt. Morgan* at Wyndham's Theatre, Miller gave this metaphor his familiar sociological turn when he said:

> But there is a sense of paralysis, and I believe this is seen by a great number of people. I do not know anyone in favour of people sleeping out on the street, but there they are.
>
> . . . Back in the crash, there was a whole machinery of denial in operation to persuade people that things were not as bad as they were. Today we are denying it all more subtly, and we are doing it by *expressing* it more, in more and more hours of documentaries about drugs and homelessness. It is a different form of denial, and it is more seductive than the old one.[11]

This paralysis is emblematized in *Mt. Morgan* by the body cast that confines Lyman Felt (and from which, significantly, he escapes in order to enact his fears and memories and triumphs, which are the action of the play), and is most extreme and blatant in *Broken Glass,* in which the wife is literally paralyzed, mysteriously unable to move from her bed, just as her husband is emotionally and sexually paralyzed by his inability to deal with the world and his role in it.

Miller tells us in his preface to *Mr. Peters* that

> the play is taking place inside Mr. Peters' mind, or at least on its threshold, from which it is still possible to glance backward toward daylight life or forward into the misty depths. (vii)

There are many similarities[12] between these two plays that Miller must have been working on more or less simultaneously. The most potent of the similarities springs from an unflinching vision of the greed of the world, the hunger of human nature, the need for Eros to triumph over Thanatos. In *Mt. Morgan,* Lyman's opening lines are part of a dream-state sales meeting: "Today I would like you to consider life insurance from a different perspective. I want you to look at the whole economic system as one enormous tit. So the job of the individual is to get a good place in line for a suck. . . . Which gives us the word 'suckcess.' Or . . . or not" (2). This vision of the rapacious baby returns in *Mr. Peters* in his mythic vision of the origins of the human race:

> *Peters:* I dreamed of another planet; it was very beautiful—the air was rose, the ground was beige, the water was green, the sky was the fairest blue. And the people were full of affection and respect, and then suddenly they grabbed a few defectives and flung them into space.
>
> *Leonard:* Why were they defective?
>
> *Peters:* They were full of avarice and greed. And they broke into a thousand pieces and fell to earth, and it is from their seed that we all descend. . . . If a baby had the strength, wouldn't he knock you down to get to a tit? Has a baby a conscience? If he could tear buildings apart to get a suck, what would stop him? We tolerate babies only because they are helpless, but the alpha and omega of their real nature is a five-letter word, g-r-e-e-d. The rest is gossip. (51)

In an essay called "About Theatre Language," published with the script of *The Last Yankee* in 1994, Miller discusses *Waiting for Godot;* he tells us that "the dominating theme of *Godot* is stasis and the struggle to overcome humanity's endless repetitious paralysis before the need to act and change." He cites the famous exchange when Pozzo finds himself unable to exit, despite many adieux, and, after a silence says, "I don't seem to be able . . . (long hesitation) . . . to depart." Estragon replies, "Such is life." Miller's commentary on this could serve as a gloss on his own recent plays: "This is vaudeville at the edge of the cliff, but vaudeville anyway, so I may be forgiven for being reminded of Jimmy Durante's ditty—'Didja ever get the feelin' that you wanted to go? But still you had the feelin' that you wanted to stay?'" (91).

Near the start of the play there is this remarkably Beckettian exchange: sitting in the ruin of a New York nightclub, Calvin presses Peters for an opinion of the place:

> *Peters:* "Well, let's see. . . . Oh, the hell with this, I'm leaving. *Starts to go.*
> *Calvin:* You can't!
> *Peters:* Don't you tell me I can't, I have very low cholesterol!
> *He turns and starts out.*
> *Calvin:* What about your wife?
> *Peters:* God, I almost forgot. *Sits meekly.* Thanks for reminding me. . . . You always need a reason to stay. I have to stay because of my wife. Why because of my wife?
> *Calvin:* You're meeting her here.
> *Peters:* Right, yes! *Short pause.* Why am I meeting her here?
> *Calvin:* Probably because that was the arrangement.
> *Peters:* But why here?
> *Calvin:* What's the difference? One has to meet somewhere. (7)

Later in the play, as his confusion becomes more profound and troubling, and as the play becomes intensely vaudevillian, he tells Leonard,

> *Peters:* . . . What's begun to haunt me is that next to nothing I have believed has turned out to be true. *Breaks off in a surge of fear.* IF SHE DOESN'T COME, DOES IT MEAN I CAN'T LEAVE?! WHERE IS MY POOR GOD-DAMNED WIFE!
> *He is on the verge of weeping. The piano plays loud and fast, for a moment, "If You Knew Suzie" and stops.*
> *Leonard:* Is she ill?
> *Peters:* We are both ill; we are sick of each other. (36)

The punchline, as well as the method and the song, is heartbreakingly vaudevillian.

The conclusion of *Mr. Peters' Connections*—and the meaning of the title becomes richly poignant with echoes of E. M. Forster's modernist motto: "Only connect"[13]—simplifies meaning without simplifying the play retroactively:

Rose [his daughter]: Please stay.
Peters, straight ahead: I'm trying!
Rose: I love you, Papa
Peters: I'm trying as hard as I can. I love you, darling. I wonder . . . could that be the subject! (56)
For a moment he is alone in the light. It snaps out.

This subject is, of course, a plea for the triumph of life over death, of Eros over Thanatos, to "stay" a little longer, to resist the inevitable darkness. In his preface to the play Miller explains that "the action of the play is the procession of Mr. Peters' moods, each of them summoning up the next, all of them strung upon the line of his anxiety, his fear, if you will, that he has not found the secret, the pulsing center of energy—what he calls the subject—that will make his life cohere" (viii). He could as well be talking about Lyman Felt, or even Willy Loman ("Ben! I've been waiting for you so long! What's the answer?").

This suggests the immense coherence—and connections—in the body of Arthur Miller's dramatic work, now spanning more than half a century. What a chorus: Willy Loman, Mr. Peters, Jimmy Durante, Sigmund Freud, Samuel Beckett, Arthur Miller and the rest of us, all discovering that "the secret was vaudeville."

Notes

1. *The American Clock* and *The Archbishop's Ceiling* (New York: Grove, 1989). Miller writes in the introduction that the play was "begun in the early seventies and did not reach final form until its production at the Mark Taper Forum in Los Angeles in 1984" (xii).

2. *I Can't Remember Anything* in *Danger: Memory!* (New York: Grove, 1986), 24–25. All references are to this edition.

3. "We put forward the hypothesis of a death instinct, the task of which is to lead organic life back into the inanimate state; on the other hand, we suppose that Eros, by bringing about a more and more far-reaching combination of the particles into which living substance is dispersed, aims at complicating life and at the same time, of course, at preserving it. Acting in this way, both the instincts would be endeavouring to re-establish a state of things that was disturbed by the emergence of life. The emergence of life would thus be the cause of the continuance of life and also at the same time of the striving towards death; and life itself would be a conflict and a compromise between these two trends." Sigmund Freud, *The Ego and the Id,* in *The Freud Reader,* ed. Peter Gay (New York: Norton, 1989), 645–46. Note that I am not proposing a Freudian reading of Miller's work, but using Freud's construct as a convenient and illuminating shorthand.

4. All quotations, unless otherwise indicated, are from the performance script,

revised between September 8, 1998, and April 2, 2000. The manuscript was generously provided by Barlow-Hartman, Public Relations.

5. John Simon's review in *New York* suggests this same connection in vividly negative ways: "The play is a senescent retrospect . . . a rather vulgar bit of masturbation. There is, though, a certain slyness in this disguised piece of self-exculpation." Simon goes on to call Lyman Miller's "semi-autobiographical hero." *New York,* May 8, 2000.

6. The edited transcript of the interview with Patrick Stewart follows this essay.

7. According to an interview, this is the first time Miller has reworked his own text. "I've worked on this play more than any other. I've never worked on anything this extensively. And I love it, because now we can really investigate everything far more at our leisure than before; so much of the primary work has been done at the Public." Stephen Garrett, "King of the Mountain," *Time Out, New York,* March 23–30, 2000.

8. Matt Wolf has also noted the connection between the two plays in his review of the London production of *Mr. Peters' Connections:* "At times 'Mr. Peters' Connections' does try one's patience: the closer Mr. Peters comes to the bedridden vulgarian, Lyman Felt, of 'The Ride Down Mt. Morgan,' the shoddier this later play seems. *Variety,* August 7–18, 2000, 23.

9. All references to *Mr. Peters' Connections* are to the Penguin edition, 1999.

10. Consider Esther's line to her husband Victor in *The Price:* "No wonder you're paralyzed—you haven't believed a word you've said all these years" (New York: Penguin, 1985), 106.

11. Alan Franks, "A Ride Down Mt. Miller" *Times Saturday Review,* November 2, 1991, 6.

12. Some of the most obvious shared images are the African American nurse (Adele, the homeless woman who haunts the margins of *Mr. Peters,* puts on a nurse's cap in one scene), the constant sexuality of the central male mind, and the atmospheric ambiguity of the where/when-are-we questions the scripts insist on. There are echoes of earlier plays—as when Mr. Peters says, "Pan Am captain twenty-six years. I'm really much older than I look. If you planted an apple tree when I was born you'd be cutting it down for firewood by now" (4), unless of course a storm had blown it down, as it had the apple tree planted for Larry, the lost pilot of *All My Sons.*

13. The epigraph to Forster's 1921 novel, *Howards End.*

Interview with Patrick Stewart

By phone from New York, during the Broadway run of *The Ride Down Mt. Morgan*
June 27, 2000, 10 A.M.

Toby Zinman: I know you've said the role [of Lyman Felt] holds great appeal for you; why?

Patrick Stewart: It won't surprise you if I say it is the writing in the play that is the magnet for me. Given my stage background and the work I did for twenty-five years of my life, I'm drawn to exciting, vigorous, muscular writing, and that's the immediate appeal of *Mt. Morgan.* And especially the language of Lyman Felt, the character that I play—it's vivid and colorful, it's ironic and humorous and passionate—it's funny. And I was enchanted by the appeal of the writing. The apparently amoral aspect of the character was also attractive to me . . . the challenge the role presents in showing a man whose actions by most conventional moral standards would be said to be unacceptable; and by the end of the play he has truly brought devastation on two families. Yet he continues to justify himself and explain himself and plead that fundamentally what he was doing was for the good of everyone. Fascinating. I was attracted to those motives in him.

TZ: I remember your saying to me in Washington [I had interviewed Stewart when he was in Washington, D.C. playing Othello; see *American Theatre* magazine, Feb. 1998, 12–15, 68–70]—and I'm reading now:

> I think an actor can bring his own life to what he does to fully animate it, to fully light the fires. If acting in plays does not light fires, we should stay home and read them. If a script doesn't make the blood pulse faster through your veins, why do it? (15, 68)

Are you Lyman Felt? Crassly put. [Laughter]

PS: [Laughter] No, no, it's a fair question. There is much of me in

Lyman. I acknowledge that, and I do empathize and connect with much that he says and does. In fact, there are times when I feel that Lyman is simply an intermediary between me and Mr. Miller.

There is a speech in the second half of the play where Lyman says, "I know what's wrong with me. I could never stand still for death! Which you've got to do by a certain age, or be ridiculous—you've got to stand there nobly and serene and let death run his tape out your arms and around your belly and up your crotch until he's got you fitted for that last black suit. And I can't, I won't! . . . So I'm left wrestling with this anachronistic energy which God has charged me with and I will use it till the dirt is shoveled into my mouth! Life! Life! Fuck death and dying."

Well, that absolutely represents me, and I *know* that it represents Arthur. And every night, when I get to that moment, because I'm alone on the stage standing in a spotlight, I feel that right there in shadows alongside me is Arthur. Yes, I feel that too. I'm not ready to stand still for death either—I won't be noble and serene and just let it happen. That speech represents power for me, the life force of Lyman Felt—and I hope I share it.

So far as the morality of the character goes, I have had to keep myself at a distance from that—I feel I'll be prepared to discuss that when the run of this play is over. I cannot in any sense sit in judgment on Lyman—I couldn't finish the play. There is one thing I know that Lyman has never experienced, and I think he's a loser in this respect: which is that no one woman in his life has ever known him fully. It's always seemed to me that one of the great adventures of being in a relationship is the possibility of being as fully known by one person as you can be. In the play, of course, Lyman argues that that ain't possible—you never can be known fully—you cannot be known by the other. But it's something I have ambitions to achieve, and Lyman will never have that. Well, he may have—we are left with a tiny ray of light at the end of the play. I might just mention this, I quote Arthur in this—it's something I think of often: we were working the end of the play, the director, David Esbjornson and Arthur Miller and myself, alone in the Ambassador Theatre, and I was going over what we called "the Mt. Morgan" speech at the end, which Arthur had actually worked over several times. We got to just about the point when Arthur had decided we should remove the last three lines of the play—which he had added during the previews at the Public Theatre—and now he said we no longer need them because I've said this elsewhere. And so now the play ends with, "Imagine the three of them sitting out there on that lake talking about their shoes." Arthur said, "I've got it: he's at the foot of the right mountain." I asked him what he meant. And he said, "All his life Lyman has been climbing a mountain. He was climbing the wrong mountain. Now he's at the foot of the right mountain." Actually, even as I repeat that, it makes me tremendously emotional [his voice is audibly choked up]—because there's great power in the thought of that man at last arriving at the place he should have been years and years ago. And that there is the possibility of a new way of being in the world available to him at that moment.

TZ: The kiss the nurse gives him at the end seems to me to be a kiss of forgiveness—or if not forgiveness exactly, acceptance, in the way that the play seems to accept Lyman Felt even as it argues with him or exposes him; it felt to me that Miller's sympathy was contained in that last image. Am I reading that right—was I feeling that right when I saw it on stage?

PS: I think so. That moment has been very much in development through the run of 120 performances. Ironically, now that we're talking about it, I think I got closer to it last night than I had before. When he believes the nurse is leaving, the terror, the fear of abandonment, the loss of both wives and daughter and friend, as each one leaves the stage at the end, finally overwhelms him. He's been holding it at bay, he keeps the nurse there, he needs to have somebody with him, and he's terrified of the dark that would be represented by being alone, and staves off the rising panic by having a conversation with the nurse by saying, tell me what you talk about. He doesn't really want to know that; he needs to have a conversation with somebody, he needs to keep that connection with another living person going. But the conversation comes to an end, and of course it includes her describing how they sit talking about their shoes on the ice. But in the way I've been moving towards playing it in the last few days, and I think finally getting there last night, when he thinks the nurse has gone, the emotion, the terror, the panic all within him starts to come out, and he begins to break down. That's what the nurse sees when she turns, so the kiss that comes—I can't speak for Oni Faida Lampley [who played Nurse Logan]—it seems to be not so much a kiss of forgiveness but comfort. The nurse sees someone in pain and as a nurse, as a woman, as a fellow human sufferer, gives the one thing that intuitively might be helpful. And she's right, of course. And it's that which brings him back from that brink of despair to a more positive, hopeful conclusion.

TZ: Yes, I so vividly remember the look that crosses your face as that happens—a kind of new light. It's really a very lovely moment.

Were you involved in any of the changes to the script? I read the original version and then read the revision and was surprised at how much it's been altered. Did you participate in that?

PS: You mean the original version in which the father is a character? No, no, the bulk of that work was done by the time I saw the script, whenever that was, eighteen months ago at the Public Theatre. Arthur had made those revisions—the father had gone. At the Public Theatre, the one major change was that there was quite a substantial scene in the second half which was with Leah in the hospital immediately after she's had the baby, and I went to the director first of all and said, "I don't know why this scene is here." And from the point of view of Leah—well, in the scene Leah seemed to be saying, "Well, now I've got what I want, I really don't need you anymore," and it didn't seem to be consistent with the character. I talked to the director about that. We were also both concerned about the length of the second half, which even now is still longer than the first and is generally thought not to be a good thing in the theater. You try to get it the other way around. I've got to tell you, it was a tough morning when David and I invited Arthur to come and have some lunch with us or a cup of coffee across the street at a café on Lafayette Street, in order to say to him, "We don't think this scene should be in the play." [Laughter] It's a tough thing, with a man like that, to say, we don't think this should be here.

TZ: How did he react?

PS: He listened sternly to what we had to say, and he made the very best response, which was, "Let me think about it." And he came in the next day and said, "It's gone. It's gone. You're right, we don't need it." Later, I was to go to him a few times and say, could we adjust this sentence, I'm not sure this is clear, is there another way of saying this? I actually said to him, there are two tiny lines that I'd like Lyman to say, and after he agreed to it, I actually had him initial the changes in my script [laughter].

TZ: My goodness, he must have been so grateful for such deferential treatment.

PS: I don't think it's the deference so much as the seriousness about the play, not taking it lightly. And it was also a thrill to get Arthur Miller's initials on a script on a word that I had added. So he is serious about that, I think, when he realizes that the people he's with have one objective, which is to make the experience of his play as good as possible, and that's what it's always been.

And you know, here's the other thing: he likes actors. Not all playwrights do, which may be surprising. But Arthur does, and when I began to realize that, it's very relaxing. On numerous occasions, he said to me [uses American accent], "I don't know how you do it! I sit there and I watch and I don't know how you do it!" Well, that's so *charming.* "I couldn't do it, it would kill me!" He likes actors, he knows that a play is not complete until it's been given flesh and blood, and sometimes that flesh and blood requires that there's input from the actors and the director.

TZ: It occurred to me that the premise of the play—although this is ambiguous—that since many of the scenes are imagined by Lyman and then staged for us, that in a variety of ways, some of which you've already talked about—Lyman is Miller's surrogate. The character, being played by an actor, who is actually the playwright, making up the whole business.

PS: Correct.

TZ: When I originally read the play in the published version, I thought that the ride down Mt. Morgan is suicidal. That it was a way of escaping from the box he'd trapped himself in. But when I saw it on stage, it seemed much more an act of arrogance that he had done that.

PS: I don't see it like that. When did you see it?

TZ: Right after it opened.

PS: The Mt. Morgan speech, which Arthur worked on for a week, almost daily, I think is very clear now. It wasn't clear last year [at the Public]. The ride down Mt. Morgan, the actual car ride is done in a desperate attempt to reconnect with life. He says very clearly at the end [quoting from memory], "What I really thought, Leah, was if I walk in, at two, three o'clock in the morning, out of a roaring blizzard like that, you might believe how desperately I needed you, then I might believe it too. I believe in my love then life will come back to me." That's what the ride down Mt. Morgan is about. It's an attempt to find life. Then he says, "Tom, I didn't mean to crash but I did." So he's admitting there's a self-destructive element in this. Who knows? But what he was trying to do is risk death in order to reconnect with life because death has been the great fear in Lyman's life. That's what he's been keeping at arm's length, fighting off.

TZ: I just read *Mr. Peters' Connections,* which seems so much a continuation of this. And then I started to think in some ways that it was all Willy Loman reworked, in different personalities.

PS: That's right. But this shouldn't surprise us. Writers have been doing this for hundreds of years. . . .

Robert Scanlan

The Late Plays of Arthur Miller

Since he turned seventy in 1985, Arthur Miller has finished nine new plays *(I Think about You a Great Deal, I Can't Remember Anything, Clara, The Ride Down Mt. Morgan, The Last Yankee, Broken Glass, Mr. Peters' Connections, Resurrection Blues* and *Finishing the Picture);* he has extensively revised two big plays of the seventies (*The Archbishop's Ceiling* and *The American Clock*), published a magisterial 614-page autobiography (*Timebends*), written two screenplays that have been made into completed films (*Everybody Wins, The Crucible*) and seen his novel *Focus* made into a movie,[1] collaborated on a new opera based on *A View from the Bridge,* and published a novella *(Homely Girl).* In addition, during this same period, Miller has participated in important revivals of the "Big Four" canonical plays *(All My Sons, Death of a Salesman, The Crucible, A View from the Bridge)*—each of which has triggered a new round of major awards—and he has seen several of his plays, old and new, made into television movies. His lifetime total of plays, by my count, now stands at thirty-six (ten of which are one-acts). In these same years (which most ordinary people would call their old age) Miller has kept up his usual steady stream of articles and essays—a practice that has been a regular and distinguished feature of his entire writing career. A new collection of these occasional pieces was published on his eighty-fifth birthday *(Echoes Down the Corridor).* In short, Arthur Miller, even in his old age, has been the hardest-working and most productive playwright in America: he simply has no rivals.

The plays of this period have been given a mixed press. The British, by and large, have been the ones to hail them as the visionary works of a master, while the American press has been grudging and whiny about them, habitually dismissing Miller as a relic of a bygone era. No wonder that Miller has grown fond of premiering his work in London, where he is spared the airy disdain of young and undistinguished theater critics, or the lingering hostility of old established ones. Miller has paid a heavy price in America for his 1963–64 "Lincoln Center plays"—*After the Fall* and *Incident at Vichy,* which were both abused by critics in their day, but have fared much better than predicted over time—again, especially in Great Britain. Since then, run-of-the-mill critics have thought it safe and fashionable to glance condescendingly over their shoulders at what Miller might be up to, but to dismiss almost a priori the continuing new work *(The Price, The Creation of the World and Other Business, The American Clock, The Archbishop's Ceiling).* These important middle plays deserve careful critical reconsideration (and fresh and probing productions), but I will confine myself on this occasion to defending six of the latest nine—all written since Miller turned seventy.

It is almost as if Miller's huge success with the Big Four, written in the years between 1947 and 1956 (basically, Miller's thirties) is being held against him. Is it fair to compare his current work continually to his achievements of that era? What other American playwright could stand up to such comparison? It is especially ironic in Miller's case because there is no standard by which to make the comparison, except his own success. And what we conveniently summarize as success is in itself a complex sociohistorical dynamic that is only tenuously related to the intrinsic merits of individually wrought plays. *The Last Yankee,* for instance, could be said to be a better-crafted play than the rickety *All My Sons; Broken Glass* could easily be praised as more painfully disturbing and emotionally complex than *Death of a Salesman; The Ride Down Mt. Morgan* might arguably have far more social and psychosexual significance than does (or did) the melodramatic *View from the Bridge;* and how feeble would *A Memory of Two Mondays* appear in a matchup with *Mr. Peters' Connections?* Such comparisons—tinged as each might be with more than a hint of validity—are just as absurd as the ones that disparage the later work as "not up to" the earlier. The real question is who has written (or was capable of writing) a better play in this same span of time. American playwriting since 1985 is not a field full of obvious strong rivals to Miller's plays of the same period.

Once we break the grip of self-competition (the critic's fame-struck tendency to stand Miller in his own shadow), we clear our minds for a better appreciation of the late plays. Without exception, these six plays attempt what our recent poet laureate, Robert Pinsky, dubbed "an explanation of America," and they do so in plain domestic terms. In other words, all six of the plays I refer to can be read as parables about the state of the nation. Miller has further made it his business to root each parable in deep and believable personal psychology. And as always, he has situated that psychology in uniquely American settings, carefully and artfully chosen for their resonant metaphorical value. This represents an act of great consistency and fidelity—consistency of aim and method, and fidelity to his talent—which I find insufficiently appreciated in the plays themselves, and too lightly valued within contemporary theater culture.

I suppose that the believable personal psychology to which Miller remains committed is what earns him the occasional contempt of the critically au courant. Miller himself certainly felt compelled to account for himself on the topic of realism in a striking essay he appended to the published version of *The Last Yankee.* In this essay he says (among many notable things) that "the play's language . . . has a surface of everyday realism, but its action is overtly stylized rather than 'natural.'" It is clear it was the harrying critics who goaded him into saying such a thing, since it is pretty obvious he constructed (some would say contrived) the plot of the play just as he constructed or contrived every other of his plots. What playwright ever does anything else? *All* plays are artifacts, and in that respect *entirely* contrived. But there has been, for many years now, an open challenge to the idea that it is a playwright's business faithfully to observe the people of his time and place, and to record and interpret the texture of those times—that is, to strive for a historical perspective, to take a stab at explanation (and thereby express a belief in meaning).

A distinguishing characteristic of the plays Miller has written since his seventieth birthday is their unwavering faith in certain concomitants of playwriting. Miller has kept faith with two major aspects of his craft, the human subject and the deep formal commitments of full-blown (I would say "orchestral") composition. Let me review the human content first. Six of his late plays can be divided into two groups according to two equally humanistic preoccupations: (1) the "damaged wives" series: *The Ride Down Mt. Morgan, The Last Yankee, Broken Glass* and (2) the old-age plays of puzzlement and retrospect *(I Can't Remember Anything, Mr. Peters' Connections),* which bracket the other three. *Clara,* a one-act that leads off the series, stands curiously alone and is difficult to classify, though its central motif of denial is arguably the common thread in all six plays. *Clara* depicts a stunned father in the apartment of his murdered daughter—a scene we are all reluctant to acknowledge as "everyday" in our time. This bewildered father is depicted trying, with the help of a cynical homicide detective, to overcome his inability to name his daughter's Hispanic boyfriend (and probable killer). *Clara* is stark and disturbing, and it appears poised to be a reactionary backlash play, a disastrous payback for naive and misplaced liberal values. But *Clara* is also clearly an exploration, a sort of waking day-mare, a fleshing-out of the sort of anxiety attack one might expect in the father of a grown daughter who lives away from home. But if Miller was suffering from critical neglect—or worse, critical disdain (trivialization)—during the Reagan eighties, he might understandably have ruminated on circumstances that question the grounds of long-standing liberal convictions. As a parable about giving up old radical views—in effect, fighting denial—it leverages on the idea of a shattering disillusionment, but the play is too slight and too schematic to be taken quite so seriously. It toys with a thought it does not fully express, and there is no indication that Miller set enormous store by it.

Miller's one-acts all seem to be daydreams, protracted fantasies, exploratory five-finger exercises. They probe a theme by indulging (or giving form to) a provisional "what if?" scenario. Many artists, and certainly playwrights, develop ideas this way. Daydreams operate by a sort of laissez-faire pact with the imagination—just to see what it will yield. Calling such unregulated escapades to eventual account is the typical Miller moral gravitational pull, and his one-acts are either paired with another "take" on similar material or expanded—one might almost say corrected—into a subsequent full-length play. *Clara* was paired in 1987 with the far better one-act, *I Can't Remember Anything,* the first important play about old age, but also a stark parable about the dwindling away of American radicalism. In this small play, an old man (and stubborn ex-radical) living alone in the Connecticut countryside is called upon by an old friend, now widowed, who suffers from a severely lapsing memory. The two old friends visit, talk, look after each other, squabble and take stoic stock of the passing of time as it affects meaning in their lives. The play is full of amusing banter embroidered on a grim bed of nostalgia, loneliness and encroaching senility. Both characters—one with and one without a working memory—are rendered equivalent by the relentless action of time; they are fading from history, and they both know it. Played sentimentally, the play would fall apart. Its deftness lies in its tough stoicism, and this mustn't be, in performance, a veneer hiding even a trace of self-pity. The central subject is the people in the play, and compassion for them is the prevailing tone.

By the time the two one-acts (eventually published together as *Danger: Memory!*) were finding their first production at Long Wharf, Miller had already been working at least six years (perhaps longer) on *The Ride Down Mt. Morgan.* This is the first of the three consecutive plays about marriage (the other two being *The Last Yankee* and *Broken Glass*) that are the heart of Miller's late work. The series grows increasingly potent and profound in its gradually deepening exploration first of sexual fidelity, then the deeper emotional rights and obligations between men and women, and finally the sometimes deliberate, but more frequently involuntary damage men and women inflict on themselves and on each other. At the core of all three plays are real, carefully individuated people—the hardest *matière* to import into the artifacts we call plays. Miller never shirks the duty to create characters, and he invariably takes on the obligation to build into his characters depths of humanity that will earn for them the same "rights to compassion" that real human beings possess. This humanistic obligation is not easy to meet, and very few working playwrights can pull it off. Furthermore, the sheer difficulty of the task makes any modish aesthetic rationale for avoiding it suspect.

Mt. Morgan's plot is the most obviously schematic of the three. The framing situation of a wealthy bigamist who has "crashed" his expensive sports car while careening down a slippery slope named after a bank is all too clearly a consciously devised metaphor. The Penguin edition draws unnecessary attention to the play's deepest potential flaw by crudely announcing in the promotional blurb that the play "is about the unbridled excesses of the 1980s." Miller wrote (in the *Last Yankee* essay mentioned above) that "if my approach to playwriting is partly literary, I hope it is well hidden." Not so here, where the circumstantial device of the underlying plot won't stay hidden as it governs the aesthetic progress of the play. Still, within the parable, Miller has, as always, created people, and they fully redeem the play. Once granted, the premise of the play opens an intense debate about the love of men and women, the role of sexual attraction and sexual consummation in the lives of adults of both sexes, and the many measures by which betrayal is matched against duty and entitlement. The play is uncharacteristic in Miller's work for its essentially comic form, but there is every justification for a dramatic exploration of infidelity to engage the long tradition of theatrical sex farces.

The great strength of the play remains the stubborn conviction at its core that the erotics of sexual experience—lust, and the will to self-gratification—unlock a master psychological paradigm for a more general greed that shapes large, intractable social patterns in America not easily treated in plays. Far from missing the parable, critics have tended to be put off by the fact that Miller persists in composing plays this way. He grounds his central action in a framing metaphor, then conducts a detailed inquiry governed by a rigorous psychological plausibility his American critics disparage as "realism." Miller works hard at the level of character and at the level of dialogue to sustain his surface realism, but he uses it invariably as a means of entry into a structure of analogous meanings that gradually build an emblematic portrait of the contemporary American psyche and the contemporary American social landscape. It is one thing to fail at such a vast project, but Miller has been pilloried by some even for attempting it.

The Last Yankee follows the same pattern exactly and with greater success: the play is set in a state mental hospital, where two American men meet as they come to visit (and perhaps retrieve) their clinically depressed wives. The wives have befriended each other within their protected ward, and, in their solitude and isolation from their husbands and the terrible pressures of their professional worlds (one is a carpenter of persistently modest income, the other is a successful businessman), the women have made some simple, commonsensical inroads into treating their respective mental and emotional disabilities. The men are uneasy with each other, and even more uneasy with the fragile state of their wives, which both embarrasses and angers them, but they gradually are led to see their own central roles in the catastrophe that has visited each of the women. We see them struggle between acceptance and denial of this responsibility, but the play is also framed around a deliberately antithetical pair; Miller is pointing to a culture of ruthless competition, within which people are endlessly goaded into measuring their own worth by almost exclusively monetary benchmarks for success or failure. The depressive collapse of both wives—the one harried by a barely sufficient income, the other flush with money, but emotionally abandoned—links the myopic visions within each household and suggests how each alone is insufficient to a solution. Again, illuminating a large social dynamic without sacrificing a close-up view of individuals is the basic ambition of the play. It is a huge ambition for any play, and it works with elegant efficiency here.

Miller stays true to a tradition of playwriting he learned by studying Ibsen and the ancient Greek tragedians—something he did quite thoroughly in the 1930s as an undergraduate at the University of Michigan, as Enoch Brater, among others, has shown.[2] He has never wavered in his attempt to build an insistent moral intentionality into every play, to regard "theatre as a civic art rather than a purely commercial one," as he put it in one of his essays. It is precisely this commitment that seems to put off his critics. There is an ideological aversion, not an aesthetic one, to plays like *The Ride Down Mt. Morgan* and *The Last Yankee.* American critics have not been tolerant of plays that can be described, at one remove from their literal level, as being about an entire country in denial—a country steeped in the consequences of its own bewildering mismanagement of resources and its endless conflicts over money and success. British critics are far more sympathetic both to the dramatic procedure and to the underlying portrait of America.

Broken Glass is the achieved masterpiece of the series. No recent work in the theater has explored with equal insight the terrible brutality of hatred within the recesses of the individual psyche. *Broken Glass*—an allusion to the Nazi Kristallnacht of 1938—is a timeless masterpiece about many interlaced topics, but its central theme is the internalization of prejudice and the pathology of the appalling conversion of prejudice into self-hatred. This great play has yet to achieve its definitive production in America, for it was mishandled in the premiere production that moved to Broadway. At the core of *Broken Glass* there is a heroic role to enact, for the play depicts the struggle of a lone woman's psyche to escape destruction. Her blind internal determination to resist, surmount and survive oppression makes *Broken Glass* Miller's strongest play about being Jewish (and he has written several). But it also transcends that reductive label.

Broken Glass is, on its domestic level, a marriage play set in New York in 1938. More broadly, it reaches back to a unique historical moment of inattention in America, the immediate aftermath of the German horror (not much attended to in America) known as Kristallnacht. The familiar Miller elements are all here: the local individuals with their inexplicable ills, and the barely perceived sociohistorical context of their distress. The play portrays a heroine afflicted with a sudden and baffling paralysis. She and her husband seek help from their neighborhood doctor. It is unfair to summarize this rich and subtle play glibly—which limits of space are about to force me to do—but the busy doctor eventually unearths the inner cause of his patient's distress: a deep and enigmatic fracture between herself and her husband, revealed to her in an awful moment of shock and insight by a published photograph of public humiliations inflicted on elderly Jews by Nazi thugs in Austria. This horrifying image of hatred in action unearths, by the sort of resonant analogy that Miller has made his stock-in-trade, the deep and unsuspected self-hatred in her husband that has frozen his heart, emotions and libido. It is hard not to connect this probing play with an extended passage in *Timebends* in which Miller recounts an incidence of childhood panic at having to reveal (in a public library) his father's Jewish identity by stating his name: Izzy. The incident bewildered Miller when he was a child, but his retelling it in *Timebends* might well have started him on the path of exploring the psychopathology of discrimination. Miller digs his way to the inner place where persistent discrimination is internalized as self-hatred in the victim. The self-hating Jew in the play could just as easily be the self-hating American black man, the irrascible, denigrated Irishman, the degraded Arab, or the self-destructive Native American. The heroine of the play, however, is intent on retrieving her life from such pathologies, and she prevails.

In order to work at all, such dramas as these must play with a ring of truth at each of their nested levels. The simple, literal story must have a deep psychological credibility that earns through sheer compassion and insight a claim on our full attention. In this regard, Miller is still our master playwright. No one conjures more specific people than he, or writes better dialogue than he, and no one seems to love the shape and flow and play of each scene as much as he evidently does. But he never works without a larger aim as well, and the orchestral sweep he obviously considers basic to his art includes a larger situation of his domestic dramas, in fact a full social vision as the only rationale for writing a play at all. Consider this quote from his autobiography:

> The nihilism—even worse, the yawning amusement—toward the very concept of a moral imperative . . . would become a hallmark of international culture. . . . For myself I wanted to stand with those who would not give way, not because I was sure I was good, but because of a sense that there could be no aesthetic form without a moral world, only notes without a staff—an unprovable but deeply felt conclusion.[3]

Whether the moral and social burden of each play is validated for individual playgoers remains a matter of individual experience; but these plays—and certainly their author—would seem to have earned the right to be taken seriously, to be attended to. As of this writing he is still creating serious, searching plays about the texture of experience, and the immediate quotidian realities that make life pleasant or unpleasant, meaningful or tormentingly empty. His most important late plays circle a central theme of sexual relations between adults; they chronicle, among other things, the connection between sexual contact (or lack thereof) and depression, illness and psychological denial. What did the men he portrays think they were doing? How could these women let the situations of their lives degenerate so? What forces of mutual destruction are inherent in marriage? How do ambition, success, children, careers and lust fit into this puzzle? Not one of these is a "dated" theme—quite the opposite.

The one-act *Mr. Peters' Connections* is a theatrical summation of all that has preceded it in the recent past. It is a brooding, personal, curmudgeonly fantasia that I can't help referring to as "The Old Man's Nap." It revisits more boldly than any intervening play the aesthetic and autobiographical ground of *After the Fall,* written thirty-four years earlier. The play places a consciousness remarkably like Miller's own at the center of a collage of broken memories, wavering intentions, stereotyped figments, dead lovers, lost friends, forgotten relatives and grave intimations. The somnambulant protagonist is lost and self-assertive at the same time, as he is led into a twilight space that is a vestibule between life and death. The protagonist is tired rather than exhausted, world-weary rather than defeated or spiritually depleted. If he has fears and regrets, they are engaged fears and regrets, not defeated ones; a feisty, irrascible ego survives—in fact it predominates, and though the stage directions indicate that Mr. Peters frequently weeps or skirts the edge of tears, it is hard to miss the grouchy and intractable distemper of a born egomaniac. The self-centered protagonist who got Miller into so much critical hot water in *After the Fall* is back as Mr. Peters, and he is haunted by visions of lust and regret, by angry convictions and bewilderment, by ambition and the certainty of futility:

> I am older than everyone I ever knew. All my dogs are dead. Half a dozen cats, parakeets . . . all gone. Probably every woman I ever slept with, too, except my wife.
>
> God, if no one remembers what I remember . . . if no one remembers what I . . .
>
> What's begun to haunt me is that next to nothing I have believed has turned out to be true.[4]

These are just a few of the pronouncements that escape from this old man who is shagging after his own churning consciousness, but all his speeches are addressed, in the sense that they are delivered to be heard, and to be heard by coherent, existent, conventional people—in fact, theatregoers. A principal action of the play is to be heard, and this is Miller's action as well as his fictional protagonist's. In *Mr. Peters' Connections* Arthur Miller is writing about old age, and he is sure of his connection to an art form he knows better than anyone. His every move in every script makes it clear he is confident. He knows better than any critic or pundit that a commonsense voice, guided by its own quest for the truth, has a right to speak common sense to its compatriots. That is the Miller style, and it rides on the Miller talent. Why refrain from the free play of such a talent?

There is nothing to be gained for younger talent than Miller's in refraining from anything, either. It would be far more rebellious, bold and risky on the part of young playwrights to follow where Miller (like Ibsen before him) has dared to tread: into the nitty-gritty of our lives, carefully observed, minutely listened to, unglamorously placed where we actually live, intuitively and unflinchingly explored. Old age is not for the squeamish, but more of us than ever before are about to be old. Miller is there just ahead of us, with his eyes wide open, his artistic power intact. Marriage has never suffered more as an institution than in recent decades in America; again, Miller is and has been there, exploring the guilt of abandonment and divorce, the comic agony of desire and the timeless tragedy of betrayal. Sex—especially as experienced by men who are attracted and attractive to women—has never been more coyly evaded as a serious topic than it has since feminist criticism has so effectively tried to destroy the swaggering "macho" mythology.

Finally, Miller has never let go of the project—inherited from the Depression—of exposing the narcissistic hedonism and crude self-indulgent rationalizations necessary to justifying naked greed in private and civic life. Both *The Ride Down Mt. Morgan* and *The Last Yankee* challenge the self-declared triumph of capitalism (which transpired while Miller worked on these plays) by exposing hidden costs to human dignity and human feeling that no other playwright has been willing or able to bring up (Tony Kushner has tried). One need not take ideological sides on the underlying issues to attend to them in dramatic form, but there does seem to be an ideological bias to dismissing these plays (as so many critics have) as tediously outdated because of the social parables they contain. That very denial is one of the central images of the late plays: it is always paradoxical (and suspicious) to deny that a play about denial is relevant. Is it old-fashioned and irrelevant to examine in a public work of art America's still-accelerating success mania and its human cost?

In England, they seem to think such work is important, while in America the sense of civic concern is apparently enervated beyond repair. Nobody wants to hear anything that sounds like an inquiry into cause and effect in public matters, which is the same as saying that nobody has the stomach for facing up to guilt and responsibility in public or private life. Miller's situation resembles Ibsen's in Norway in his old age. Universally recognized for the power of his moral imagination, he was an uncomfortable curmudgeon for his contemporary countrymen: his prophesies and his poetic visions were unsettling, accusatory and unwelcome. One would think American critics would pause at least to

Ruby Cohn

Manipulating Miller

Arthur Miller's plays are produced in theaters all over the world, and many companies often introduce individual elements of staging. Even on the London stage, where Miller has been more fulsomely appreciated than in New York, and where actors can just manage a convincing American accent, there was, for example, a distinctively British cut to the men's suits in *The Last Yankee.* However, that is a single detail, as compared to the major inventions of the famous 1983 Miller production in the People's Republic of China. Miller himself has written an engaging account of that adventure in his *Salesman in Beijing,* illustrated by the rehearsal photographs taken by Inge Morath, who had studied Chinese for eight years before the project. Not having seen Miller's Beijing *Salesman,* I rely on his own account, in order to highlight the cultural cleavage between Brooklyn and Beijing, and the consequent manipulation of the play to make it accessible to a Chinese audience.

As Miller, who was directing, prepared the production in Beijing, a nineteen-year-old Chinese tennis player defected to the United States and was granted asylum. In response, China canceled cultural exchanges, and there was a possibility that the government-sanctioned *Salesman* in Beijing would be closed before it opened. However, Miller and his Willy Loman, Ying Ruocheng, left that matter to fate while they grappled with the difficulties of their performance space. Seating thirteen hundred, and sporting a stage of mismatched, splintery boards, the large structure did not exactly welcome the intimate scenes of the Loman family and friends. Although the Chinese set was patterned on the original design by Jo Mielziner, staircases had to be repositioned and furnishings reconceived. Moreover, the theater was rented for other events until three days before the first preview of *Salesman,* so the actors could not grow accustomed to the set as it took shape.

During the reign of China's Gang of Four in the mid-1970s, only eight approved plays were permitted, while theater workers were often sent to factories or rice fields for "re-education"—if they were lucky. This meant that in 1983 theater craftsmen had to compensate for a hiatus in their practice. Any Western play was alien to the Chinese theater tradition, and this foreignness was customarily underlined by whiteface and wigs, which Miller resisted for *Salesman*. Among other staging problems, lighting loomed large. Even for sophisticated theaters of the West, *Salesman* presented an unusually large number of lighting cues, but the Beijing theater could accept only eighteen cues in sequence before it became necessary to replug the apparatus.

Wisely, Miller did not brood about such matters until he familiarized himself with his environment. It was the actor Ying Ruocheng who had chosen *Death of a Salesman* for Beijing performance, partly no doubt so he could play Willy Loman, and it was he who had assembled the cast for seventy-year-old Miller to direct. Having worked in Western theaters and films, Ying thought that Miller's drama would be meaningful to his compatriots. Yet the very title presented difficulties. By 1983, with Mao dead and the Gang of Four gone, private salesmen were beginning to appear in the streets of Beijing, but *traveling* salesmen in the American sense were unknown. Moreover, the salesman Willy Loman is deluded, but also heroic. Yet the tradesman, the nearest Chinese equivalent to a salesman, was literally a "low man" in both the Confucian and Marxist codes of conduct in the People's Republic of China. It was the task of the actor to cut through cultural biases and awaken sympathy toward his character, but in rehearsal Miller felt that Ying, for all his skill and sophistication, was unconsciously condescending to his character. In the scene where Willy evokes the noble heritage of traveling salesmen like Dave Singleman, Miller informed Ying that Willy had in the past sold to rugged individuals like R. H. Macy and Louis Chevrolet. "Willy is not altogether romanticizing the past here, you know. Remember, these men [the salesmen] actually referred to themselves as knights of the road" (*Salesman in Beijing,* 174). Ying then recalled that in China armed men used to accompany wagons of merchandise to protect them from bandits. "And they were away from their homes for months and months at a time and had a certain mythology about themselves" (175). After railroads rendered them obsolete, they used to perform feats of strength at local fairs, perhaps evocative of their more glorious past. Relying on this detail of Chinese social history, Ying was able to perform "a certain nobility in his suffering" (175).

Miller's title reveals that his salesman dies, and one would think that death is universal. Indeed it is, but suicide is not. Ying explained to

Miller: "A suicide in China is enticed by a spirit belonging to a person who committed suicide before, the Soul-Snarer. This spirit cannot be reborn in human form unless he helps another to kill himself" (196). Nothing very relevant to salesmen there. However, Ying also explained that suicides were performed by hanging, and the prospective suicide looks through his noose toward his destination of a beautiful landscape with lovely vistas. The view through the noose enabled Ying to play Willy's suicide as a significant sacrifice.

Miller the director did not begin by clarifying his title in the way that I have described. That came late in rehearsals, after the actors had memorized their lines. Quite early, however, Ying worried about his audience's ability to appreciate the motive for Willy's suicide in insurance-less China. In the Chinese English newspaper Miller read an account of the People's Insurance Company of China, which was doing "a fabulous business insuring property and vehicles as well as crops in transit" (55). Miller comments wryly: "Ying is surprised and happy to learn about insurance but still intends to explain how it works in the program notes" (56).

During rehearsals the actors learned their lines from Ying's translation of Miller's American English, which the director followed with his own text. He was encouraged that the rhythms, pauses and laughs were not dissimilar. However, the ethics were radically different in that the actors wanted to know whether particular characters were Good or Bad. This was especially true of the woman in Willy's Boston hotel room and the two women picked up in the restaurant. When Miller affirmed that none of these women was a prostitute, that is, Bad, the actresses grew more attuned to their characters. In contrast, when Willy and Charley played card games—changed from casino to gin rummy—the rhythms of dialogue and playing were impeccable from the start. Miller complimented the two actors, only to learn that they had spent three years playing gin in the evenings when they were sent to work in rice fields.

Chinese is a more highly imaged language than English, and only late in the rehearsal process did Miller learn of Ying's ingenious substitutes for Miller's untranslatable phrases. Here are a few examples: Willy boasts to his sons: "Knocked 'em cold in Providence, slaughtered 'em in Boston." In Ying's version this became: "I tumbled them backwards in Providence-ah, and they fell on their faces in Bos-i-ton" (29). Or, conversely, Willy complains to Linda that people laugh at him: "a salesman I know . . . I heard him say something about—walrus. And I—I cracked him right across the face." Walruses are evidently unknown in Beijing, so Ying substituted "a barrel of oil" (162). For the cliché "business is business" Ying found a similar Chinese saying: "Kin is kin, money is money." Another cliché is on Bernard's lips when he tries to comfort Willy: "Sometimes, Willy, it's better for a man just to walk away." And Willy responds: "But if you can't walk away?" Ying explained that "walk away" is meaningless in Chinese, so he changed Bernard's advice to "It's good to be able to pick things up but also to be able to put things down." And Willy responds: "Suppose I can't put them down?" The audience has by this time "identified themselves with Willy as a man who picks up all sorts of things without being able to put them down" (243). Perhaps Ying's crowning invention came in Willy's comment about his brother Ben: "That man was a genius, that man was success incarnate!" Ying explained: "Genius in Chinese is conveyed by a double symbol–Heaven-Talent, *Tian-Cai,*" which becomes "a slightly ludicrous" conflation of "heaven," "success" and "making a buck" (241). Entirely appropriate for rich, dead Ben.

From the beginning of the two-month rehearsal period Miller decided that he would not imitate American films, but would set his play in some domain of the imagination, rooted in emotional reality, that would be filtered through the setting and costumes. The Loman house gradually took form, with its downstairs kitchen and two upstairs bedrooms. In Mielziner's original set an elevator was required for the early scene shift from the adult Loman brothers in their upstairs bedroom to their teenage selves, busy with sports downstairs. Since elevators were unavailable in Beijing, Miller designed a hinged slab in each of the brother's beds, which would slope downward and allow the actors to slide unseen to the ground floor. The Chinese designer refined this: "the two slabs on which the adult actors lie under bedcovers are propped up by T's, which are pulled out of vertical positions by stagehands underneath and the actors [slide] to the stage floor" (210). Miller reflected ironically that in New York this elegant solution would have cost an extra thousand dollars a week for the two stagehands.

With good will, costumes and props were gradually if sometimes quixotically affixed to their characters. Willy's suitcases, as big as footlockers, were shrunk to size at the very first rehearsal. Later a four-foot punching-bag also had to be jettisoned for one of proper size. Gradually, the actors grew familiar with an American football and papier-mâché helmets. While Willy's boss shows off his new wire recorder, the actual Chinese tape-recorder was essential but unreliable. Breaking down during the second preview, it was miraculously resurrected backstage by a technician who spliced wires in utter darkness.

Wigs occasioned the widest cultural divide between the director and the theater staff, and Miller had to exert some authority before he could persuade actors and wig-makers to relinquish them—or at least some of them. Even Ying resisted Miller on this matter, and for him they compromised on a wig that looked like Ying's own full head of hair, but graying. Other wigs were whittled down to Ben, Howard and Charley. In Miller's words: "I have not done too badly, so I thank the wiggers profusely and make my short speech once more about our not trying to imitate Americans" (185–86).

Imitation or imagination, the Beijing *Salesman* was successful enough to be kept durably in the repertory, and Miller closes his *Salesman in Beijing* trying to believe his own words, "that it all happens in some country of the mind where people with Chinese faces and straight black hair speak and behave as though they were in another civilization" (254).

Little did Miller think that, back in his native country, indeed in his native city of New York, he would feel as though "another civilization" had devoured his most popular play, *The Crucible.* In the 1940s and early 1950s, when Arthur Miller earned his reputation, there was no off-Broadway, much less off-off. By the 1980s, some of Miller's plays were considered classics, and the theater avant-garde considered him part of the Establishment. One avant-garde company, the Wooster Group, named for its off-off-Broadway venue in Soho, courted controversy virtually from its inception in 1975. It was born in rebellion against Richard Schechner's Performance Group. Its 1977 production, *Rumstick Road,* was castigated for taping private telephone conversations. In 1981 the Group's *Route 1 & 9* featured white actors in blackface performing Pigmeat Markham comedy routines. Labeled racist by the New York State Council of the Arts, the group had its grant withdrawn. Deprived of these funds, the Wooster Group's artistic director, Liz LeCompte, then turned almost desperately to the dramatic canon: "Real plays. Just to do them, what the hell. I can't remember why I reread *The Crucible,* but I did. . . . I remembered, I guess, 'Your justice would freeze beer,' and I found the script and brought it in and we all sat around upstairs and I said, 'I want to do this play. . . . I think I was most attracted to the play because of the language, the imitation language, and the screaming of the girls. Those attracted me so much that my mouth would water just thinking about doing it" (Savran, 176).

What LeCompte doesn't say is that for the Wooster Group, "doing" a play meant manipulating a popular artifact in juxtaposition to a new performance reality. The group had worked in this way with Wilder's *Our Town,* T. S. Eliot's *Cocktail Party* and O'Neill's *Long Day's Journey into Night.* But these playwrights were dead, whereas Miller was very much alive. Ultimately, his objections to the Wooster Group's manipulation of *The Crucible* gained them more notoriety than they had ever had.

In London, where I caught the Wooster Group show, the program stated: "The Wooster Group texts stand as an alternative theatre language which redefines the traditional devices of story-line, character and theme. Each production reflects a continuing refinement of a nonlinear, abstract aesthetic which at once subverts and pays homage to modern theatrical 'realism.' The Group has developed an idiosyncratic work process. 'Source' texts are quoted, reworked and juxtaposed with fragments of popular, cultural and social history, as well as with events and situations which emerge from the personal or collective experience of Group members. These various elements are fused into a collage or score—the final text" (program notes for the London Riverside performance of *The Road to Immortality*). During the process of fusion, the performance can change from night to night, and paying members of an audience can be subjected to a very raw rehearsal.

None of the accounts I read testifies to a straight read-through of *The Crucible.* Although the Wooster Group was informed that *The Crucible* was not available for performance in New York City, their work continued, and LeCompte juxtaposed Miller's play with Timothy Leary's record *L.S.D.* The texts of Leary and Miller shared an opposition to authority, forms of intoxication and persecution, and the final emergence of a hero. At the same time their texts were seen as sequential in that *The Crucible* allegorizes anti-Communist hysteria of the 1950s, whereas *L.S.D.* epitomizes the counterculture of the 1960s (Savran, 179–80). In an early version of *L.S.D.* the Wooster Group piece opened on actors quoting some twenty minutes of the Leary record, and this was framed by an actress reciting recollections of Ann Rower, the Leary babysitter. This was followed by some forty-five minutes of collage of the ends of the four acts of *The Crucible,* with provocative casting. A white actress (Kate Valk) in blackface played Miller's Tituba, and still in blackface she also played the Proctors' servant Mary Warren. (Later she coated her blackface with whiteface.) A fourteen-year-old boy played Governor Danforth, and the teenage girls were played by wrinkled old women. All the actresses wore seventeenth-century costumes, and their voices were unmiked. The male actors wore contemporary work clothes, and their voices were miked (Auslander reads this politically). In January, 1983 LeCompte wrote Miller's agent, requesting permission to perform excerpts from *The Crucible,* and she was informed that a lawyer would have to see the piece.

In fall 1983, while the Wooster Group was charging admission for this piece in progress, a member of the group sought out Miller at a Chelsea Hotel function, and he agreed to see it that evening. LeCompte has enumerated what she thought to be Miller's fears: (1) that the audience might perceive the performance as a parody; (2) that the audience might perceive the performance as the whole play, rather than excerpts; (3) that the performance might militate against a Broadway production. Within a month Miller refused permission for the excerpts. In three letters over the course of the next year LeCompte tried to assuage Miller's fears while the company continued to work on the piece, which evolved into four parts. *The Crucible* excerpts were condensed to twenty-five minutes, and they were largely confined to the second part. At some point during the exploration, the cast took acid before rehearsing *The Crucible* excerpts, and an undrugged LeCompte videotaped them. Part of the video was then included as the third part of the performance. On October 31, 1984, Mel Gussow in the *New York Times* published an unfavorable review, mentioning "a brief send-up of the Arthur Miller play." Shortly afterwards the Wooster group received a cease and desist order from Miller's attorney. Acting on legal advice, LeCompte substituted gibberish for Miller's lines, but she did not change the staging or the costumes.

By December 1984, after an exchange of recriminations by the Wooster Group and Miller's representatives, the actor-writer Michael Kirby persuaded LeCompte to substitute his script for Miller's lines in part 2 of what came to be called *The Road to Immortality.* A sympathetic critic described the result: "The new section followed the shape of *The Crucible,* but rescored the original so that the few remaining fragments of Miller's script were obscured either by music or by the Kirby text. When a performer 'accidentally' spoke a line of *The Crucible* or made a reference to one of Miller's characters, he or she was silenced by a buzzer" (Savran, *TDR,* 101). In January 1985, the Wooster Group received another cease and desist order from Miller's attorney, and the show was closed. Not, however, for long, since it toured in 1985 and 1986—at least in Europe, where I saw it. The same sympathetic critic declares: "The dispute between Arthur Miller and the Wooster Group bears witness to the status of interpretation as an act that cannot be separated from the work itself. Thus, from now on, *L.S.D.* will be in part 'about' Miller's withholding of rights for *The Crucible*" (*TDR,* 109). This might be true for LeCompte and the thirteen members of her cast, but I am dubious as to whether audiences absorbed anything of that saga. Reviews in Edinburgh and in London mentioned *The Crucible,* but already the Miller-Wooster confrontation was receding into the past. LeCompte in an interview casts light on the confrontation:

"What we were trying to do I guess was weave the social issues of Miller together with a lot of memory distortions to get a piece which was about the erosion of moral certainty in a search for so-called higher values" (Grant, 13). *The Road to Immortality (Part Two)* not only dramatized "the erosion of moral certainty," but was itself morally uncertain. And proud of it. Perhaps its title should have been *The Road to Immorality.*

My last example of Miller manipulation also juxtaposes an avant-gardist with a Miller play, but George Coates Performance Works is as rooted in the San Francisco Bay Area as the Wooster Group is in New York City. The George Coates Performance Works is basically George Coates himself, stretching toward a quarter century of unique performances. For his following in Silicon Valley, Coates's name is synonymous with high tech; for New Music buffs he is a producer of avant-garde opera; for intermedia aficionados he is an exemplary figure. In most of Coates's works he has borrowed the Czech *laterna magica* technique whereby live actors emerge from their film or video images. He calls the technique "reframing" because his productions tend to redirect audience experience by causing events, objects and characters to flow into one another, obliterating narrative linearity. Sometimes Coates parodies a newsworthy item, like virtual reality or Internet surfing. At other times he free-associates around a specific figure—William Blake, Lewis Carroll, Ludwig Wittgenstein. Coates evolves his pieces through long rehearsals, where he works closely with composers, musicians, video operators, sound and lighting designers, as well as actors. He rarely tours, and has to be seen on his home ground.

That home ground is part of his theatricality. In the late 1980s, San Francisco artists scanned blueprints for spaces that could accommodate them, especially after the 1989 earthquake. Homeless professionally, Coates examined a space that had been rejected by ballet, opera, equity theater—a deconsecrated church with sixty-foot-high arches and a vaulted ceiling. For a decade that has been Coates's magnificent home ground. He entitled his first show there *The Architecture of Catastrophic Change,* but it was for him the antithesis of catastrophe.

George Coates has occasionally directed a play from the dramatic canon, but he always marked his production idiosyncratically, as when he cast stand-up comedians in *Waiting for Godot.* In 1999 he acquired the rights to a play that was decidedly foreign to the dramatic canon—*Up Your Ass* by Valerie Solanas. In 1966 Solanas had given her play to Andy Warhol to produce, and when he apparently lost the only copy, Solanas shot him. (The subject is at the core of the movie *I Shot Andy Warhol.*)

Warhol died in 1987 from surgical complications perhaps related to the shooting, and Solanas died a year later, destitute in a derelict hotel near what was to become Coates's theater.

What has all this to do with Arthur Miller? Solanas's play is, in her words, a satire on "men, married women and other degenerates," and Coates, an old hand at applying for support, knew that *Up Your Ass* was an unlikely candidate for a grant funded by the National Endowment for the Arts. Familiar with Miller's anti-censorship stance as president of PEN, Coates thought of pairing Solanas's reviled play with a revered Miller work, but he would request a grant only for the latter. He looked Arthur Miller up on the Internet and was delighted to find unfamiliar titles. Given Coates's interest in architecture, he was immediately attracted by *The Archbishop's Ceiling,* and he emerged enthusiastic from his reading. Serendipitously, Miller visited San Francisco at this time, and in Coates's effort to seek his permission for the pairing of the two plays, Miller mistook him for his driver. While waiting for the actual driver, Coates had about a half-hour with Miller, and he talked hard and fast. Viewing the two plays as statements against censorship, Coates was not yet sure of *how* he would pair them: perhaps on a double bill, or perhaps intercutting them. Miller was receptive to Coates's approach, although he had never seen his work. Perhaps recalling his Wooster Group experience, Miller told Coates that he had carte blanche to fit *The Archbishop's Ceiling* into his program, as long as he used all of the play and not merely excerpts.

In the event, Coates left both plays intact. He directed a song-studded, drag king version of *Up Your Ass* on Friday and Saturday nights, and a textually faithful *Archbishop's Ceiling* on Thursday and Sunday nights. He received an NEA grant for the Miller play.

Written in 1977 during the Cold War, *The Archbishop's Ceiling* is set in a baroque archbishop's palace in an unnamed Eastern European capital. The palace is the privileged abode of a government-approved writer, Marcus. The play opens on an American writer, Adrian, suspiciously searching for electronic surveillance devices in the furnishings and even in the high ceiling of the archbishop's palace. Maya enters with coffee. The two have been lovers, and Adrian has tried to fictionalize their affair but has been unable to complete his novel. Soon Marcus enters with the country's greatest writer, Sigmund, and a young Danish beauty who knows little English. The drama gradually focuses on Sigmund, who has just completed an oppositional novel. The ruling party wants to force Sigmund into exile. So, for their several reasons, do Marcus, Maya and Adrian. Almost predictably for a Miller hero, Sigmund ultimately rejects their urging; he will remain in his own country, a thorn in the side of the regime.

The Archbishop's Ceiling assigns ambiguous motives to its male characters, and to Maya, who has had affairs with each of them. The play accumulates tension in the characters' uncertainty as to whether the archbishop's ceiling is bugged. Given the possibility of surveillance, the four voluble characters slip in and out of self-censorship; only in a corridor near the palace entrance is it safe to speak freely. Since most of the dialogue is heard within the archbishop's room, however, we are not quite sure when the characters are speaking sincerely or when they are "acting" for their possible audience.

In Miller's text the "safe" area is a dimly lit corridor that leads upstage left into darkness. In Coates's production a brightly lit passage leads downstage right directly into the audience; we are closest to the characters when they speak freely. Otherwise they may be censoring themselves—as a conservatively-minded U.S. Congress has encouraged artists to do if they wish to receive NEA funding.

In addition to this modified staging, Coates introduces a very San Francisco element into his production. The male-bashing farce *Up Your Ass* thrives on a baker's dozen of female performers, some of them drag kings. Coates siphons off five of these performers for the Miller play. His American Adrian wears an un-American mustache and goatee; the genius Sigmund wears a full beard. Not unlike Chinese wigs denoting Westerners in Beijing, these hairy additions denote gender. But the powerful Marcus sports no facial hair, and his voice is high-pitched for a man. Onstage all three actresses of male roles imitated masculine strides and positions. The few embraces were perfunctory and passionless. Gender-bending is, of course, a comic device, which fits oddly into this serious play, and it may be unintentional that the best acting came from the two actresses in women's roles.

Coates obeyed Miller's stipulation; he presented *all* of *The Archbishop's Ceiling.* Yet I'm not at all sure that Miller himself would prefer Coates's production to the Wooster Group excerpts. However, I think Miller should be proud that his plays speak to avant-garde artists, however off-key their hearing may be.

Works Cited

Auslander, Philip. *Presence and Resistance: Postmodernism and Cultural Politics in Contemporary American Performance.* Ann Arbor: University of Michigan Press, 1992.

Grant, Steve. "Wooster Source." *Time Out,* August 27–September 2, 1986.
Miller, Arthur. *The Archbishop's Ceiling.* London: Methuen, 1984.
———. *The Crucible.* New York: Viking, 1953.
———. *Salesman in Beijing.* New York: Viking, 1984.
Savran, David. "The Wooster Group, Arthur Miller and *The Crucible.*" *Drama Review* (summer 1985): 99–109.
———. *Breaking the Rules: The Wooster Group.* New York: Theater Communications Group, 1988.

Deborah R. Geis

In Willy Loman's Garden
Contemporary Re-visions of *Death of a Salesman*

More than fifty years after its first Broadway production, Arthur Miller's *Death of a Salesman* has become a cultural icon. On one level, the "legacy" of *Salesman* can be discussed in terms of re-productions or revivals of the work itself, particularly when directorial, design and casting choices allow us to view it from a fresh perspective. For example, the 1998 revival that originated with the Steppenwolf Theatre Company in Chicago and later moved to Broadway was remarkable for a number of reasons, not the least of which was the new depth that Elizabeth Franz's portrayal of Linda Loman gave to a role that has sometimes been dismissed as one-dimensionally supportive and passive.[1] Franz allowed us to see—for the first time, at least for this viewer—the quality and scope of Linda's suffering, particularly as Brian Dennehy's Willy bullied her in the first part of the play.

A second level of discussion of *Salesman*'s legacy might be the clear influence that it has had upon subsequent works for the American theater. Regardless of whether Sam Shepard intended this to be the case, for example, one can see the father-son tensions set amid the gleaming, unfulfilled promises of the American dream of his *Curse of the Starving Class* as a hyperreal, bombastic take on the family drama driven by the same energies, the same idealism and despair as *Salesman*. Perhaps more explicitly, it is difficult to read or watch David Mamet's *Glengarry Glen Ross* without making connections between its imagery of salesmanship and that of Miller's play, particularly in Mamet's character of Shelly Levene, the failed real-estate salesman who tries desperately to make a comeback in order to rescue his family relationships as well as his own pride.[2] August Wilson's *Fences,* too, invites many comparisons to *Salesman* in its portrayal of Troy Maxson's vexed relationship with his son Cory and particularly with his long-suffering wife, Rose.

What interests me most in this essay, though, is a third level at which we might consider the impact of *Salesman* upon American literary and dramatic consciousness: its more direct appropriation as intertext for a surprising number of new theatrical works. In other words, rather than simply evoking Miller's play by some general thematic means, these works export actual characters (or references to actual characters) from *Salesman,* or they quote, parody or otherwise appropriate Miller's text in explicit references to it as either "real" or as a literary work with which the characters are familiar. This type of intertextuality creates a more dialogical approach to Miller's "masterpiece," one that allows for interrogation and deconstruction of its assumptions about culture and character. While in some sense the appropriation of *Salesman* is still a type of homage, these works enact critical rereadings of Miller's play that enable us to review both *Salesman* and these new texts from a postmodern perspective.

Rosalyn Drexler's 1984 play *Room 17C* begins, in a sense, before *Salesman* ends, as Willy has not yet committed suicide; rather, it exists in a kind of parallel universe that allows Drexler to rewrite Miller's work to her own liking, and even to recombine it with an entirely different literary text. Rosette Lamont describes Drexler's plays as creating a "semiotics of instability" in which she "destabilizes the accepted forms of discourse, of the dramatic genre as a whole" (ix). In *Room 17C* Linda Loman has now taken over Willy's job as a traveling salesperson and has proven to be far more successful at it than he ever was. Drexler gives her Linda the last name of "Normal" rather than "Loman," the near-anagram underscoring the complicated trajectories of characters (both here and in Miller's play) who aspire to "normal" American ideas of success. In her opening stage directions, Drexler shows that although Linda has crossed from the realm of the domestic to the traditionally masculine realm of the wage-earner we should not infer that she has therefore become liberated from the positions that Miller assigned her:

> Linda has taken over her husband's destiny to be a successful salesman. Her life is still not her own. Her husband keeps calling to check up on her. She has to harden herself. In some way she still is playing his "masochistic" game. Whatever she does pains him. He threatens her with his suicide, but it is she who will die (in the line of duty, burned to a crisp with her sport's "knock-'em-dead" line). (2)

Willy, then, exists as an offstage character, a voice on the phone; the first we hear of him is in a missed connection, as Linda at the beginning of the play tries to reach him but gets no answer. Asserting her financial independence, she tells the operator that it is not a collect call, but one that should be charged to her room. Slightly later, she characterizes Willy as "a traveling salesman and a parasite," saying (with a cynicism that stands in sharp contrast to Miller's Linda), "Well, he's fired now. Got a gold-plated watch to commemorate his masochism," adding that now she's the one "who attends to business" (5).

Paralleling Willy's hotel room liaison in *Salesman,* Linda has a romantic encounter . . . with Sammy Gregor, a "man-sized cockroach," obviously drawn from Kafka's Gregor Samsa in *The Metamorphosis.*[3] Drexler takes pain to emphasize that the cockroach should not be played in "cute" Disneyland fashion with a bug costume; rather, he should exhibit a "bug persona" (nervousness, creeping, crawling) but that for the actor, "a well-worn brown suit will suffice" (2). Linda is attracted to Sammy because of his romantic qualities, his sensuality, his free spirit, his ability to banter with her. Her comments to him continually emphasize his otherness: she calls him "loathsome" (3), says she's "not Walt Disney" (9), and tells him, "I will not let you turn this trip into a Japanese horror film" (10).

Yet Linda also makes it clear that she sees a link between Sammy and Willy: not only—as I mentioned earlier—does she characterize Willy as a "parasite," but she even describes a family photograph in which Willy, also in a brown suit, resembled a cockroach: "At any rate, he was more than willing to be there [at her feet], his body flattened, his head at a tilt as if waiting for some final blow" (11). She points this out after Sammy—in a move that echoes Gregor's fetishizing of the photograph in Kafka's story—tells Linda that he saw her framed photo wrapped in her lingerie, and Linda responds that "family photographs reveal too much" (11). What becomes clear in such interactions is that while Sammy and Willy bear more than a superficial resemblance to one another, Sammy is of a different "species" because of his ability to "read" Linda in ways that Willy (at least as we saw him in *Salesman*) was never able to do. At the same time, Linda's initial physical repulsion toward Sammy (which never wholly subsides) is modified by some sense that there is a possibility for a mutual orality (they eat rare hamburgers from room service together; they engage in verbal sparring) that she and Willy have failed to share. Indeed, when she does get Willy on the phone, she talks to him in a series of clichés that she seems to have absorbed from him and from the discourse of striving for the American dream of successful salesmanship: "Where's your backbone, dammit? Sit up straight, Willy, or no one'll know you're at the table" (8).

In Linda's phone conversations with Willy, Drexler plays directly with the audience's awareness of the plot of *Salesman* in order to create an ironic dialogue between her text and that of Miller's play. When Linda hears that Willy is depressed, she says, "No, no, no! Don't kill yourself, darling! It'd be anti-climactic" (8). And later, when he calls back to tell her that he can't find the instant coffee (confirming that he has not switched roles with her very successfully), she tells him, "Oh, I forgot to remind you to check the water heater. Pan has to be emptied. No, the hose does not lead directly to the gas line. Boy, do you sound depressed" (12). Although Linda constantly reaffirms to Willy how much she misses and loves him, it is clear that she is reciting the lines of a script that she has followed many times before, one that is just as familiar to her as one of her sales pitches. At the same time, since the audience knows the script of *Salesman,* we are caught between horror at the inevitability of Willy's demise and amusement at the extent to which Linda's cynicism rebels so profoundly against the role that Miller wrote for her: does Miller's Linda carry any subtextual resentment of Willy, or does Drexler create an entirely subversive reading of her character?

The key moment of disappointment in his father for Biff comes, in *Salesman,* when he surprises Willy in Boston and finds him with a woman in his hotel room. Drexler translates Linda's version of this story rather differently; as Linda explains to Sammy, "They haven't gotten along since Joey [Drexler's parallel to Biff] walked in on Willy when he was with some woman, somewhere." She continues, "Talk about men putting women on a pedestal! Joey had his dad living on Mount Everest. Poor kid, thought he had to take sides, defend me; I couldn't have cared less" (14). Here Drexler radically reverses our assumption that news of her husband's philandering would be devastating to Linda; she refuses to play victim, yet we also get the sense that her cynicism is born of years of disappointment and ultimately has caused her to withdraw emotionally. In what appears at first to be a repetition of Biff's trauma, Joey walks in and finds Linda with Sammy—and indeed, his shocked reaction at first mirrors that of Biff with Willy—but in this case, it is Linda who rewrites the scenario. Joey makes a speech calling her "the lowest of the low," extending his discourse to apply to womankind: "Woman is a perilous craft, and crafty though she is, cannot avoid the rocks in her path, so ready is she to abandon herself to the elements . . . to wreck what has formerly had direction and buoyancy" (18). Crucially, though, Linda responds, "I hadn't realized that I had raised a woman hater, Joey; and an excessively literary one to boot" (18). By calling attention to the textual nature of Joey's language—as she did by calling Willy's suicide attempt "anti-climactic"—Linda forces a Brechtian distancing between a character's words and deeds. This is a relentless act of demystification that can be read psychologically as her own deepening cynicism and as her enactment of an ongoing critique or revision of the text in which her character is "supposed" to find herself. Joey's education has included "learning" the texts of misogyny couched in literary form, yet it is Linda's direct critique of Joey's text that allows her to assert a different kind of maternal power.

The ending "Requiem" of *Salesman* contrasts the voices of Charley, who responds to Biff's remark that Willy had the wrong kind of dreams with his "Nobody dast blame this man" speech; Happy, who vows to fulfill Willy's dream; and Linda, who says that she can't cry and that she has made the last payment on the house—"We're free" (138–39). Drexler's Linda seems to have found, briefly, a kind of freedom with Sammy at the end of *Room 17C,* but it is short-lived. At the end of the play, Joey and Sammy manage to escape when the hotel catches on fire, but Linda expires from smoke inhalation when she stays to answer another phone call from Willy. Sammy, who turns and addresses the audience, gets the last words as his monologue evokes the cockroach's mythical ability to survive the unthinkable: "Even mushroom clouds cannot divert my way of life" (19). He attributes this ability to his lack of imagination: "Linda had imagination. Imagination can accomplish the end of the world" (19). He then sings the "popular roach anthem," which turns out to be set to the tune of "America the Beautiful" (19–20). Drexler thus provides a complex response to *Salesman*'s nostalgic yet tragic commentary on the pressure for bourgeois success in America in the years after World War II as conveyed through Willy's longings and failure. The survivor in Drexler's play is Sammy, the character who has deliberately chosen an "alternative" path; Linda's "imagination" is seen as both what allowed her to dream and ultimately what brought about her destruction.

Paula Vogel's *The Oldest Profession* was first produced in 1981 and was given subsequent productions in Canada and New England in 1988, 1990 and 1991. When the opening scene reveals five women between the ages of seventy-two and eighty-three sitting on a New York City park bench, it rapidly becomes clear that we are witnessing four still-active prostitutes and their madam as they discuss everything from cooking to their customers' fetishes to stock options. By the end of the play—which is structured as a series of blackouts, with one more of the five women missing (i.e., deceased) with each new blackout—Vogel has not only introduced Willy Loman as an offstage character, but has also used the "oldest profession" as a contrapuntal text to *Salesman*'s commentary on capitalism and the body. Vogel's exploration of the politics of commodification draws explicit connections between Willy's failed career and the complex emotional trajectories of these women who have sold their bodies for a lifetime.

Probably the most important idea to underscore about Vogel's play is the matter-of-factness with which she—and the characters—treat what they do: the professional role as prostitute is portrayed as a job like any other job, with its employee gossip, its moments of tedium and pleasure, its preoccupation with sick days and vacation days. By suggesting that prostitution is not altogether different from other careers, Vogel pointedly implies that the reverse is also true: that other jobs are not altogether different from "the Life," thus echoing Brecht's portrayal of the prostitutes in *The Threepenny Opera.* Moreover, Vogel takes on the taboo subject of sexuality in older women and shows their course, despite their impending mortality, as an optimistic one in that they feel they have more, not less, to offer their clients than their younger competitors.

As with Drexler's play, we never actually see Willy Loman, but his offstage presence is weighted by the mythology of Miller's play. We first hear about Willy when the women discuss how to make ends meet by coaxing more money out of the clients, and more time and productivity out of their own work schedules. Ursula, who is the most aggressively concerned with efficient moneymaking, comments that "Lillian here stays in bed with Mr. Loman much too long" (142). Our understanding is that Willy, like many of the other customers, has been a client for many years; Lillian, who is now seventy-five, has developed both a routine and an intimacy with him that may extend beyond mere business. Vogel takes the sense in *Salesman* of Willy's loneliness on the road and extends it into imagining that Lillian, like the woman in the hotel room in *Salesman,* provides a sustenance that is both a transaction he pays for and a relationship that has longtime intimacies parallel to those of a marriage or close business partnership.

What is important here is that we get all of this from the prostitute's point of view, not Willy's: Lillian is the agent of the exchange, not its object.[4] The turning point comes when we hear that Mr. Loman seems not to be in his right mind: Lillian reports that he "paid with these" and pulls from her purse (145) a pair of "long silk stockings circa 1945," complete with seams, echoing the stockings that Willy gives the woman in *Salesman,* while Linda mends hers at home. She explains that he seems to be lost in the delusion that they are still in World War II: "Mr. Loman thinks that stockings and chocolate are a better bet than our currency . . . as long as the 'Japanese are beating the pants off our boys in the Pacific Theatre'" (145). The tone of the stage direction that follows is an interesting one, generating both the emotion of the dramatic moment (and all of the information that we already carry with us about Willy) and a subtle, slightly flippant undercutting of the moment's poignancy: "There is a respectful silence as the women realize that Mr. Loman has lost his marbles" (145).

The implication is that Willy has survived in a way he did not in *Salesman*—that is, he lives through his suicide attempt and presumably through either the death of Linda or the dissolution of his marriage—but that the cost has been considerable, as despair, loneliness and old age have made him succumb to the delusions (the pull of the past) that we saw haunting him in Miller's play. When Lillian asks Mae (their madam) what they should do about Willy, she replies, "I don't know. He's been left alone for too long" (145). She adds that the management of Jefferson Square, the apartment building where most of the clients seem to live, will send Willy off to a nursing home if they find out that he is losing his faculties: "They think they've done their responsibility just because they've installed handlebars by the toilet and the tub . . . Jefferson Square's designed for folks with all their fixtures in working condition" (146). Just as Willy was displaced from his salesman job, we see that he will inevitably be displaced, too, from his current home; he has been relegated to the status of a "fixture," an object of long-standing existence (like the text of *Salesman* itself?), but one that is no longer "in working condition"; thus, his past seems to be about to repeat itself even as he believes himself to be still in 1945.

Mae asks whether Willy has any relatives who could look after him, but Lillian replies that all he has are "[t]wo good-for-nothing sons who are only God-knows-where" (146). Vogel suggests that despite (or perhaps because of) all of their guilt about their father, Happy and Biff have ultimately deserted him, thus putting the lie to Happy's insistence at the end of *Salesman* that he is "gonna win it [his dream] for him" (139). This is a cynical reading, but certainly not unsupported by Miller's text.[5] As before, Vogel lets the stage direction carry both this cynicism and the emotional weight of all that Willy has lost. When Mae says that she'll stop by Willy's apartment that night to talk with him, they "pause, as if a requiem for Mr. Loman. Then Mae, shaking her head, gets back to business" (146). The image of a "requiem," of course, echoes Miller's title for the concluding scene of *Salesman;* here, though, its relegation to the status of a pause before Mae "gets back to business" is both poignant and (within the world of the play) pragmatic.

It is not simply through the inclusion of Willy Loman as an offstage character, however, that *The Oldest Profession* responds to *Salesman*. Vogel's play is set on a "sunny day shortly after the election of Ronald Reagan in 1980" (130). At the beginning the women debate issues of government spending and the market economy. Ursula—politically, the furthest to the right of the group—argues (despite her own advanced age) that "Social Security has no place in a free market" and condemns "big government spending and borrowing" (135). On the surface level their exchanges are amusing because of the extent to which they demystify the prostitutes and reflect on the similarity of their economic concerns to those of "ordinary" bourgeois citizens. At the same time Vogel sets up a parallel between Willy's gradual exclusion from his profession in the midst of a postwar boom economy[6] and the situations of these senior citizens in 1980 at the dawn of the Reagan era: they face gradual marginalization, pushed along by their own baby-boomer children. Mae, threatened by the competition her women face, waxes nostalgic about the past in a way that imagines participation in an idealized "family":

> When I see the new generation of prostitutes working right on the streets—gypsies, all of them—on their own with no group, no house to call their own, no amenities for customers, no tradition or . . . or finesse . . . where's the pride in the name of prostitute? . . . Remember the House where we all first met? A spick-and-span establishment. The music from Professor Joe in the parlor; the men folk bathed, their hair combed back and dressed in their Sunday best, waiting downstairs happy and shy. We knew them all; knew their wives and kids, too. (139)

Willy, throughout *Salesman,* paints an image of a rosy past only to rub up against such moments in the present as when thirty-six-year-old Howard shows off his new recording machine to Willy, calling him "kid," eventually telling him that he is fired. Caught as he is in the myth of the individual's climb toward success, Willy attempts to pass that same drive on to his own sons, but, as we know, his efforts are mostly in vain, as Biff in particular confronts his father's failings. In Vogel's play, despite Mae's glowing account of the past, we can never get too far away from the notion that the prostitutes' bodies are being bought and sold. Toward the end of the play, when Edna and Vera are the only two left, Edna reflects a glimmering of a new political consciousness when she talks about her sympathy with "union struggles for lettuce workers in California" (171), but it comes too late, for she vanishes shortly after, with the next blackout, leaving Vera alone on the bench, sole survivor of her profession, until the blackout that concludes the play. David Savran has argued that the women in *Salesman* are associated "with a dark and disruptive natural realm that must be subjugated and rigorously controlled" (36). By making the prostitutes' voices central, Vogel reverses the terms of that discourse.

While Drexler and Vogel create characters who live in a parallel universe with the Loman family, Donald Margulies provides a different take in his 1989 play *The Loman Family Picnic.* He gives us a family in Coney Island, Brooklyn, 1965, living lives that bear remarkable resemblances to those of the Lomans; but he also makes *Salesman* into a book that Mitchell, the eleven-year-old son, has studied in school and has now decided to rewrite as a musical.

The sets of identical picture windows in the neighboring apartment buildings that we see as Margulies' play opens suggest that the drama here is being replicated, in various forms, among other unseen families, all of whom have bought into the promise of prosperity and fulfillment that the era offered them. But the events of the play imply that by 1965 the pressures of Jewish assimilationism, the American dream, the Cold War and the legacy of the Holocaust have dramatically challenged the images of the American family that were already under stress in Miller's play. Indeed, the climactic moment is when Herbie, the father, tries to take the money that Stewie (the oldest son) has just received from friends and relatives for his bar mitzvah and use it to pay the bill for the event. "Why didn't you tell me I'd have to pay for my own bar mitzvah?!" Stewie wails (249), and the moment is both comic and heartbreaking.

Making the bar mitzvah central to the play is one of the ways in which Margulies unearths the "repressed" Jewish subtext of *Salesman,* which Miller rendered "universal" but which can clearly be read as a play about a Jewish family.[7] The family depicted in Margulies' play reflects, as does Tony Kushner's *Angels in America,* the generational distancing from Jewish tradition as Stewie, fed up with the rabbi's refusal to tell him what his *haftorah* passage means, agrees to go through the motions of his bar mitzvah, but vows that once it's over he'll never set foot in the synagogue again. Doris (the mother), whose immediate concern is that the post-ceremony party be a success, seems content with Stewie's agreement to go through with the ritual, but she is the character who reveals the greatest consciousness about what Jews in their position should and shouldn't do. She fears having her sons stand out too much, and the events of World War II provide her with a peculiar logic for this: "Look what happened to the Jews in Europe. Better you should have friends and be popular, than be showy and alone" (200). When Mitchell tells her that his teacher thinks he'll be bright enough to attend an Ivy League university, she responds, "City College was invented for people like us" (203), arguing that their relatives would "despise" them if they seemed to be exceeding their middle-class aspirations: "Dream, my son, but not too big" (203). Doris's description of their apartment building underscores the paradoxes of ethnic identification and assimilationism:

> I love our high-rise ghetto . . . Hanukkah looks like Kristallnacht here: a bonfire of orange-flame menorah bulbs burning in thousands of windows. A brick wall of electric flame! We're not alone. You know how good that feels? They moved us up, closer to heaven. Jews upon Jews who are glad to be here, who came as far as we did, from Flatbush, from Williamsburg, from East New York. Jews who escaped the Nazis, who escaped their relatives, who fled the schvartzes. Millions of miles of wall-to-wall carpeting that, if placed end to end, would reach us from here to Jupiter and back. Instead of stoops they built us these little terraces. Sometimes I have to restrain myself from doing the cha-cha over the edge just to see what it would feel like going down. (217)

The jarring juxtapositions that Doris makes (high rise/ghetto, Hannukah/Kristallnacht, local/international "immigrants," escaping Nazis versus one's own relatives versus the participatory racism of fleeing African American neighborhoods) are so extreme as to be comic, but are not altogether unbelievable; through them, Margulies illustrates the mixture of self-abnegation and residual guilt and horror about the Holocaust that characterized the rise of secular Judaism in his parents' generation. The presence of these sentiments, so raw here, calls attention to their absence or displacement in Miller's play. In one of several surreal moments in *The Loman Family Picnic,* Doris even refers to their relatives who were killed during the Holocaust as if they have appeared as guests at Stewie's bar mitzvah: "[T]here's Grandma's Uncle Izzy. The one who died in the war . . . The one in the striped pajamas. *(Calls.)* Uncle Izzy! Go in to the smorgasbord! You must be starving!" (236). Like *Salesman, The Loman Family Picnic* is populated with ghosts from the past: but Margulies makes it explicit that at least some of these ghosts represent a specifically Jewish past that cannot be entirely laid to rest.

One of the ghosts that haunts Doris is her Aunt Marsha, who killed herself at twenty-three and who returns periodically to offer Doris advice; she provides a parallel to the visions that Willy has of his brother Ben in *Salesman*. Like Drexler, Margulies seems to be responding to Miller's sidelining of Linda's unhappiness by bringing the suffering of his "Linda" character to the center of the play. Here Doris is the classic housewife that Betty Friedan described in *The Feminine Mystique,* full of dreams (mostly about movie stars) but forced to play the "good" wife and mother: "I love my life I love my life I love my life" she repeats "through gritted teeth" (214). When we see her at the opening of the play, she is cutting her wedding dress to shreds. Later, she appears in it to go trick-or-treating with her sons, dressed as the bride of Frankenstein; her entrance in the torn-up gown echoes Mary Tyrone in O'Neill's *Long Day's Journey into Night,* another family play about repression and miscommunication that is clearly an additional intertext for Margulies. Doris's escapes into fantasy (the ghosts, the movie stars) show that she, like her son Mitchell, seeks refuge in the world of the imagination (recall Sammy's closing words about Linda in *Room 17C*); at the end of the play, she acts out various scenarios in which she announces to Herbie that she is leaving him, but the play concludes with her serving him his tuna plate as usual, followed by her tight-lipped "Don't" as Herbie starts to apologize for attacking Stewie for the bar mitzvah money echoed by "silence" (264). Margulies thus gives us a glimpse into the cost of the repression that his Linda-equivalent suffers, but implies that her appropriate role has been so deeply ingrained that she is unable to make the transition from imagining alternative scripts to playing them out in her real interactions with her husband.

Herbie's alienation from his family is even more explicit in *The Loman Family Picnic* than Willy's is in *Salesman*. When we see him arrive home at the end of a long day of work, his family doesn't even wake up to greet him, so he speaks "facetiously" to the sleeping family members about his role as provider (206–7). His excitement at having met a man in his store (Herbie sells lighting fixtures) who wants him to manage his showrooms in New Mexico is deflated by Doris's flat-out rejection of the idea: "There are no Jewish people in New Mexico" (227). Strikingly, Herbie's final explosion in the play comes from his frustration at feeling that he has nothing of his own: "THIS IS ME?! THIS IS MY LIFE! THIS DRAWER IS MY WHOLE LIFE, RIGHT HERE; THIS DRAWER!" (252). Herbie's anger is right there on the surface; his broadly drawn character—insofar as it becomes nearly comical or parodic—evokes less empathy than Willy, yet one could also say that Herbie, too, reveals the despair in attempting to perform the role of the "good" husband/father/salesman and failing at each role in some crucial way.[8]

Margulies' portrayal of Herbie's relationship with his sons provides some telling parallels to Miller's depiction of the Willy/Biff/Happy relationships. At one point Herbie suggests to Mitchell that they go outside and throw a football; when Mitchell responds incredulously that they have never done that before, Herbie is quick to assure Mitchell that he was only joking, making it impossible for us (or Mitchell) to know what impulse was behind his initial suggestion. Here, as in the climactic moment when Herbie tries to take Stewie's bar mitzvah money, the jealousy and loss buried in Willy's behavior with his sons is made manifest in Herbie's interactions with his; Doris's disavowal of this feeling at the beginning of the play makes it clear that Herbie is torn between wanting his sons to succeed and resenting his own inability to experience the promise they embody. In a scene that recalls *Salesman,* Mitchell and Stewie in their bedroom hear Herbie talking to himself; here Mitchell seems to be worried about his father, but Stewie is annoyed that Mitchell has awakened him yet again to tell him what their father is doing. As in *Salesman,* we see a keen sense of loss and despair at a father's unreachability; the key shift, though, is that Margulies has Herbie address his monologues in this sequence explicitly "to us" (221–23). While Willy is lost inside his own mind and enacts microdramas (with Ben, for example—we recall that Miller's original title for the play was *The Inside of His Head*),[9] Margulies has Herbie—as well as the other characters—acknowledge our presence, a gesture that both limits our psychological absorption in the characters and creates a kind of complicity with them.

The most important turns to the audience come at the moments when Mitchell, in an effort to deal with the unhappiness of his family life, tells us about the musical version of *Death of a Salesman* that he has started writing after reading the play in school; it is in these moments that Miller's work as an intertext becomes most explicit but also most hilariously poignant in Mitchell's fascinating (mis)readings. He explains to us that when Miss Schoenberg, his teacher, assigned them the play, he read it three times because he was so struck by the "similarities" with his own family—"Except Willy Loman, the guy in the play?, the salesman?, doesn't sell lighting fixtures" (213). He says that he tried to bring up the point in class that if Willy committed suicide, his family wouldn't have been able to collect the insurance money, but that "Miss Schoenberg said not necessarily" (213). Mitchell's concern here is to make the play real, as he also talks about how Arthur Miller and his family lived on almost the same spot as he (working thus on the assumption that Miller, too, must have been writing about his own family). Mitchell's transformative creative act is to replace the expected oral book report on *Salesman* with "something else, something different":

> So, I'm writing this musical-comedy version of *Death of a Salesman* called *Willy!* With an exclamation point. You know, like *Fiorello!? Oklahoma!? Oliver!?* So far I've come up with a couple of songs. Like, when Biff and Happy are up in their room and they hear Willy downstairs talking to himself?, they sing this song called "Dad's a Little Weird" which goes: *(Sings)* "Dad's a little weird, he's in a daze. Could it be he's going nuts, or is it just a phase?" *(beat)* Well, it's a start. What do you think? (214)

Even now, when noncomic musical adaptations are more common (cf. the Broadway musical version of James Joyce's *The Dead* by Richard Nelson), Mitchell's decision is comic because of his innocence about the crossing of genres. He loves musicals: at one point, he is singing along with the record of *The Pajama Game* and "knows every word by heart" (223). While on some level Mitchell recognizes the similarity of the Loman family tragedy to his own, he desperately wants to rewrite Miller's play in the hope that reshaping its vision will, in turn, allow him to revise his own family life. He plans on adding a picnic scene, set in Prospect Park:

> Everybody's young and happy. Biff's wearing his varsity T-shirt and he and Happy are tossing around the football, and Linda's setting the picnic table with laminated paper plates and potato salad and coleslaw, and Willy's at the barbecue in a "Kiss the Cook" apron, flipping the franks. He's got the day off for a change, and he sings something like "Oh What a Beautiful Morning," only that's already been done, but you know what I mean. "What a Picnic!", something like that. And Willy's dead brother Ben is there, and Charley and Bernard from next door. Even the woman from Boston is there, disguised as a park attendant and laughing all the time. *(A beat.)* They're all happy . . . Yeah, and the whole family sings in harmony, really beautiful, like on the *Sound of Music* record when they sing "How do you solve a problem like Maria?" *(A beat.)* You know, this picnic idea I really like. I love picnics. *(A beat.)* We never go on any picnics. (230–31)

Of course, in *Salesman* the idealized family is a false vision of the past. Mitchell's picnic scene would make his own family fit the images of joy, togetherness and spontaneity that have been conveyed to him via television and via Rodgers and Hammerstein musicals (he is also therefore misreading even these musicals themselves, which also have their disturbing sides, such as the Nazi threat in *The Sound of Music*).

Just at the height of Mitchell's own family turmoil—immediately after Herbie fights Stewie for the bar mitzvah money and then expresses outrage over having nothing to call his own—Mitchell steps forward to sing a song from his picnic scene. This time he is accompanied by actual music, and the other members of his family (Stewie, then Doris and Herbie, and eventually even Marsha) step in to take their roles. In other words, at this point Margulies merges Mitchell's fantasy text with the play-in-progress, at least for this one scene, thus underscoring both the power of Mitchell's imaginative world and its painfully ludicrous differences from (and resemblances to) both Miller's play and the events of the family drama we see enacted. The pastoral picnic scene that Mitchell had initially described turns into something more: Mitchell and Stewie sing a duet (accompanied by a soft-shoe) about their father losing his mind and Doris sings Mitchell's version of Miller's "attention must be paid" speech: "Attention! / Attention! / You must pay attention / To such a man as your dad" (255). When Herbie enters, his song-and-dance number begins with his bragging about his success at work that day, but his "routine becomes more and more frantic" as he sings:

You shoulda seen me
Faking and lying,
Shpieling and dealing,
Nobody buying.
Schmoozing and losing,
Never stopped trying.
Fretting and slipping
And sweating and schlepping
and yelling and crying
But knowing I'm dying.

(257–58)

Doris comforts him with lyrics about putting his feet in her hands; the family rejoins in a chorus, sung "with great urgency" (258) about the picnic, but they disperse to the sound of thunder, as Mitchell, alone on stage, sings, "It was a perfect day / For a picnic, / Till the clouds made the sky turn dark," adding, "There'll be another day / We'll have our chance to play" (259). The sequence suggests that Mitchell has "paid attention" to the tragic elements of Miller's play as they slip into his musical, just as the troubled dynamic within his own family impinges on the creative re-vision he attempts to stage. The increasingly "frantic" and "urgent" quality of the singing and dancing reflect Mitchell's longing for the transcendence that the musical genre promises him, yet what emerges instead marks the same loss of innocence that characterizes the experiences of Biff and Happy in *Salesman* as they realize that the childhood dream of the seamless, carefree family is only an illusion. Mitchell's recourse is to translate into his work of art the largely futile attempts to sustain that illusion.

Like the character of Mitchell, the three playwrights I have discussed grapple with the appeal and power of *Salesman* as a dramatic text at the same time that they show the desire to incorporate it into new visions. In Drexler's and Margulies' plays, Linda's barely submerged feelings of loss and strength are foregrounded, while in all three works Willy's presence becomes more powerful in its effects on other characters as his physical time on stage is minimized. The Boston woman or her surrogate is cast in a more sympathetic light while, strikingly, the sons are rendered more cynically but remain, like Biff and Happy, bewildered inheritors of their parents' legacy. Dynamics of gender and ethnicity and their larger relation to issues of capitalism, of "selling," all of which underlie the interactions of Miller's characters, are brought boldly to the surface in these three plays. In the plays' metadramatic moments these playwrights show themselves aware of the challenges posed by a response to a canonical theater work. Their gift is the ability to make its familiarity strange and yet to nurture the seeds that Willy planted at the end of *Salesman* into new and intricate creations.

Notes

1. Some critics have confused their abhorrence for Linda's unquestioning support of Willy with a disdain for her character. Dennis Welland writes that "Linda is just too good for Willy and thus too good for the play" ("*Death of a Salesman,*" in *Twentieth Century Interpretations of* Death of a Salesman, ed. Helene Wickham Koon [Englewood Cliffs, N.J.: Prentice Hall, 1983], 29), while Brian Parker reviles the "essential stupidity of Linda's behavior" ("Point of View in Arthur Miller's *Death of a Salesman,* in Koon, 54). In his discussion of the treatment of women in Miller's plays, C. W. E. Bigsby points out their tendency to be portrayed as "conservative forces" (146) and suggests that Linda's "culpability lies in her acquiescence" (182). See *A Critical Introduction to Twentieth-Century American Drama,* vol. 2 (Cambridge: Cambridge University Press, 1984). Even Miller, describing the attempts to cast Linda for the first Broadway production, wrote that they "needed a woman who looked as though she had lived in a house dress all her life, even somewhat coarse and certainly less than brilliant" ("The American Theater," in *The Theater Essays of Arthur Miller,* ed. Robert A. Martin [New York: Viking, 1978], 46). He later described Elia

Kazan as shaping Mildred Dunnock's performance, though, to create a Linda filled with "outrage and protest rather than self-pity and mere perplexity" (*Timebends: A Life* [New York: Grove, 1987], 189).

2. Many commentators have discussed the connections between *Death of a Salesman* and *Glengarry Glen Ross.* See, for example, Richard Brucher, "Pernicious Nostalgia in *Glengarry Glen Ross,*" in *David Mamet's* "Glegarry Glen Ross": *Text and Performance,* ed. Leslie Kane (New York: Garland, 1996, rpt. 2000), 211–25; David Richards, "Lives of the Salesmen: From Miller and Mamet Lessons for the Stage," *Washington Post,* May 29, 1984, H1; Ruby Cohn, "Oh God I Hate This Job," in *Approaches to Teaching Miller's* Death of a Salesman, ed. Matthew C. Roudané (New York: MLA, 1995), 155–62.

3. Drexler also takes on Kafka in her play *Occupational Hazard* (1988; rev. 1992), an adaptation of his story "A Hunger Artist"; the play is included in Rosette Lamont, ed., *Women on the Verge* (New York: Applause, 1993), 1–44.

4. For a discussion of the Boston woman and the women in the bar in *Salesman* as objects, see Janet Balakian, "Beyond the Male Locker Room: *Salesman* from a Feminist Perspective," in Roudané, *Approaches to Teaching,* 117.

5. Miller wrote that he later regretted that "the self-realization of the older son, Biff, is not a weightier counterbalance to Willy's disaster in the audience's mind" ("The Salesman Has a Birthday," in *Theater Essays,* 14).

6. See Linda Kintz's discussion of the relation of Willy's plight to the white man's fall from the middle class in late 1940s urban America ("The Sociosymbolic Work of Family in *Death of a Salesman,*" in Roudané, *Approaches to Teaching,* 108–10, esp. 110).

7. Several critics have discussed Salesman as a "Jewish" play. See, for example, Dan Vogel, "From Milkman to *Salesman:* Glimpses of the Galut," *Studies in American Jewish Literature* 10 (fall 1991): 172–78. Bigsby points out that the salesman in "In Memoriam," the short story that Miller wrote at seventeen that later inspired *Salesman,* is Jewish (173). Welland, on the other hand, defends the idea of making Willy "ethnically neutral" (30), an argument now difficult to buy if we consider that whiteness is never "neutral" and that any performance or even any dramatic text bears markers of ethnicity.

8. Miller writes in *Timebends,* regarding the salesmen he knew as a child, that "these men lived like artists, like actors whose product is first of all themselves, forever imagining triumphs in a world that either ignores them or denies their presence altogether" (127).

9. See Miller, "Introduction to the Collected Plays," in *Theater Essays,* 135.

Works Cited

Bigsby, C. W. E. *A Critical Introduction to Twentieth-Century Drama.* Vol. 2. Cambridge: Cambridge University Press, 1984.

Brecht, Bertolt. *The Threepenny Opera.* Trans. Desmond Vesey, lyrics by Eric Bentley. New York: Grove, 1964.

Drexler, Rosalyn. *Room 17C. Transients Welcome.* New York: Broadway Play Publishing, 1984. 1–20.

Kane, Leslie, ed. *David Mamet's* Glengarry Glen Ross: *Text and Performance.* New York: Garland, 1996, rpt. 2000.

Koon, Helene Wickham, ed. *Twentieth Century Interpretations of* Death of a Salesman. Englewood Cliffs, N.J.: Prentice Hall, 1983.

Kushner, Tony. *Angels in America, Part One: Millennium Approaches* and *Part Two: Perestroika.* New York: TCG, 1993, 1994.

Lamont, Rosette, ed. *Women on the Verge: Seven Avant Garde Plays.* New York: Applause, 1993.

Margulies, Donald. *The Loman Family Picnic. Sight Unseen and Other Plays.* New York: TCG, 1995. 197–264.

Mamet, David. *Glengarry Glen Ross.* New York: Grove, 1983.

Miller, Arthur. *Death of a Salesman.* New York: Viking, 1949.

———. *Salesman in Beijing.* New York: Viking, 1984.

———. *The Theater Essays of Arthur Miller.* Ed. Robert A. Martin. New York: Viking, 1978.

———. *Timebends: A Life.* New York: Grove, 1987.

O'Neill, Eugene. *Long Day's Journey into Night.* New Haven: Yale University Press, 1989.

Roudané, Matthew, ed. *Approaches to Teaching* Death of a Salesman. New York: MLA, 1995.

Savran, David. *Communists Cowboys and Queers: The Politics of Masculinity in the Work of Arthur Miller and Tennessee Williams.* Minneapolis: University of Minnesota Press, 1992.

Shepard, Sam. *Curse of the Starving Class. Seven Plays.* New York: Bantam, 1984.

Vogel, Dan. "From Milkman to *Salesman:* Glimpses of the Galut." *Studies in American Jewish Literature* 10 (fall 1991): 172–78.

Vogel, Paula. *The Oldest Profession. The Baltimore Waltz and Other Plays.* New York: TCG, 1996. 127–72.

Wilson, August. *Fences.* New York: New American Library, 1986.

Elinor Fuchs

Theorizing *Salesman*

In a major reorganization of the courses offered at the Yale School of Drama, a one-term seminar previously required only for students in the Department of Dramaturgy and Dramatic Criticism, "Issues in Dramatic and Theatrical Theory," was made part of a new core curriculum of three year-long courses required for all dramaturgs, directors and playwrights. As the teacher of dramatic theory at Yale, I suddenly found myself with three times as many students, and sixteen extra weeks of classes to plan.

We were already into the second term before I hit upon a strategy to teach what I was calling "Theorytheory," a playful term that at least suggested the metatheoretical nature of the undertaking. Six weeks were blocked out for this project at the end of the term. The problem was not what to teach, but how to make the teaching active enough to engage theater practitioners. I approached five of our more theory-oriented dramaturgs with an invitation. Each of them would become responsible for "curating" one of the five remaining weeks. Under their direction, we would break the class up into five groups consisting of members of all three class disciplines: directing, playwriting and dramaturgy. These groups in turn would teach their assigned material to the class as a whole, and write and perform a scene or scenes based on *Death of a Salesman*.

Our weeks would be divided in the following manner. In the introductory session, I would explain how the "classic" theory of Marx, Freud and Saussure fed into the recombinations and critiques of the poststructuralist generation of theorists, who in turn fed into more recent adaptations worked by theater and performance theorists. Five weeks would follow on basic feminist theory, gender as performance, race-based theory, queer theory and postcolonial theory. Each group would meet at least twice with its curator before its appointed week to discuss the material and plan and rehearse the brief performance intended to put the week's theoretical readings "on their feet."

The group was enthusiastic about basing the class scenes on *Death of a Salesman,* a play so familiar that students might think they had little more to learn from or through it. This idea appealed to me as well. Just because of its familiarity, I had often opened my graduate course in dramatic structure with an examination of the play's formal patterns. Thinking they knew all there is to know about *Death of a Salesman,* the students were surprised to discover the precision and elegance of its design. It was possible that *Salesman* might offer as much to students applying theoretical ideas as to students using tools of structural analysis.

The account that follows is culled from the five final project reports written by the student curators.

Basic Feminist Theory

The readings for this week laid out the distinctions among three fundamental branches of feminist thinking: liberal (advocating political and economic equality with men), cultural (based on a belief in innately and universally different male and female "cultures") and materialist (focussing on class, racial and other differences among women as well as men). Its student curator was Erika Rundle, a first-year dramaturg who majored in semiotics and theater at Brown University, and earned an M.A. in communication and rhetoric at Rensselaer Polytechnic.

> *Rundle:* My group consisted of five students who had varying degrees of familiarity with feminist theory. The women in my group enthusiastically welcomed the introduction of this material into a course on dramatic theory. The men, less familiar with the material, were not hostile to feminist theory, but approached the performance more as an assignment than as something that could affect their work as theater artists.
>
> We chose a scene from *Death of a Salesman* that showed Linda Loman's subjugation within the patriarchal family structure, and decided to reenvision that scene according to the tenets of liberal, cultural and materialist feminism. We thought that the differences among these types of feminism were important points that needed to be explored in class, and agreed that presenting three variations on one scene from the play could facilitate discussion of different approaches to feminist thought.
>
> The group decided to deconstruct the scene (abbreviated here, but not in class), that occurs near the end of act 1, in which Linda's voice is repeatedly silenced by Willy.[1]

Willy: Go back to the West! Be a carpenter, a cowboy, enjoy yourself!
Linda: Willy, he was just saying—

Willy: I heard what he said!

Happy, trying to quiet Willy: Hey, Pop, come on now . . .

Linda: Willy, dear, he just decided . . .

Willy, to Biff: If you get tired hanging around tomorrow, paint the ceiling I put up in the living-room.

Biff: I'm leaving early tomorrow.

Happy: He's going to see Bill Oliver, Pop.

Willy, interestedly: Oliver? For what?

Biff, with reserve, but trying, trying: He always said he'd stake me. I'd like to go into business, so maybe I can take him up on it.

Linda: Isn't that wonderful?

Willy: Don't interrupt. What's wonderful about it? There's fifty men in the City of New York who'd stake him. *To Biff:* Sporting goods?

Biff: I guess so. I know something about it and—

Willy: He knows something about it! You know sporting goods better than Spalding, for God's sake! How much is he giving you? . . . .

Linda: Maybe things are beginning to—

Willy, wildly enthused, to Linda: Stop interrupting! *To Biff:* But don't wear sport jacket and slacks when you see Oliver.

Biff: No, I'll—

Willy: A business suit, and talk as little as possible, and don't crack any jokes.

Biff: He did like me. Always liked me.

Linda: He loved you!

Willy, to Linda: Will you stop! *To Biff:* Walk in very serious. You are not applying for a boy's job. Money is to pass. Be quiet, fine, and serious. Everybody likes a kidder, but nobody lends him money . . . .

Linda: Oliver always thought the highest of him—

Willy: Will you let me talk?

Rundle: The playwright in the group volunteered to write the liberal feminist scene, but admitted that he was hesitant to change Miller's text. He did not want to make fun of Miller, and was afraid that rewriting the scene would be disrespectful. The rest of the group immediately responded that deconstructing the text was part of the project of postmodern theory. Our performance was not intended as lack of respect for Miller, but to bring to light other choices for the main female character in the play, thereby pointing out her predicament and allowing us to comment on it.

One of the directors pointed out that in 1949 Miller's text could have been considered radical. She believed the play constituted a full-blown attack on capitalism and the American dream at a time when those ideologies were considered sacred. We began to look at other scenes in the play where female characters were present. In each of these scenes, women were subjected to male power. Miller, we decided, was consciously dramatizing women's oppression on stage in order to critique it. We considered the possibility that Miller had actually written a feminist play.

The two female directors decided to tackle the cultural feminist approach together. The other dramaturg and I were left to work on the materialist feminism scene. We decided to take a Brechtian approach, giving each character a monologue that would be addressed directly to the audience, breaking through traditional narrative structure. Each character would begin with the first words spoken in Miller's original scene, using that line as a start for deconstructing their characters. We imagined the male characters' monologues to be both revealing and funny, almost Woody Allen–like, while Linda's would be rather dark, but ultimately more liberating. They would proceed to analyze their characters in light of the societal strictures and expectations placed upon them.

The "liberal feminist" scene that developed from these discussions was conceived as a sequel to the original scene. In it, Linda finally confronts Willy about being constantly silenced. Willy's apology does not satisfy her, and she persists. "I want to be treated as I treat you. I don't want you to call me down from our room to fill up your milk glass . . . I want *you* to ask *me* if you can get me anything. I want *you* to soothe *my* headaches once in a while. I want to get a job to help out with our finances." Shaken, Willy tells Linda that she is his foundation and support. Linda responds as a modern-day Nora coming into a new understanding of marriage. "That's fine, Willy. But who's mine?"

Rundle: The authors of the cultural feminist scene inserted the words "I'm sorry" after every line the men spoke. The idea was that Linda would start the scene as "Miller's Linda," and by the end be transformed into a cultural feminist who could control the men in her family by uttering the very words that had previously relegated her to virtual silence. The group was enthusiastic about this idea because we thought it was subversive theatrically as well as politically. We were aware that it would require real acting and strong directing choices to work.

Although we were excited by its potential, the scene's rehearsal process was fraught with confusion and disagreement about how Linda's inner realization of her inherent power could be physically and characterologically manifested. We decided that we needed to locate the particular moment in the text when Linda would realize the "rule" to which she had been conditioned and turn it on its head for her own benefit. This moment had to be clear, and the "I'm sorrys" that followed it had to be acted in such a way that the audience would be able to divine the hidden rule as well. This was an ambitious agenda, and much less of it was realized in performance than we had hoped.

The four monologues written for the play's central figures directly incorporated references to feminist theory. Here, in part, is Linda's, written by Rundle:

Linda: Willy killed himself today. I couldn't cry. I was torn between sorrow and liberation into a strange kind of silence. Yes of course I had been silenced by Willy my whole life, but I realized when he died that he had been silenced as well—and that we were, all of us, Willy, Happy, Biff, and I, silenced by an insidious ideology that we lived and suffered under like an invisible iron claw.

Patriarchy and capitalism seemed natural to us; there was a right way to do things if you wanted to get on in the world and be someone. Why, it wouldn't even have occurred to us then that we could name these things, they were so much a part of us, and we a part of them. But we were, in fact, their agents. Myself perhaps one of the most ardent. These ideologies shaped us all—in fact created the whole idea of what it means to be a family—and prescribed all our roles within it according to an economy that was ultimately tragic. We merely acted out our roles, not knowing we were always being directed—by a master narrative of progress, hard work and femininity that kept me in the kitchen, nourishing a monster; by Elia Kazan and a male-dominated theater structure of playwrights, designers, producers, agents; by a bourgeois Broadway audience with ingrained ideas about acceptable forms of female rage.

Because I was a white, lower-middle-class, post–World War II suburban housewife, I believed in the American dream. But I see now that all of us together held up a kind of false consciousness about how happiness could be gained in a system that was built only to tear us down, to buy and sell our souls and convince us that success meant getting the highest price we could for them. Well, Willy did pay, in the end. He was worth about twenty thousand dollars.

I am free of Willy now—the Law of the Father if you want to get technical about it. I own my own home now. My plan is to sell off what all our painful labor bought us—to a corporate developer, and at a profit. They've been itching to build another high-rise apartment building on our land in Brooklyn. I'm leaving the city and going somewhere where I'll have room to think, a room of my own, where I can dig beneath all the lies and dreams we lived by and make a map for myself, a map for rereading. I am choosing to think and to live, this time, with all my intelligence, and with vigilance.

Gender as Performance

Amy Strahler, also a first-year dramaturg, and perhaps not by coincidence also a Brown graduate (Brown is known for its strong emphasis on theory), with experience as a dramaturg for Center Stage in Baltimore, worked with Rundle in refining the choice of readings for both of these first two weeks. Her week focused on the materialist position that gender is socially constructed performance, including the assertion that "woman" as a set of "real" attributes and qualities does not exist.

Strahler: As it turned out, my group consisted of four men—two directors, one dramaturg, and one playwright. I was not daunted by the absence of women in the group until I received a call from one of the members. He was extremely angry that we were using *Death of a Salesman* as the text for our deconstruction, feeling that it was sacred to American drama and should not be tampered with. He also felt that the idea of relating any of the theories we were planning to study to any aspect of theater was a waste of time.

I tried to explain my own evolution into and away from postmodern theory—how I studied it at length as an undergraduate and eventually moved away from it, feeling unsure about the results of applying such theory to performance. I told him I too had questions about the effectiveness of feminist theory in the theater, but that I still felt it was important to be aware of the ideas it developed. He seemed a bit less reluctant. Of the three others, one was also coming at this theory for the first time, and two had been exposed to it as undergraduates.

At our first meeting, one of the directors brought props for our as yet unplanned performance: a children's makeup kit and a hand-held egg beater. He announced that these props were meant to signify "female" and "male" gender—the makeup kit identified with femininity and the egg beater being a phallic object. I was pleased that he had gone out of his way to bring these props, even if the manner in which he discussed them was oddly defensive, as though he were armoring himself against an attack for being male.

We discussed the theory at length. Though we didn't talk about *Death of a Salesman* that night, we left with a more grounded sense of the ideas we wanted to express in our performance: that gender is a performative act that we all engage in, that men and women are socially constructed in our culture to be "masculine" and "feminine," and that altering one's gender identity can be viewed as subversive, politically threatening and socially deviant.

At our second meeting, we laid out all our props on the table. We had an amazing array: a blow-up baseball bat, a sequined purse, a *Star Wars* action figure, a pair of silver high-heeled shoes. One of the directors suggested that we take a small section of text from *Death of a Salesman* and, without altering the language, repeat it over and over again, with all of us moving through the roles in a circular fashion. Like the onion in *Peer Gynt,* we would show the identities in the scene as layers of constructions that had no essential core, no ultimate identity. The props would be used as signifiers for masculine and feminine attributes, but this did not mean that we could only use the prop for its intended meaning. Rather, if we were playing a male character but were holding the makeup kit, we would have to use the kit in some way that made it "masculine." This device was intended to further the project of scrambling our assumed essential gender identities.

Searching through the play we landed on the scene where Happy picks up a girl while waiting for Willy in the restaurant. At Happy's urging, Stanley, the waiter, makes the contact:

Stanley, going to the girl's table: Would you like a menu, ma'am?
Girl: I'm expecting someone, but I'd like a—
Happy: Why don't you bring her—excuse me miss, do you mind? I sell champagne, and I'd like you to try my brand. Bring her a champagne, Stanley.
Girl: That's awfully nice of you.
Happy: Don't mention it. It's all company money. *He laughs.*
Girl: That's a charming product to be selling, isn't it?
Happy: Oh, gets to be like everything else. Selling is selling, y'know.
Girl: I suppose.
Happy: You don't happen to sell, do you?
Girl: No, I don't sell.
Happy: Would you object to a compliment from a stranger? You ought to be on a magazine cover.
Girl, looking at him a little archly: I have been.
Stanley comes in with a glass of champagne.
Happy: What'd I say before, Stanley? You see? She's a cover girl. (94)

Strahler: Using this text over and over again, we each stepped in on a rotating basis for Happy and the girl. We cut Stanley, whose line was spoken by the entire group, as were the stage directions. We played with gender in a Brechtian fashion, exposing the gender acts that each of us had to perform in order to become the character. Each time the scene began, it was bigger and more grotesque than the time before. When we had cycled through ten times, with each of us playing both characters at least once, we stopped. By then, the scene had grown into a rape scene, with

> Happy completely dominating the girl physically, even though the actors playing the roles at that point were both male. For an attempt at a kind of alienation effect, we performed the scene one more time after that, but this time we played it absolutely "straight." I stepped in as the girl and one of the directors played Happy. Another played Stanley. It was almost impossible to accept the scene as "realistic" after this explosion of the text.
>
> Once we had gotten a scene down that we knew would illustrate our ideas, we were much more confident about the whole task. Even those members who had originally wanted to bail out admitted that they were looking forward to showing the performance in class. I do not think this project would have been successful without incorporating the theory into an actual piece of theater.

The class found the changes made on the short *Death of a Salesman* scene increasingly disturbing. What was most remarkable was the "straight" reprise of the scene as the conclusion to the ten variations. The realistic behavior seemed to be simply one more variation in a range of performance styles. The group successfully demonstrated its theme, that "natural" gender behavior could be seen as constructed and rehearsed as any other.

Race Theories

The third and fifth weeks of our project were curated by two second-year dramaturgs: Rebecca Rugg, who had earned undergraduate and graduate degrees from Cornell and the University of California at Riverside, and had had a wide previous exposure to contemporary political theory; and Christiane Salomon, who came to Yale from Brazil with an M.A. from the University of São Paulo in comparative literature and literary theory.

The students created two scenes for this class, one in the form of a trial, focusing on the ethnicity of the Lomans' intellectual young neighbor Bernard, that explored the issue of the unstated (but universalized) Jewishness of the play's Brooklyn world. As this is a familiar theme in *Death of a Salesman* criticism, we decided to focus on the second scene.

> *Rugg* and *Salomon:* Our main concern, as we began to plan the class, was that we were all white people basking within safe Ivy League walls. While considering our seeming distance from race theory, we realized that our formulation cast whiteness in a position of neutrality. But in fact race theory should be of importance to everyone in the class, because we all not only "have" race already, but attend graduate school in a racially polarized

city and culture. We decided that our primary task was to stir a certain awareness of our own racial identities in context.

In trying to bring the issue of race to the Lomans, we came upon the same point—the Lomans, too, already have race, but don't "know" it. The issue became how to render whiteness visible, how to move it away from a position of neutrality. Then we remembered that growing urbanization is a key element within the play. We decided to use a scene in act 1, where Willy and Linda discuss the development of the ugly apartment buildings around their formerly nice backyard.

Willy: Why don't you open a window in here, for God's sake?

Linda, with infinite patience: They're all open, dear.

Willy: The way they boxed us in here. Bricks and windows, windows and bricks.

Linda: We should've bought the land next door.

Willy: The street is lined with cars. There's not a breath of fresh air in the neighborhood. The grass don't grow any more, you can't raise a carrot in the back yard. They should've had a law against apartment houses. Remember those two beautiful elm trees out there? When I and Biff hung the swing between them?

Linda: Yeah, like being a million miles from the city.

Willy: They should have arrested the builder for cutting those down. They massacred the neighborhood. *Lost.* More and more I think of those days, Linda. This time of year it was lilac and wisteria. . . . There's more people! That's what's ruining the country. Population is getting out of control! Smell the stink from that apartment house! And another one on the other side. (11)

The curators noted that in the past they had always been on the side of the beleaguered Lomans when reading this "urban blight" scene. They saw they could "turn this scene around," and expose the new urban landscape as in fact the growth of a racially diverse community. Miller himself gives the hint to this reading with Linda's line, "Well, after all, people had to move somewhere." This short scene excited great interest in the class, increased by the imaginative way the classroom itself was used. Our room was on the first floor of the Drama School "Annex" building, one of Yale's oldest, with leaded casement windows giving onto an unsightly back alley. As a native of Brazil, Christiane spoke Portuguese. Another dramaturg in the group, Allison, had majored in Russian in college. The group decided that these two women would in effect represent the scene's unrepresented, the "out-of-control" population that had surged into the neighborhood.

As the actors playing Willy and Linda sat on the bench beneath the casement windows discussing the neighborhood's decline, Christiane and Allison left the classroom and stationed themselves in the alley beneath the windows. The scene was played without change, but noisily interrupted:

> *Willy:* Why don't you open a window in here, for God's sake?
> *Linda, with infinite patience:* They're all open, dear.
> *Willy:* The way they boxed us in here. Bricks and windows, windows and bricks.
> *The neighbors start a fight.*
> *Neighbor 1:* What the fuck is going on?
> *Neighbor 2:* Cala a boca sua imbecil. Se você não entende minha linguaga o problema é todo seu. Sua filha da puta. Só fica aqui me enchendo o saco.
> *Boombox is turned on.*
> *Neighbor 3 explodes in Russian.*
> *The sound of rap music gradually starts to take over their discussion.*
> *Neighbor 2:* Já te falei pra calar essa boca. Vai dar pra quem te come. Sai daqui, sai, sua idiota.
> *Linda:* We should've bought the land next door.

This experiment in alienation nicely modeled ways in which the somewhat abstract readings of the week could be brought to bear on the practice of theater. It revealed the class's "normative" identification with the Lomans' sense of loss, and complicated the play's—or at least the audience's—undertow of nostalgia.

Queer Theory

The fourth "Theorytheory" week was dedicated to the branch of theory that even our initial planning group found difficult to define. Two of our most experienced curators disagreed on the extent to which "gay" and "queer" overlapped. The curator for this week was a second-year dramaturg, Cynthia Brizzell, who had made the unusual move of leaving NYU's theory-intensive graduate program in performance studies after earning her M.A. to work more directly in theater at Yale.

> *Brizzell:* My group, all of whom identified as "straight," did not have much prior exposure to queer theory, so my first goal was to help them find a meaningful point of access into this work. The group kept asking for a simple, clear definition from which we could work. This was more difficult than I thought, because to me the whole point of "queer" is that it defies

simple, clear definitions. I tried to help them to experience Sedgwick's postulation that queerness is a self-defining act and that one could, for example, engage in queer identity without engaging in homosexual acts. But what identity does queer hold when it is not also, in some part, also a homosexual identity? We did finally agree that queer theory questions the very idea of master narratives, but narrowing beyond that point was impossible.

In our next meetings we engaged the Miller text exclusively. We didn't want just to make either of the brothers gay; we were sure that our classmates would find that too easy. We also didn't want to equate gay and queer quite so simply. We were amazed at how easily Biff could be read as "queer" with only slight shifts in emphasis and framing. And in the end, we felt that we had found another way of understanding Miller's text without actually subverting it because the character of Biff is already one who questions master narratives.

As in the other scenes, the "queer" group found provocative passages in *Death of a Salesman* that were deepened and made more complex when read through and against the theoretical texts. The group picked several of these relating to Biff, editing them so as to highlight the "queerness." Their performance relied on a knowledge of the theory as developed in the classroom work, and on a chorus of critical statements that they occasionally interleaved into the Miller text.

Chorus 1: If the continuum—
Chorus 2: of sexual orientation—
Chorus 3: is a blur—
Chorus 4: how do we know—
Chorus 5: when we've reached a certain point?
Willy: Like a young god. Hercules. And the sun, the sun all around him. Remember how he waved to me? Right up from the field, with the representatives of three colleges standing by? And the buyers I brought, and the cheers when he came out.
All: Loman, Loman, Loman!
Willy: God Almighty, he'll be great yet. A star like that, magnificent, can never really fade away! (62)
Chorus: Biff is two years older than his brother Happy, well built, but in these days bears a worn air and seems less self-assured. He has succeeded less, and his dreams are stronger and less acceptable than Happy's. (13)
Happy: . . . I think I got less bashful and you got more so. What happened, Biff? Where's the old humor, the old confidence? . . .
Biff: Why does Dad mock me all the time? . . .
Happy: I think the fact that you're not settled, that you're still kind of up in the air . . .

Biff: I tell ya, Hap, I don't know what the future is. I don't know—what I'm supposed to want. (15)

Chorus: We might think of queer theory as the project of elaborating, in ways that cannot be predicted in advance, this question: What do queers want?[2]

Biff: Dad. I flunked math . . . See, the reason Birnbaum hates me, Pop—one day he was late for class so I got up at the blackboard and imitated him. I crossed eyes and talked with a lithp.

Willy, laughing: You did? The kids like it?

Biff: They nearly died laughing!

Willy: Yeah? What'd you do?

Biff: The thquare root of thixty twee is . . . (111)

Willy bursts out laughing; Biff joins him.

Chorus: A homosexual panic defense for a person (typically a man) accused of antigay violence, implies that his responsibility for the crime was diminished by a pathological psychological condition, perhaps brought on by an unwanted sexual advance from the man he attacked.[3]

All: Loman, Loman, Loman! . . .

Willy, with full accusation: You're trying to put a knife in me—don't think I don't know what you're doing!

Biff: All right phony! Then let's lay it on the line.

Willy, to Linda: You hear the spite!

Happy, coming down toward Biff: You cut it now!

Biff, to Happy: The man don't know who we are! The man is gonna know! *To Willy:* We never told the truth for ten minutes in this house! . . .

Happy: We always told the truth! . . .

Biff, To Willy: Now hear this, Willy, this is me.

Willy: I know you!

Chorus: What it takes—all it takes—to make the description "queer" a true one, is the impulsion to use it in the first person.[4]

Biff: No! Why am I trying to become what I don't want to be? Making a contemptuous, begging fool of myself, when all I want is out there, waiting for me the minute I say I know who I am! Why can't I say that, Willy? *He tries to make Willy face him, but Willy pulls away.*

Willy, with hatred, threateningly: The door of your life is wide open! . . .

Biff: Can't you understand that? There's no spite in it any more. I just am what I am, that's all. (123–26)

All: Loman, Loman, Loman! God Almighty, he'll be great yet. A star like that, magnificent, can never really fade away!

In identifying Biff as queer, but not decisively, or even necessarily gay, the group was opening up what Eve Kosofsky calls "the open mesh of possibilities, gaps, overlaps, dissonances and resonances, lapses and excesses of meaning" in the constitution of (sexual) identity.[5] It was a subtle and delicate undertaking, and Brizzell lamented that what the group presented seemed to them much rougher and less intellectually stimulating than what they had experienced in their discussion and envisioned for the class. All the curators had this perception about their scenes; I had begun to see that to have turned out otherwise was a structural impossibility.

Postcolonial Theory

Rugg and Salomon once more collaborated on this final week of the project. The entire class responded to postcolonial theory as particularly vital and relevant.

> *Rugg* and *Salomon:* It was easy to find the right scene in *Death of a Salesman:* Uncle Ben's journey to Africa seemed ready-made for our purposes. Coming up with a treatment for the scene was harder. The group was large, and all had strong opinions about the material and creative ideas about staging the scene.
>
> We wanted to avoid replicating a colonialist dynamic in our approach to our source texts, so we decided to place postcolonialism within an American context. We all heard an echo of the Columbus story in Uncle Ben's dazzling account of riches ripped from the land. We decided to organize the classroom into a "colonial" grade school seating arrangement—that is, a space conditioned by an uneven power structure—complete with an old-fashioned teacher to run things (a second-year directing student).

Teacher, reciting with class: In 1492, Columbus sailed the ocean blue.
Willy: That's funny. For a second there you reminded me of my brother Ben.
Ben: I have only a few minutes.
Charley: You never heard from him again, heh? Since that time?
Willy: Didn't Linda tell you? Couple of weeks ago we got a letter from his wife in Africa. He died.
Charley: That so.
Ben: So this is Brooklyn, eh?
Charley: Maybe you're in for some of his money.
Willy: Naa, he had seven sons. There's just one opportunity I had with that man . . .
Ben: I must make a train, William. There are several properties I'm looking at in Alaska.
Willy: Sure, sure! If I'd gone with him to Alaska that time, everything would've been totally different.
Teacher, reciting with class:

In Xanadu did Kubla Khan
A stately pleasure-dome decree:
Where Alph, the sacred river, ran
Through caverns measureless to man
Down to a sunless sea . . .

Charley: Go on, you'd froze to death up there.

Willy: What're you talking about?

Ben: Opportunity is tremendous in Alaska, William. Surprised you're not up there.

Willy: Ben! I've been waiting for you so long! What's the answer? How did you do it?

Ben: Oh, there's a story in that. I have many enterprises, William, and I have never kept books.

Teacher: Columbus was born in Genoa, Italy. The independent city-state of Genoa had a busy port.

Willy: I remember you walking away down some open road.

Ben: I was going to find Father in Alaska.

Teacher: Christopher concluded that the earth was 25 percent smaller than was previously thought, and composed mostly of land. On the basis of these faulty beliefs, he decided that Asia could be reached quickly by sailing west. Before an audience of uncomprehending islanders, Columbus claimed that by right of conquest, their island now belonged to Spain and renamed it San Salvador . . . believed by Columbus to be in Asian waters.

Ben: At that age I had a very faulty view of geography, William. I discovered after a few days that I was heading due south, so instead of Alaska, I ended up in Africa.

Teacher: Christopher Columbus sailed west across the Altantic Ocean in search of a route to Asia but achieved fame by making landfall in the Caribbean Sea.

Willy: Africa! The Gold Coast!

Ben: Principally diamond mines.

Willy: Diamond mines!

Ben: Yes, my dear. But I've only a few minutes—

Willy: No! Boys! Boys! Listen to this. This is your Uncle Ben, a great man! Tell my boys, Ben!

Ben: Why, boys, when I was seventeen I walked into the jungle, and when I was twenty-one I walked out. And by God I was rich.

Teacher: His stop at Puerto Rico was . . . the main foundation for the claim that Columbus "discovered America." In his logbook he wrote that he had found a "New World," unknown as yet to Europeans.

Willy: You see what I been talking about? The greatest things can happen! (38–42)

Intercutting the Miller scene with the Columbus story and Coleridge's "Kubla Khan" was intended to show how the colonizer's dominant position gives him control over the shaping of history, whether factual or imaginative. In connecting the Ben scenes to the Spanish conquistadores, the students did not see themselves as "radicalizing" Miller's text, but as bringing to the surface its historical roots and geopolitical implications. Like Columbus, Ben's single focus (as Willy imagines Ben) is the extraction of wealth; human interactions with those from whom he was attempting to wrest it would have been purely opportunistic. Similarly, Willy sacrificed his own better values to "success," and was in turn sacrificed to the same harsh law.

Conclusions

The results of these weeks of the "Theorytheory" project are not easily summarized. The students were both enthusiastic and resistant. Many of the readings were difficult, but at some level obvious. The actual exposure of the students to the theoretical material in the six-week unit was too relentless, but at the same time too meager. There was a surprising unanimity from the curators that the historical feminist theory categories now seem tired ("old news" wrote Strahler). Yet this response should be examined more closely, as it was also true that the gender-related categories made the students, and especially the men in the group, not just impatient but uneasy, as if the subject were too personal and volatile to be aired in a mixed-gender classroom.

As Brizzell wrote about queer theory, and about the theoretical project in general, "These theories opened my eyes in so many ways that I cannot imagine who I was before I studied them," yet she notes that for many of her colleagues the work "was like tasting medicine." She had confidence that the medicine would take, and that the students would be "better dramatists, and better people" for the experience. But Rugg wondered whether even if students had not read "high theory"—its revelations were not part of "everyday consciousness"—their impact diminished because they had already "seeped into popular culture." In any event, the overwhelmingly white and American-born student body entered most readily into discussion in those areas with which they associated themselves least, race and postcoloniality.

Our experiment represented an effort to teach "theory" actively, to enact it as we studied it, the only way that seemed possible in a conservatory setting. Each working group learned far more from its own exercise than the larger group was able to absorb. Intense small-group discussions did not lead to a high level of classroom discussion; the groups' hopes of replicating in the classroom their own levels of excitement in their working sessions were by and large disappointed. Rather, excitement was proportional to effort expended. The outpouring of effort made by each group almost guaranteed a certain passivity in the weeks when the students were not "on." Ironically, the very activity the planning sessions produced may have resulted in lessened activity in the classroom.

Beyond any questions about the structure and conception of the project, I find myself questioning the possibility of passing on the sense of revelation that I too, like some of the curators, experienced on first opening myself to the great post-sixties theoretical project. The moment when paradigms of the self went crack, when the solid floor of assumptions about reality opened beneath one's feet, may not be recapturable as such for the next intellectual generation, for whom the explosion of simultaneous provisional realities, channels, nodes, zones, tracks, rhizomes and modes of being has become normal life. Still, to live in this "normalcy" is not necessarily to think it: students find little opportunity to translate their personal adaptations to postmodern culture into conscious thought about dramatic texts. Here was one clear value of our "kidnapping" Miller, the introduction of certain methods of thought for reinvesting the "classic" text with new questions and productive new difficulty.

That Arthur Miller's *Death of a Salesman* should survive the cultural shifts of the past half century to earn the reverence of students in their twenties and early thirties is surely one mark of its emergence as a "classic." Like other classics, it has an uncanny ability to anticipate its audience horizontally across different cultures, and vertically through successive generations. But we were not sure of that when our pedagogical experiment began. We thought it possible that our investigations would trump Miller's text, exposing its midcentury limitations. To their surprise, each group of students in succession discovered that the very issue on which they might have found Miller wanting was already anticipated by the text. Even Willy's silencing of Linda and his distaste for his neighbors, the students concluded, might be more Willy's problem than Miller's. Finally, our exercise reinscribed the play as a large and open work, capable of responding with remarkable generosity to a range of critical and aesthetic values not yet thought at its inception.

Notes

1. All scenes cited here are taken from *Death of a Salesman,* in *The Portable Arthur Miller,* ed. Harold Clurman (New York: Penguin, 1971). Page numbers are indicated in the text.

2. Michael Warner, *Fear of a Queer Planet: Queer Politics and Social Theory* (Minneapolis: University of Minnesota Press, 1993), vii.

3. Eve Kosofsky Sedgwick, *Epistemology of the Closet* (Berkeley and Los Angeles: University of California Press, 1990), 90.

4. Eve Kosofsky Sedgwick, *Tendencies* (Durham: Duke University Press, 1993), 9.

5. Sedgwick, *Tendencies,* 8.

Enoch Brater

William Bolcom's *A View from the Bridge* and American Opera
A Discussion

Enoch Brater: Bill Bolcom's involvement with Arthur Miller's work is quite extraordinary. The project that most concerns us in this discussion is the opera that he wrote based on *A View from the Bridge.*

Bill, why don't you begin at the beginning, and trace for us, if you would, the history of your relationship with Miller.

William C. Bolcom: I never had thought of making an opera of an Arthur Miller play. I had always had a feeling that most of the time the only reason to make an opera, which is a huge amount of labor, is if it really needs to be done. The usual problem is that people decide they would love to do an opera of something they love because they want to let you know how much they love it, and that's a very laudable thing. But does your love for it actually enhance anybody's understanding of the piece? Is there any real need to put it into opera? The point is that when you transfer any work into another medium, you have to say, "There's something that we can give that may have been an unrealized dimension of the original."

EB: How did you begin your project on a Miller play?

WCB: What happened was this: about 1993 or 1994 we settled on the subject *A View from the Bridge.* I got the first draft of the libretto in 1994. Arthur and Arnold Weinstein had sketched together a pretty good idea of what they wanted to do. What we ended up doing in many cases was going back to the very first version of the play written in verse in 1955.

EB: And all in one act.

WCB: It was one act of two. There were two plays. The other one was called *A Memory of Two Mondays,* to which in certain ways it was related. *A View from the Bridge* had a bit of the verse-play atmosphere about it, which meant that it was not a great big hit. But it was full of interesting things. It also did not fill out the character of Eddie Carbone's wife, Beatrice. She was hardly in it, and we needed to have more tension between Beatrice and Eddie.

EB: Bill is exactly right. It was written in verse as a one-act play. Miller said he wrote it very quickly. He based it on a story he heard that had a profound effect on him. He wanted to write it down as fast as he could so that he wouldn't lose its flavor. He hoped to share with his audience the tremendous emotional impact it had on him. The play, which was done originally in New York with *A Memory of Two Mondays,* was not a hit. Miller then revised the play.

WCB: Put it into two acts.

EB: And decided against using verse dialogue. It was done in London, under Peter Brook's direction, and it was a big hit. Then it returned to New York to successful reviews. So Bill is talking about going back to Miller's original one-act version.

WCB: Going back to the original because the verse-play was closer to what you might find yourself singing. It would have some of the same concentration of language as in an opera libretto. What it comes down to is that you really have to rethink a play for the new medium as totally as you can and yet retain the same thing, which I think we did successfully, partly because we had absolute cooperation from Arthur in every way.

The key point was that I needed to find out what I could do to this play, or with this play, that would justify having it turn into opera. I don't think that Miller's been well served by some of the movies of his plays. The plays are still the strongest form of his own theater. He depends on something that opera and theater share, and that is the presence of bodies out there, somebody performing and somebody watching.

That's one of the reasons why we could retain certain things that the film versions of the various plays could not. Films do not require audiences to have cathartic experiences. For example, the wonderful revival of *Death of a Salesman* with Brian Dennehy had that terrific cathartic thing at the end that you experience when you have a really strong performance. There are men sobbing in the seats because it's their lives up there on stage—all the things that don't happen when you're in front of a screen. But you can have it with opera, too.

Anyway, back to how we got to the business of doing this play. Every so often people decide they want to make an opera out of something. I think it's happened to Miller many times that people call up and say, "I've done a whole opera on your piece." Then, of course, the thing is, "Do you approve?" Then poor Arthur is stuck with having to say, "Gee whiz; this is terrible. I just don't know what I'm going to do." In fact, this happened with *A View from the Bridge*. Around the time when he was married to Marilyn Monroe, a couple of young protegés of Alan J. Lerner decided to do a musical of *A View from the Bridge*. Arthur hated it. End of all that work.

This happens quite often to Arthur. So he often has called in Arnold Weinstein, who can look at the setting with him. Somebody had come up with a *Death of a Salesman* setting, or at least a good deal of it. So they sat down, listened, and looked at it. The guy had brought a demo tape and everything else, and they both decided that *Death of a Salesman* is not in any way helped by being an opera. Arthur says, "Do you think anything of mine could be done as an opera?" Arnold says, "Well, the one that really should be an opera—because there are things you can realize as an opera that may not have been realizable as a play—is *A View from the Bridge*. As it happens, we have a commission going at the Lyric Opera Chicago. How about doing *A View from the Bridge* there?"

So Arthur calls up, and Arnold calls up, and they both say, "We would like to have you do *A View from the Bridge*." I said, "That sounds great." Then I heard that Bruno Bartoletti, the musical director of the Lyric, had come back from a trip and said, 'Oh, I think Bill should do—What do you call it in English, *Uno sguardo dal Ponte!*" So that's how I was snookered into doing this thing. There was no choice. I was flanked by both sides. I had to consider the thing seriously. And of course the first question is, what makes it justifiable as a sung work? The answer is the chorus. This is something that Arthur would have liked to have been able to do, had he had the money, in a theater production, to realize the chorus *as* a chorus. This is just simply beyond the ken of a Broadway theater. Once the chorus speaks, you've got to pay them enormous amounts.

So first we have to look at the chorus. Then again, we did use in many ways the dialogue from the first 1955 version because lots of the language was already singable.

So between all of those things, and Arthur always overseeing everything and Arnold doing wonderful, concise renderings of what was there, pulling things together out of bits and pieces of dialogue and making arias out of them—all of the words are related directly to

Arthur's original dialogue. He didn't necessarily invent; he did, however, reshuffle.

So how did we transform the material? Well, the language had to become more concentrated. It had to feel like dialogue, and yet it couldn't be dialogue because you were slowing down the diction of the sentence by the simple virtue of singing it, and you had to find the lyrical line underlying it. There are parts of modern operas in which you have essentially text set to music, but you try to do that as a need to get from A to B to C. What you really want are lyrical moments that justify the point and presence of music. So it was really a matter of trying to find those nodes, those places where the music and word can coalesce and the reason for music can be there. Alfieri in *A View from the Bridge* is a one-man chorus, and there's no real problem in Alfieri becoming the leader so that the chorus then has an active role.

As we got closer and closer to the premiere, I had already put together many sketches. The actual writing out of the opera and the orchestration took about a year and a half. So we were just pulling these things together until we had a whole grab bag of possible ideas. By rereading and rereading and rereading and living with the texts, certain ideas just come suddenly to you that are related to the text and seem to reify the verbal content. Again, whenever I needed something, I would turn to Arthur or Arnold, and there were times I needed it. In one place, however, I just went back to the 1955 play. I needed an aria for Alfieri at a point right after Eddie does this terrible thing with shaming Rodolpho in front of Catherine. So I found two speeches in the original 1955 version of *A View from the Bridge* and I shoved them together, and that was my aria. So this is how you do it. I have to have the sense of how it all goes. Even though I have sketches of what I'll be doing, I only know the size and proportion when I'm starting from the top and going to the end, and that's essentially how you work it out. So what we did was kind of fun. We ended up composing the whole thing pretty much by fax.

I still have my old piano, my clunky old piano, which I bought for a hundred bucks and fixed up with a friend. It's now sitting in the Chelsea Hotel in Arnold's apartment. Scott Griffin, a young man who is also a producer and works at Carnegie Hall, is very adept at playing the piano. So the year I was working nearly constantly on *A View from the Bridge,* I would fax pages to Arnold of the vocal score as I completed them. Arnold would call up Scott, Scott would come up and run through them, and bawl out the voice part. Meantime, Arthur was in New York City quite often because the Signature Theatre was doing a season of his plays. So Arthur could keep up, and he'd say, "Well, I like this. I don't like that." He was very approving of pretty much everything I did, but there were questions here and there. So I'd fix it up. That's fine. That's what you want. It was very natural, very low-key. He never worried that we were going to violate his play because that play is going to be done just fine. It's probably being done in some language right now. Nothing we've done is going to get in the way of that. But the play had to be rethought in order to make it into a proper opera. In fact, Arthur went on record saying that the problem with the other opera of one of his plays—*The Crucible*—was that it was too close to the play, that it hadn't been transformed enough to become an opera. It hadn't become lyrical in a heightened way, which has to happen to an opera. How can I explain what that is?

What makes an opera different from a play or a movie or a TV show is that in those media the text is up here in the consciousness, and the subtext is down here in the deeper part of the consciousness. Imagine, if you will, that with opera, the two are switched around. So the subtext is actually the surface, and the verbal context feeds the subtext, which is why it becomes an opera. One of the marvelous cases of this sort of transformation is what Verdi did with *Othello* when he turned it into *Otello*. The handkerchief aria, which is one of the key parts, is almost completely new.

EB: A lot of critics have commented on the choral element in Miller's play; Alfieri is the choral element in *A View from the Bridge*. But when Miller was writing the play he thought of the citizens, the whole community, as being the chorus, the way the chorus works in classical Greek theater. I wonder how you dealt with that.

WCB: If you saw the opera, you might have noticed that the chorus is practically always there. This is a very tight community with houses with very thin walls; and what Mrs. So-and-So was doing two doors down you heard about rather loudly through the window. So there was no sense of real privacy. Everybody is there all the time.

One of the central images in the opening of the opera is the fact that this sounds like a case that a lawyer might have faced thousands of years ago; a person having this terrific jealousy about a person he doesn't have a right to, i.e., his niece, and having sexual urges toward her and not willing to articulate them or admit them to himself. He dies without ever consciously realizing what he's felt. As he saw it, the only thing to do was to try to protect Catherine—he could not admit to himself his own attraction to her. Much came from his denial.

The director, Frank Galati, did a wonderful thing in rehearsal. He had the soloists perform for the chorus as if they were an audience, the chorus answering to the soloists as if we were having a call-and-response from the chorus. That gave it a cohesion and a sense of dialogue between the two; and where Alfieri might have spoken as an explainer, as a lawyer, the chorus has a dialogue with the principals the same way as in an ancient Greek play; people warning the characters against something that's going to happen.

EB: Were any of the people involved in the project attracted to it because it concerned a very passionate Sicilian world, one we might associate with Italian opera?

WCB: It was going to be tied into the tradition of Italian opera, but there was a big difference. These are Americans. It's 1950 and they go to the Brooklyn Dodger games. So what was important was the incursion of American culture on all these Italians: the fact that they still had the operatic sense of impulse, but translated as much as anything else by where they were, who they were, what they were dealing with, the texture of American life, and the conflict between two Sicilians who really were immigrants.

EB: One of the revealing aspects of the collaboration you had with Arnold and Arthur on this project was the playwright's willingness to provide new text when you thought it was necessary.

WCB: I was interested in having real honest-to-goodness places where it all coalesced and the person had a song about how they felt. This is the old opera tradition. A dramatic situation arises that causes a particular emotional state of mind; this is then expressed by the aria, which, you see, is rather static—the person stops and sings about what they're feeling. The music can do certain things that you can't do in a play. You can't come right out and say, "I love you" in a play anymore; it's too corny, but you can do it in opera. People sing it all the time.

We came to the ending of an act—Eddie has done this terrible thing, Marco has been arrested, and I said, "You know, Marco needs an aria." We had to do this for two reasons. One is that he needs to express his state of being, who he is, where he is. The other is that you can't interest a terrific person in the part unless there are enough arias and places for them to be front-and-center. They want that very badly.

I called up Arnold and said, "I need an aria for Marco," and in three days Arthur sent us a first draft of an aria for Marco because he could see that this was necessary. I needed another one for Catherine Malfitano playing Beatrice and, again, Arthur wrote that.

EB: I teach a course on Arthur Miller and we read *A View from the Bridge.* Students in my class always want to know about the title of the play; whose view is it, what view is it? What do you think that you and Arnold brought to the "view" that Miller dramatizes in this play?

WCB: I think our view was essentially the same. Arthur really felt that it was. However, Arnold has a certain atmosphere in his work that is Arnold's and Arnold's alone, and I think that's probably true with mine. So in that way, of course, we had to intrude our own personalities. I once made a speech to the cast. I said, "I have to tell you that I have done my very best to give the best readings I could to you. I realize at the same time that you were forced to read the play as I've done it, only because I was the one who decided what the notes are, how quickly you do them, whether you go up on this word or down on the next word, and all those other things. It's my own kind of arbitrary way of doing it. I feel in certain ways that I hamstrung you. I would, for example, in an opera have to do something that no good director would ever do, which is say, 'Read lines to the actor.' You never do that in theater, and I have to do it as an opera composer."

EB: I'm curious about the nature of the performers as collaborators in the opera's first production at the Lyric in Chicago in 1999. Did they transform your work in any way?

WCB: Occasionally. With singers you have to think of the physicality of the situation. With women singers—this is a question of physics; it's crazy—when you get above the staff in the singing, the danger is that the vowels all turn into "ah." So you try with your setting to make sure that key words, your money words, the words that carry the meaning, are not done up at the top of the stratosphere, which is sometimes the emotional peak. So this is the kind of thing that you try to calibrate as carefully as possible.

I reworked the soprano part for Catherine Malfitano, and there were times I heard it back and said, "I like this line better." I've done this for every singer I've ever worked with. You can't be arbitrary about it. I don't want to ruin the sense of something. I want to make sure that all the theatrical values will come through. We saved a good number of the laughs, which are important in Miller. One of the biggest mistakes in his plays is that too many directors do it all downbeat. Arthur's full of humor, from one end to another, in his most tragic plays. One of the things that happens in *Death of a Salesman* about thirty seconds before Willy Loman runs his car into the telephone pole or whatever it is, is a big laugh. And the laugh doesn't destroy the tragedy of the event. You have to keep those two things in balance.

EB: When we talked earlier you said you had a revealing anecdote about Arthur Miller and Arnold Weinstein. Would you like to conclude by telling us what that was?

WCB: About three months after the first draft of the libretto was given to me, I went to Chicago with Arthur Miller and Arnold for a big launching of a program called *Toward the Twenty-First Century in Opera.* A lot of the local money folks paid for a string of new pieces and new works and twentieth-century masterpieces to be performed at the Lyric Opera. They don't do these at a loss.

Here's Arthur saying, "Well, why are they having me come out and meet these people? We haven't talked to the backers yet." I said, "Arthur, it's a done deal. We have the money out in front." And he said, "Well, don't you still feel a little nervous about not going in front of these people, maybe showing them a couple of tunes to see what we're doing?" I said, "No, because we don't have to. They trust me. They trust you. It's going to be all right." He said, "Well, when do you think they'll be absolutely able to see this thing?" This is in 1995. "In four years," I said. He said, "We're gonna be doing it in October of 1999? I'll be eighty-four!" And he started laughing. He said he'd never had that amount of time to wait for anything. You start with a play, and in a few months you get together with your people, get your money, get your backers, get your actors, and then you put it together within the same calendar year. An opera, forget it; it's gonna take forever.

Enoch Brater

A Conversation with Arthur Miller
October 26, 2000

Enoch Brater: Let's begin with Ann Arbor. Why did you come to study at the University of Michigan? Why didn't someone like you go to City College in New York, which would have been a very logical path in the middle of the Depression?

Arthur Miller: Well, I did go to City College for about three weeks in the evening; I was working during the daytime. But I couldn't stay awake, so I decided I'd work for a few years and make enough money to go to school in the daytime. I was a little better at staying awake in the daytime. Anyway, coming to Michigan was partly because at that time it was probably the only university in the United States that had an active interest in creative writing. At least I knew of no other. There was that, and there was also that the tuition was so cheap, and money was difficult to come by. So those are the reasons.

EB: Did your family think it was odd that you were coming all the way to the Midwest, leaving New York and all that world behind you?

AM: I looked at it as a kind of adventure. I thought of it as the Wild West. I was amazed that in Detroit they had the same cars we had in New York! For a young guy, it was a great adventure. People didn't jump into airplanes in those days and fly off to some place. Moving around was a good deal more difficult.

EB: When you were a student here, how often did you get back to New York?

AM: I got back during the Christmas vacation, and that was about it. I usually had to work during the spring vacation, and in fact that's when I wrote my first play. So I got back once each year.

EB: Tell us about the *Michigan Daily*. Why did you stop writing for the *Daily*?

AM: Well, because I started to win prizes for my plays, and I wanted to spend more time writing plays. I lost my impulse to do journalism be-

Arthur Miller speaking via satellite hookup at the University of Michigan, Rackham Auditorium. (Courtesy U-M Photo Services)

cause I tended to want to make the stories better, and that left fact behind a good deal of the time. I found I wasn't really made to be a reporter. The only thing about journalism was they had a payroll, and that wasn't the case in the theater. You were completely on your own there and could easily starve to death, but I decided to pursue the theater because I loved it.

EB: What drew you to Professor Rowe's class, the Kenneth Rowe who was an important person in your life at Michigan? How did you get connected with him?

AM: I had a wonderful teacher named Erich Walter who later became the dean of the university, and Professor Walter directed me toward Kenneth Rowe. In fact, it was actually in Walter's essay class that I wrote my first play. It was only later that I went to Professor Rowe. It was a great event in my life because Rowe, while I'm sure he wanted to teach me a lot, taught me really only one thing, and that was that I could hold the stage with dialogue. He acquainted me with the history of the theater and with the development of various forms, and it was a quick way of getting educated.

EB: Let's talk a little bit about the plays that you started writing once

Enoch Brater in conversation with Miller on October 26, 2000. (Courtesy U-M Photo Services)

you left Michigan. What were you writing just before *The Man Who Had All the Luck* was done on Broadway in 1944?

AM: I wrote the Hopwood plays; there were, I think, three plays. Then when I got out of school, I wrote a tragedy of the conquest of Mexico by Cortez and the fascinating story of Montezuma [*The Golden Years*]. Of course, I was ignorant of what was going on in Broadway and commercial theater—mind you, there was no non-commercial theater at that time. You either made it on Broadway or you didn't make it at all. And I wrote this tragedy which had, I don't know, probably twenty-five characters in it, which was an absurdity as far as getting it produced in the commercial theater. Commercial theater regarded an eight-character play as being excessive. So I couldn't get that produced, but I had hoped that the Federal Theatre, which was, of course, a theater subsidized by the government, would be able to do it. But the Federal Theatre folded within six or eight months after I got onto it. So I never did get that play produced at all except many years later in England, where they did it on television.

EB: You had a lot of jobs during that period. Do you remember much of your work days at the Brooklyn Navy Yard?

AM: That was during World War II. I was rejected for the army because of a wounded leg that I had as a result of playing football stupidly in high school. I wanted to do something that was related to the war effort, so I took a job there. But at the same time I was writing programs for radio, the DuPont radio program called *Cavalcade of America,* also several others. And I'd do that in the daytime and work eleven hours at night in the Yard. I was a shipfitter's helper and finally became a shipfitter. It was a terrific experience. It was wonderful work, although I never did understand how we managed to get ships out of the Yard and onto the high seas without sinking, because few of us knew very much about anything. The Yard before the war had six thousand workers in it who were highly trained people. During the war it had sixty thousand, and we were all loafers from every kind of a position in society and nobody knew a ship from a hole in a wall. How we managed to repair and build ships is still an amazement to me. But they floated!

EB: After *The Man Who Had All the Luck* failed on Broadway, what brought you to write the novel *Focus?* Why did you move into fiction at that point?

AM: I decided I didn't belong in the theater because I couldn't recognize on the stage anything that I had imagined when I was writing that play, and it was partly my fault that it didn't work. It was also the production—they didn't know quite how to deal with this style, which was a kind of presentational style. Nowadays it's not all that extraordinary. In those days it was practically unheard of, and I think that the audience was totally bewildered by the play. I just decided there was no hope for me as a playwright. So I decided to write prose. I wrote this novel, which incidentally fifty years later was made into a film. If you wait long enough, everything happens.

EB: You wrote *All My Sons* at a critical point in your life. That play put you on the map in the American theater. It's been reported many times that this was going to be your last attempt to write a play. Did you think that *All My Sons* was going to be a big hit on Broadway?

AM: Oh, no. I was writing radio at the time. That's how I made my living, and I wrote the play over a period of about two and a half years, thinking that I would do a play that I would believe in—every page of which I would believe. If that didn't work—if I couldn't get it produced, or if it were produced and failed—then I would go into another kind of work because I was not interested in hanging around, as many of my friends were forced to do, waiting for the lightning to strike and for a production to happen on plays I had written or wanted to write. So that was a long job that I imposed on myself, and when I finished I was happy to see that three producers wanted it at once. So it worked, and that was a great gratification.

EB: How did you get to Willy Loman? What gave you the idea for this character?

AM: Really, it's a ball of wool that many threads go into; it's no one thing. Willy Loman for me is, of course, first of all, a character, but he was also the vessel for many feelings and ideas that were floating around in my head for the past decade or more. Some of it goes back into my childhood. So it was not an idea; it was a segment of my flesh, so to speak. *All My Sons* was written in the style that it is in order to be sure that it would work. I no sooner finished it than I wanted to get away from that style and indulge in a more *written* piece of work. The idea behind *All My Sons* as a style is that nobody wrote it. I had suppressed or removed any sign of metaphor or a signal that there was a literary mind behind all of this. I wanted it to seem as though it were really happening. The opposite view goes into *Death of a Salesman,* where I wanted to write for the stage and where the style would be right in the forefront. So it's a completely opposite attack on material.

EB: One time when we talked about *Salesman* you remarked that the play was too affective; that you thought you were writing a hard-boiled play but the audience was crying. Do you still feel the same way?

AM: I guess I do. I am happy, of course, that it affects people so profoundly, but originally I was a little disturbed that it was sweeping people away rather than making them see life a little clearer. But I suppose you can't make people see unless they feel, and in fact the next play, *The Crucible,* is a completely different kind of an emotional piece of work; it's cooler, it's more classical and it was that way in part because I was reacting against the emotionalism in *Death of a Salesman.*

EB: Just last week I was talking to my students about the conditions that gave rise to *The Crucible* and living through that horrible period Lillian Hellman called "Scoundrel Time." The students were of course fascinated. It was really remarkable that when I was talking about McCarthyism, you could have heard a pin drop. The students had a lot of questions about this and about your life at that time. One of the things they wanted to know is what it was that made people like you and someone like Lillian Hellman stand up to those right wing people when it was so very difficult for so many others to resist?

AM: I think it's probably a temperamental thing more than anything else. I don't know about her, but in my case, I had always had a difficulty abiding the interference of others in my work. That's why I never hired out to Hollywood, excepting one time for a short job. I was desperate for money, and I worked for a few months on *The Story of G.I. Joe,* which was a film made back in the forties. That was Robert Mitchum's first film. The idea that you would write scenes and somebody owned the paper you were working on was an abomination, and I think that my feeling of being violated was part of the reason or mainly the reason why I wouldn't knuckle under to these people. It seemed to me that it was the very opposite of Americanism anyway. But I've written a piece, published in *Echoes Down the Corridor*—it was a lecture I gave at Harvard—about the circumstances of my life in that period. It's fairly complicated.

EB: When you started to write a film script, *The Misfits,* was that your first experience with writing a big commission for Hollywood?

AM: Well, it wasn't commissioned. I wrote *The Misfits* completely on my own. I had written a short story or a lengthy short story which was published in *Esquire* magazine, and I thought it would make a wonderful film, so I wrote the film. Then John Huston saw it and wanted to direct it.

EB: We saw a film clip earlier with Burt Lancaster and Edward G. Robinson in *All My Sons.* What did you think of those earlier adaptations of your plays from the forties and fifties?

AM: On the whole I didn't like them. I think that Lancaster was very good, and Robinson was, but they treated the material quite sentimentally. Likewise, *Death of a Salesman* in the screen adaptation had a marvelous actor who could have done it beautifully, Fredric March. It was marred because they couldn't confront the hard facts about what these plays were about, and they mucked them up. They sentimentalized them and they blatantly reached for emotional reactions when there shouldn't have been any. I've written about some of the distortions that went into the *Death of a Salesman* script. I'll just mention one or two. They made Willy crazy, and they worked at making him crazy so that you could dismiss the whole thing. I think it was because it was the beginning of the real right-wing turn in this country, and the studios were very sensitive about any criticism of the American ways. I say that advisedly because the truth of the matter is that they no sooner finished making the film than it was attacked by the American Legion and a few other such organizations. The studios made another film called *The Life of a Salesman.* This was at Columbia Pictures. It consisted, really, of some professors at City College in New York lecturing us about how wonderful it was to be a salesman, and that there couldn't have been a better life for anybody. They were going to show this piece of stupidity to the audience along with *Death of a Salesman.* It was so bad that they couldn't really show it, so they scrapped it. But that'll give you an idea of what the atmosphere was like. It was incredible. And by making Willy crazy, they made the whole thing ineffectual; therefore, he didn't represent anybody who wasn't crazy. I haven't fared very well in the films, except for *The Misfits,* which I like.

EB: Tell us about *The Crucible,* which was produced by your son Robert.

AM: Now that is another story. *The Crucible* I think is a wonderful movie, with a strong director [Nicholas Hytner]. And the star is a master actor, Daniel Day-Lewis [Miller's son-in-law, Rebecca Miller's husband]. So I had better luck with that one.

EB: Recently there have been powerful productions of plays like *Salesman* and *A View from the Bridge* and *The Price* in Chicago and New York. You've seen some of those productions. How would you account for this renewed interest by a younger generation of actors and directors in plays from an earlier time in your life?

AM: I don't know. A new generation comes along that hasn't seen these plays, and they just rediscover them. It's the only explanation I have, because they've been around a long time. My plays are done all over the country all of the time; it's just that in New York the commercial theater is such that you can't really do a top-level production without it costing a million dollars, and my plays have a lot of characters in them. So they're expensive, and that's another reason why it took an economic boom for these plays to get on. Theater is intimately involved with the economy, politics, the society as a whole. It's not an art that can be set aside in one corner and thrive; it's mixed up with the way we live.

EB: One of the questions that students have asked is, if you were thinking about writing plays like this today—*Salesman* or *All My Sons* or *The Crucible*—what would you change in those plays?

AM: I don't think I'd change anything. They seem to do what I wanted them to do, what the material required. I think there's a mistaken idea that if a play is about a previous period, that it's outdated. We do Shakespeare all the time, and it's about life 450 years ago. Things get outdated because the writing in them is superficial, but I don't think anything gets outdated because people are wearing different costumes or perhaps using different locutions in their speech. The modernity of a work is based on its inner feelings, its original grasp of ideas.

EB: Students also wanted to know about the female characters in your plays. They seem very much a part of their time: dramatic figures like Linda Loman and Kate Keller. If you were dealing with those kind of female characters in today's world, do you think you would update them, put them in a different context?

AM: You know, there's been a remarkable production of *All My Sons* at the National Theatre in London. In that production, which I saw, the mother of the family knows the story from the time the curtain goes up. She believes that her husband, in effect, was responsible for the death of their son in the war. Finally, a production was done in which that woman was played with an intensity that made her the center of the whole play, which is what I always believed anyway. We have done the play largely as a fight between the father and the son. In fact, the mother, the woman, is the center of that play; likewise, in *Death of a Salesman.* In Robert Falls' production the character Linda Loman was very differently played. She is a fierce protector of her husband and also of herself, and she is not the passive weakling that she generally is portrayed as. Of course, it's the way the play was written. But finally—it took a half of a century—she is played the way she should be played.

EB: Why do you think that so many writers of your generation with a Jewish background have been involved so often in telling a story about America? So many writers of your generation and Jewish background have had a major impact on the theater and on the literature of the United States. How would you account for that?

AM: Well, because this country has always been a wonder to any immigrant group. It's been the way to heaven compared to almost any place on the planet. For poor people, America has always been the way to realize themselves, and of course the Jews were in a specially bad position in Europe because of anti-Semitism, which is historic and goes back a millennium. Here the hope was that one could be judged by one's character and one's work. The Jewish writer here simply carried through, I think, what the ordinary Jewish people were feeling; that is, that they were discovering an incredible blazing society that had all kinds of endless hope in it and was full of incredible failings which they wanted to understand and eliminate. So the field of activity here was open, for the first time of course, in two thousand years. The Jews came to the United States and had a free range of imagination before them, whereas before they were constrained and had to pretend that they were not there. Here they could come forward and announce themselves. So the writers, I think, simply carried through what generally Jews did in this country.

EB: Our audience has some questions for you.

Audience Member 1: My question for you involves the collaborative art of theater. It's one of those arts where you can't simply do it all on your own; you need to rely on performers, directors, producers, etc. Could you share with us some experiences where you discovered something new about your play or experiences where you were disappointed with the performance of your play?

AM: The theater is a performance art like music. You can read a score, a musical score, and make judgments about it, but until you hear it, your experience is only partial. The play is at the mercy of the actors and the director and the designers and all the other arts that go into a production. I have had terrific experiences with actors and I've had some dreadful ones. You hold your breath when you cast a play because you don't know whether you're dealing with a sane person or a maniac, or a talented person or somebody who simply seems talented. It's like life; you don't know what you're getting into when you cast a play. I think that I've learned something sometimes about a work of mine. I like to think that the actors make it better than it is, and I often get very moved by their work. I remember performances from which I still get a tingling in my spine when I think about them, but I don't want to mention names because some of these actors are still around and they've got enough trouble. So I'll just say that in general, on the whole, I've been very well served by them.

Audience Member 2: My question is this: Because of your great courage during the McCarthy era, when you were summoned before the HUAC committee did you have a certain righteous indignation? Where did you find the courage to confront bullies like those who were sticking up for McCarthy and following the crowd and the prevalent political times? Or did you have thoughts like other people would in your position, such as how is this going to affect my career? What can they do to me? What were your feelings right before you were forced to go before the committee?

AM: First of all, I was not dependent professionally on any corporation or big organization for my livelihood, unlike people who worked in Hollywood. The blacklist on Broadway theater in New York existed, but it was very spasmodic and weak, and I could always go back and write a play unless they put me in jail. So there was that. People who are totally dependent on the film studio knew that their career was over if they resisted these investigations, and that's terribly important. I suppose by the time 1956 rolled around, which was the time that I got sucked into it, I had already felt as I did for twenty years or more. Professor Brater earlier read from my testimony and from my editorials in the *Michigan Daily* that I was a confirmed anti-Fascist; and I felt that the civilization could go under if we had dictatorship, and that was a feeling I had for two decades by the time I was called. So I didn't feel I had much choice in the matter. But as I would emphasize again, I could follow through on my feelings because I knew I could always sit down at the typewriter and write a play, which a screenwriter could not do or an actor or a director who worked on films.

Audience Member 3: I was wondering what playwrights and possibly screenwriters you enjoy reading and what people would you recommend for a young playwright to be reading nowadays.

AM: If I were to try to educate anybody, I would start with the Greeks and Shakespeare and Ibsen and Strindberg, and I could name probably thirty other people. In contemporary terms, you should know what Brecht was up to, what some of our contemporary writers are doing. The British writers at the moment are terrific dramatists. The variety is endless. There are many, many ways to attack a dramatic problem, and offhand it would be hard for me to emphasize one over the other.

Audience Member 4: I'm wondering if you feel at all disappointed in the fact that your more recent work seems to have been taken much more to heart in Great Britain, where they seem to understand what you're doing much more than here in America.

AM: First of all, remember that the British theater still is basically a subsidized theater. This is not simply a financial situation, but it fuses the spirit of the audience, the theater, the actors, everybody else. They don't expect a play to make a million dollars next month. They are very relaxed about that aspect of theater. They also have a theater culture which in a sense we don't have. We have a lot of productions, but one wonders how many people in America think that going to the theater is really essential to their mental existence. There are a lot of people in England who feel that way. I'm not sure that it's diminishing or not; some people think it is. But at the moment there is still a certain intense interest in what happens in the theater. I don't find that here. There is interest on the part of would-be actors or writers and so on, but generally speaking educated people don't look to the theater in America for any kind of illumination. That's the difference.

How that developed, I have my ideas. I think it developed basically since the mid-fifties with the birth of the British National Theatre, which of course was and is a subsidized theater. They do shows which they feel are valuable. Some of them they know will have a limited audience, but they're still valuable. We can't do that here because we have to make a profit. I think that this is vital to understanding the difference, and I think it may also have affected the reception of my work in both countries.

Audience Member 5: You have often commented about being one of the few American writers that still has a connection with the Great Depression. Could you comment about the struggles in writing *The American Clock* and why you call it a vaudeville?

AM: The play originated because I read Studs Terkel's *Hard Times,* a series of recollections by people who had lived through the Depression. It evoked all of my own memories, and I decided I'd try to do something in the theater that mixed both my memories and Studs' writing. That's how the thing started. But behind that was the feeling that we had lost consciousness of what this country had been through in those years or the years of the thirties. They had disappeared from our awareness, and that also the values that they seemed to me to represent, those years, were being swamped by—well, let's call it what it is—just plain greed and the lust for the buck. One thing that was sometimes or more often obvious in the thirties was that people had of necessity to think socially. They had to think beyond the scope of their own little lives, and there was a kind of a spirit of being together with other people, and that life was not quite an arena in which you fought the lion; it was also a place where people cooperated a lot. They had to in order to survive. So it was an attempt on my part to remind Americans where they'd come from. That was the impetus; but it was also a certain beauty in that kind of suffering that had happened, because it showed the endurance of the human spirit, which I wanted to celebrate.

EB: What would you tell students who want to write for the theater—should they stay at it, should they work at it, or do you think it's just impossible today?

AM: You know, it was always impossible. It was impossible when I was starting out. In some ways it's easier because you have a non-commercial sort of theater. There's off-Broadway and there are resident theaters all over the country, and so on. One thing to remember about theater is that it is the most direct approach to addressing your fellow citizens. You don't need any machinery. You don't need any cameras. You don't need anything but a man or a woman standing on a board and speaking. And this, so to speak, nakedness of the form is a great thing. It is probably the most democratic of all the arts in that respect because you really don't require a lot of money to do it. You can't do anything where film is concerned without spending a fortune. You could conceivably do a lot in the theater without spending a fortune. So I want to preserve it.

The country is neglecting an enormous asset by not doing something about helping this art to survive. It can be done with practically a pittance. It doesn't need billions of dollars; it only needs some love and attention and a certain amount of money, but not all that much. I would not discourage people from writing. The more stuff we put out, the more pressure there will be probably on those in power to make it possible to produce these plays on a wider spectrum. It would be a shame if this great civilization killed off one of the most vibrant arts we've got.

Mel Gussow

Afterword
The Legacy of Arthur Miller

Once, when I asked Arthur Miller what he thought his legacy would be, he answered without hesitation: "Some good parts for actors."

Some good parts for actors? Couldn't almost any playwright make that statement? Couldn't Tennessee Williams have also said that, or, for that matter, Shakespeare? Or even lesser playwrights?

Miller explained that when actors and directors decide to do his plays, it's not because they have "great moral importance," or even "literary importance." It is the challenge of the role, for example, the many different ways an actor can approach Willy Loman. Miller allowed that there was more to be seen in the plays, that they deal "with essential dilemmas of what it means to be human." He made it clear that the plays were always intended to be generic as well as specific.

Miller has said that he could not have written *The Crucible* simply because he wanted to write a play about blacklisting—or about the Salem witch hunts. The center of the play is "the guilt of John Proctor and the working out of that guilt," and it exemplifies the "guilt of man in general." In other words, there is a moral as well as social and political base to Miller's work, and it is that sense of morality, of conscience, that distinguishes him from other important playwrights.

He is one of four major American playwrights of the twentieth century, the others being Eugene O'Neill, Tennessee Williams, and Edward Albee. O'Neill began as the pioneer experimentalist; his principal contribution was in his depiction of the disparity between reality and illusion. Williams was the great poet of our theater and Albee with searing intensity probes marriage, family and the failure of the American dream.

Miller's individual significance is for his moral force and his confirmed sense of justice, or, rather, his sense of correcting injustice wherever he finds it—in business, art, politics, the courts, the court of public opinion. He does this in his life as well as in his plays.

In a sweeping statement, Robert Brustein once said he defied anyone "to name a single work of art that has ever changed anything,"[1] overlooking the fact that Beckett—and Chekhov before him—changed one's concept of theater, and that art, even theater, can be a sentinel in alerting public awareness.

Miller's response to Brustein's remark was particularly perceptive. He said, "I think works of art change the consciousness of people and their estimate of who they are and what they stand for. Plays suggest to people how to behave, what is acceptable and what is unacceptable." As proof of the statement, his plays, especially *Death of a Salesman* and *The Crucible,* continue to speak to theatergoers around the world, in China and Russia as well as on home ground.

These plays and others are unified by recurrent themes and motifs: embattled fathers and sons, fraternal love and rivalry, the price that people pay for the choices they make in life, suicide as sacrifice, and, above all, the law, in Miller's words, as a "metaphor for the moral order of man."

It is no coincidence that lawyers figure prominently as characters in almost all his plays: Alfieri in *A View from the Bridge;* Quentin, Miller's surrogate and the protagonist of *After the Fall;* in *Death of a Salesman,* Bernard, the young man who is arguing a case before the Supreme Court and does not need to tell Willy—or anyone—about it. In a sense, Miller is lawyer as playwright, aware of all sides of a dispute but clear about where he stands, for an essential moral truth.

Were his plays only works of social consciousness, they might have faded along with the plays of Clifford Odets. In play after play, he holds people responsible for their—and for their neighbor's—actions. Each play is a drama of accountability.

Watching *All My Sons,* his first Broadway success, it is impossible not to be aware of contemporary parallels—of accidents in nuclear plants, of defective tires and cars being shielded by the companies that produce them, of drug manufacturers who put products on the market before they have been adequately tested.

There are other through-lines in his art, for example, the theme of power and the loss of power. In *The Crucible,* power rests with public opinion and the judges who run the system, but also with the individuals who first cry witch. The author is also saying, with hope, that there is an ultimate authority that will eventually rectify wrongs.

In Miller's plays, a man loses his confidence, his position, or, like John Proctor, he loses his good name. How does he behave, how will he react, can the character gain—or regain—the courage to go on, or will he find solace in embracing defeat?

Willy Loman is confronted by a loss of faith, a loss of pride and an end to possibilities. He has always thought that if he works hard and sells well, he will succeed, and that his sons will succeed after him. It turns out that is a dream based on false values. For Willy, as for Miller, the Great Depression was a turning point, in itself the end of an American vision of prosperity.

After O'Neill, the American theater was dominated for many years by Williams and Miller. *A Streetcar Named Desire* in 1947 and, two years later, *Death of a Salesman* were revelatory occasions, and, as we know, they are not only great plays but paradigms of two extraordinary careers. Sadly, Williams career was cut short, even before his death. With Miller, the career continues into the present.

It would be easy to think of Williams and Miller as opposites, Williams as a hauntingly autobiographical playwright who could transform his dreams into plays that probed the human heart; Miller as an objectifier, a kind of American Ibsen—Ibsen, who in Harold Clurman's analysis, had "a compelling force to combat meanness, outworn modes of thought and hypocrisy," and was "in quest of a binding unity, a dominant truth."

However, as Clurman added about Ibsen, his plays are also "deeply autobiographical . . . dramatizations of his emotional, spiritual, social and intellectual life," and it is that quality that gives his plays their "staying power."[2] All these things can be said equally about Miller.

It should be added that Miller is as admiring of Strindberg as he is of Ibsen. Even as he is aware of—and offended by—Strindberg's misogyny, there is another side to Strindberg with which Miller can identify: Strindberg's "vision of the inexorability of the tragic circumstance, that once something is in motion, nothing can stop it,"[3] that, as with the Greeks, it is impossible to avoid the power of Fate.

Miller also expresses a kinship with Williams. As he said, "Tennessee felt that his redemption lay in writing. I feel the same way. That's when you're most alive."

When Miller is not writing plays, he spends time building tables and other furniture. He loves carpentry and often uses it as a metaphor for playwriting: the objective is to build a better table, to write a better play. In one of our conversations, I suggested that he had already made a terrific table—*Death of a Salesman*—very early in his career and wondered, after that, what the incentive was. He said first of all that *Death of a Salesman* was his tenth play and added that each play has a different aim. A different wood? No, "same wood"—the Miller wood, firm, solid, like mahogany, seemingly impervious to the weather (but perhaps not so impervious to critics). The same wood, but a "different aim—to create a different truth," and for Miller each play becomes "an amazing new adventure." Some playwrights write the same play over and over again: not Miller.

As he has said, "I have a feeling my plays are my character and your character is your fate." Ineluctably, he is drawn to his study, where he writes far more intuitively than one might suppose, an artist sustained not only by his ideas but by his moments of inspiration. He also said, "There's an intensification of feeling when you create a play that doesn't exist anywhere else. It's a way of spiritually living. There's a pleasure there that doesn't exist in real life—and you can be all those other people."

Several years ago, Miller was in Valdez, Alaska, to receive an award at the Last Frontier Theater Conference, and he and a local official went fishing for salmon in Prince William Sound, which is surrounded by a glacier. As they passed an iceberg, Miller's companion leaned over the side of the boat, chopped off pieces of ice and brought them aboard. Miller touched glacial ice. "Eight million year old ice," he said in astonishment. "It doesn't melt."

In June, 2000 I was in Valdez for that same conference, and I, too, touched glacial ice—and thought about Arthur Miller. When he told me that story, I suggested that if ice can last that long, perhaps that says something about the survival of civilization and of art. Never one to sidestep a metaphor, he said, "You hang around long enough . . . you don't melt."

Miller is very much a survivor, an artist who has gone his own way without regard for fashion or expectation. The work, at its best, is both timely and timeless, which is why the plays continue to be done.

And there are also some good parts for actors.

Notes

1. See Martin Gottfried, *Arthur Miller: A Life* (New York: DaCapo Press, 2003), 395.

2. For these evaluations of Ibsen, see Harold Clurman, *Ibsen* (New York: Simon and Schuster, 1977).

3. For Miller's comments on Strindberg and Williams, see Mel Gussow, *Conversations with Miller* (New York: Applause Books, 2002).

Contributors

Arnold Aronson is Professor of Theatre in the School of the Arts at Columbia University. His publications include *The History and Theory of Environmental Scenography, American Set Design* and *American Avant-Garde Theatre: A History.*

William C. Bolcom is a composer and pianist who received the Pulitzer Prize for Music in 1988 for *12 New Etudes for Piano.* He has taught at the University of Michigan since 1973 and wrote the music for the opera based on *A View from the Bridge,* with libretto by Arthur Miller and Arnold Weinstein. He has made over twenty recordings of American popular songs with his wife, mezzo-soprano Joan Morris.

Enoch Brater is the author most recently of *The Stages of Arthur Miller* and *The Essential Samuel Beckett.* He is Professor of English and Theater at the University of Michigan, and has also published *The Drama in the Text: Beckett's Late Fiction* and *Beyond Minimalism: Beckett's Late Style in the Theater.* The series he edits for the University of Michigan Press, "Theater: Theory/Text/Performance," was the inaugural recipient of the Association for Theater in Higher Education Award for Excellence in Editing.

Ruby Cohn is Professor Emerita of Comparative Drama at the University of California, Davis. She has written three books on Samuel Beckett, including *A Beckett Canon,* and a half dozen on contemporary theater in Britain, France and the United States.

Patricia Denison is the Acting Chair of the Department of Theatre at Barnard College, where she is also a member of the English Department. She is the editor of a collection of essays on the British playwright John Osborne.

Peter Ferran, cofounder of the Brecht Company in Ann Arbor, Michigan, is Professor of Fine Arts (Theatre) in the College of Liberal Arts, Rochester

Institute of Technology, where he teaches theater arts and directs student productions.

Jonathan Freedman is Professor of English and American Studies at the University of Michigan. He is the author of *Professions of Taste: Henry James, British Aestheticism and Commodity Culture* and *The Temple of Culture: Assimilation, Anti-Semitism, and the Making of Literary Anglo-America, 1880–1980.*

Elinor Fuchs is Professor of Dramaturgy and Dramatic Criticism at the Yale School of Drama. She is the author of *The Death of Character: Perspectives on Theater after Modernism,* winner of the George Jean Nathan Award for Dramatic Criticism, and coeditor of *Land/Scape Theater.*

Frank Gagliano is a playwright and the Benedum Professor of Theatre at West Virginia University. He was the first Artistic Director of the University of Michigan's Festival of New Works, where he established the Arthur Miller Award for Playwriting.

Deborah R. Geis is Associate Professor of English at DePauw University. She is the author of *Postmodern Theatric(k)s: Monologue in Contemporary American Drama,* coeditor of *Approaching the Millennium: Essays on* Angels in America and editor of *Considering* Maus: *Approaches to Art Spiegelman's "Survivor's Tale" of the Holocaust.*

Laurence Goldstein is Professor of English at the University of Michigan and, since 1977, editor of the *Michigan Quarterly Review.* He is the author of three books of poetry and three books of literary criticism, most recently *The American Poet at the Movies: A Critical History.*

Mel Gussow, a cultural writer for the *New York Times,* is the author of *Edward Albee: A Singular Journey, Conversations with Miller* and books on Harold Pinter, Tom Stoppard and Samuel Beckett. His criticism is collected in *Theater on the Edge: New Visions, New Voices,* and he is also the coeditor of the Library of America's two-volume edition of the plays of Tennessee Williams.

Bruce J. Mann is Associate Professor and Chair of the English Department at Oakland University in Rochester, Michigan. He is the dramaturg for the Meadowbrook Theatre and the editor of *Edward Albee: A Casebook.*

Austin E. Quigley is Dean of Columbia College and Professor of English at Columbia University in New York. He is the author of *The Modern Stage and Other Worlds* and *The Pinter Problem.*

Robert Scanlan, a past president of the Poet's Theatre in Cambridge, Massachusetts, teaches in the English Department at Harvard University for the Dramatic Arts curriculum. He was for many years the Literary Director of the American Repertory Theatre, where he headed the Dramaturgy and Playwriting Programs for the Institute for Advanced Theatre Training.

Mike Sell is Assistant Professor of English at Indiana University of Pennsylvania. His published work includes *The Avant-Garde and the Limits of Criticism: The Connection, Happenings/Fluxus, and the Black Arts Movement* and the edited volume *The Ed Bullins Reader.*

Andrew Sofer is Assistant Professor of English at Boston College. His recent work includes *The Stage Life of Props,* as well as essays in *Modern Drama, Comparative Drama,* and *English Literary Renaissance.*

Patrick Stewart, who plays Capt. Picard in the popular television series, *Star Trek: The Next Generation,* has been a member of the Royal Shakespeare Company since 1967. He first played the lead role in Miller's *The Ride Down Mt. Morgan* at the Public Theatre in New York in 1998, reprising the role two years later on Broadway.

Toby Zinman, Professor of English at the University of the Arts, is also a theater critic for *Variety* and Philadelphia's *City Paper.* She is the editor of two collections of essays: one on David Rabe, the other on Terrence McNally.

Index